Shoot the Women First

SHOOT THE WMEN FIRST

Eileen MacDonald

RANDOM HOUSE
NEW YORK

Copyright © 1991 by Eileen MacDonald

All rights reserved under International and Pan-American Copyright
Conventions. Published in the United States by Random House, Inc.,
New York.

This work was originally published in Great Britain by Fourth Estate Limited,
London, in 1991.

Library of Congress Cataloging-in-Publication Data

MacDonald, Eileen.
    Shoot the women first / Eileen MacDonald.—1st ed.
        p.   cm.
    ISBN 0-679-41596-3
    1. Women terrorists—Psychology.   2. Women terrorists—Interviews.
    I. Title.
    HV6431.M332   1992
    303.6'25'019—dc20   92-3867

Manufactured in the United States of America
98765432
First Edition

Book design by Naomi Rosenblatt

When the Himalayan peasant meets the he-bear in his pride,
He shouts to scare the monster, who will often turn aside.
But the she-bear thus accosted rends the peasant tooth and nail
For the female of the species is more deadly than the male.
—*Rudyard Kipling*, "The Female of the Species"

Acknowledgments

Many people gave me invaluable help in researching this book and to them I owe my gratitude. Due to the nature of the subject matter, I am unable to mention some of these people by name.

My special thanks go to Minister Hwang at the Korean embassy in London and to Mr. Park Shinl in Seoul, both of whom gave so much of their time and effort in persuading the authorities to grant me an interview with Miss Kim; to Irene Rado Vajda and Alison Jamieson for the hard work and expertise as fixers, translators, and critics; to Tala Sive for her help and friendship in Jerusalem, and to Eric Silver; to Michel Sontheimer in Hamburg; Frances Heidensohn of Goldsmiths College, London; Oliver James; the staff of the Fawcett Library; and the Council for the Advancement of Arab-British Understanding.

Many friends and far-flung relatives generously put me up when I landed on their doorsteps—particularly Julie and Paul Ratcliffe, who were surprised to learn of my existence as the cousin of an in-law but nonetheless welcomed me into their home in Korea and provided much good tea. Also, special thanks to Linda Faith, who let me stay on numerous trips to Belfast.

I am very grateful as well to the many friends to whom I talked for hours about this book, but who never fell asleep. David Winner gave me much advice, criticism, and support. Thanks also to Lucy Homfray for her help and cheerfulness.

To Giles O'Bryen, my editor at Fourth Estate, for his calm approach in the face of all calamities, and to Annabelle Edwards, the copy editor, who was kind, helpful, and interested.

Above all, my thanks to my husband Paul, who always thought it was a good idea, and who only ever paled slightly when asked to read yet another draft.

Contents

Introduction

Several years ago, for the purposes of a newspaper story, I "joined" a group of animal liberationists, some of whose members were suspected of planting bombs under the cars of vivisectors and scientists. I had assumed that such violent attacks must have been carried out by men. Yet once inside the group I discovered that not only were women members in the majority, they were also, in effect, its leaders. I had read that women usually only played support roles in such groups, probably as girlfriends to the men. However, it quickly became clear that while the men did a lot of talking and planning, it was the women who met up late at night to carry out the actions. They seemed to have more energy and commitment than the men, and were prepared to risk more. I started to wonder whether these were common characteristics of women in movements that espoused violence.

Just before the end of the assignment, I was interviewed by a member of the British Anti-Terrorist Squad who saw fit to warn me, rather darkly, that I was "just the type" to become a terrorist. I asked him what on earth he meant, but he would not tell me. Instead he repeated the warning, saying that he would "hate me to be on the other side of the table" from him.

If I had read some of the material I have during the research of this book, I might have been able to set his mind at rest. For example, I could have checked the quantity of my body hair, and dashed off for an IQ test. Let me explain: many and various are the theories put forward as to why women should be prepared to kill or be killed, and some are downright bizarre. The work of a certain Cesare Lombroso proposes that criminal females are evolutionary throwbacks, displaying more body hair then normal women, and also a lower intelligence. Freud thought aggressive females were trying to be men. Others consider that terrorist women have a chromosome imbalance that makes them more masculine than feminine.

At the time I was innocent of these expert opinions, and the effect of the warning was to increase my fascination for women committed to violence. I am sure this is not what the officer had intended; he had been attempting to debrief me. I had always been interested in how women succeeded in what were considered to be male-dominated environments—possibly because I have spent my working life as a journalist in just such a milieu. Now, after being told that I had something in common with terrorist women, my curiosity grew, and was eventually translated into this book.

The women I have interviewed belong to a wide variety of groups to which the term "terrorist" is often applied. The members of such organizations, we are told, are mad, bad, evil, ruthless; they are animals, subhumans, cowards, beneath contempt. They blow people up in a bar, or on an aircraft, or at the Memorial Day service for the dead. No one is safe, and nothing can protect us because these killers do not care who their victims are; they disrupt our everyday life by casting a shadow of fear on our plans for the future. They care nothing for human life. Their actions defy our understanding; indeed we are led to believe that right-thinking people should not waste time trying to understand them. They do not deserve it. Our reaction to the term "terrorist" is Pavlovian. We know the sorts of brutes they are, and nothing more really needs to be said on the subject. This is one of the reasons why I have tried not to use the term in this book. It is too emotive, too loaded for a book that seeks to understand rather than to condemn.

My purpose is not to blame or exonerate any one particular group or action, but simply to point out that there are value judgments involved in such matters, and that the use of the word "terrorist"— with its commonly implied baggage train of loathing, fear, and condemnation—simply excludes proper judgment of a particularly complex issue. It is just too vague a word to be applied wholesale to such a broad diversity of people and causes. There are the nationalist, freedom-fighting movements: the Irish Republican Army; the Palestinians of the Intifada; ETA, fighting for the Basque homeland. Then there are the political revolutionaries of Europe: the Red Army Faction, successor to the Baader-Meinhof group; the French Action Directe; the Italian Red Brigades—all agitating for an overthrow of societies that they view as corrupt and capitalist, no matter that such societies satisfy the majority of their compatriots. Apart from these two main categories, there are also people who carry out mass murder on the orders of the state: government agents like Kim Hyon Hui, who blew up an aircraft full of passengers on the instructions of the North Korean regime.

Why should someone who is fighting for a nationalist cause be tarred with the same brush as someone who kills to create a society that most citizens do not want? One answer is that they use the same weapon—terror—to achieve their aims. Nationalist movements would not call their actions terrorist, though; they see them as acts of war. Even Europe's most highly organized anti-terrorist squad states quite categorically that there are fundamental differences. The head of the squad, which is based in Wiesbaden, Germany, dismissed the notion that nationalist movements are terrorist: "The IRA and ETA, and others like them, are fighting for their homelands. They are engaged in civil war," he said. They could only be described as terrorists, he continued, when the guerrillas in such movements killed innocent people, thus committing "terrorist acts."

This distinction may seem rather too subtle, but it suggests that those who deal with terrorism on a daily basis are keenly aware that the terminology is a problem. Some governments employ terror. Members of the French Resistance were terrorists until France was liberated, and then they became heroes. Only history, it seems, can decide who is a terrorist, and who is not.

None of the women I interviewed considered themselves to be terrorists—with the exception of Kim Hyon Hui, who is a special case since she was acting on the orders of the North Korean state after a lifetime of brainwashing. Of course, this is hardly surprising. The image most of us have in mind when we hear the word is of a masked, quasi-military figure with cold killer eyes, cradling a Kalashnikov or preparing to detonate a bomb. They must be inhuman, emotionless, else how could they do such things? It is a monstrous image, yet for that reason strangely comforting. These creatures have nothing to do with us. You could spot them a mile off and take the necessary evasive action. It is much more frightening to learn, as I have done, that these "monsters" often look and speak much like the next-door neighbor or the woman behind you in line at the checkout. If they are not obviously mad, bad, and hairy, if they do not have bloodshot eyes and do not much like talking about killing people, then it is harder to work out what motivates them. In attempting to understand first and judge second, one runs the risk of being accused of harboring sympathies for terrorists; but perhaps it is better to be accused of that than to cower in terror at a false image of a monster that does not exist.

What of the image of women in such groups? It seems that the majority of those who commit atrocities for a cause are men: the notorious "Carlos" (actually, Ilich Ramirez Sanchez), a Venezuelan mercenary who has worked for the Palestinians and for Colonel Quaddafi; the wicked Hindawi, who waved his pregnant girlfriend off an El Al flight with the suitcase of wedding clothes he had given her packed with explosives; the dreaded Abu Nidal group, led by a man described by the intelligence service as "the most dangerous terrorist" in existence.

However, there is also a sizable number of women (in some cases over 50 percent of the membership) in these organizations, and their very presence poses another problem for us. Men are traditionally seen as having a certain familiarity with violence—whether as defenders or aggressors, they are expected to know how to fight. Women, by contrast, are associated with nurturing and caring, and are still often revered by society as Madonna figures. They are the protectors and givers of life, rather than the destroyers. If the male members of a movement committed to violence are seen as mad, bad, and evil, how much more then are the females? In taking up arms they commit a double atrocity: using violence, and in the process destroying our safe, traditional view of women.

"Shoot the women first" was reputedly an instruction given to recruits to West Germany's armed anti-terrorist squad, and also the advice offered by Interpol to other European squads. I have spoken to several members of these organizations, and though none of them would confirm that they ever had been given such an instruction, they considered it to be a damn good piece of advice. Herr Christian Lochte, a director of Germany's intelligence-gathering network on subversives (their equivalent of the British MI5 or the American FBI), has had over twenty years experience in studying the political revolutionaries who have murdered and bombed in his country. He commented: "For anyone who loves his life, it is a very clever idea to shoot the women first. From my experience, women terrorists have much stronger characters, more power, more energy. There are some examples where men waited a moment before they fired, and women shot at once. This is a general phenomenon with terrorists."

So, are women terrorists more dangerous than men, more ruthless, able to shoot without forethought or hesitation? I asked the British Anti-Terrorist Squad if they would like to comment on the differences—if any—in the motivations and actions of women and men. The response was hardly enlightening. A Scotland Yard press officer informed me that the squad had nothing to say beyond that male and female terrorists were similar in all respects, the sole difference being that women would try to use their "feminine wiles" on the male officers once they were apprehended.

I looked elsewhere for insight into why women should represent a more urgent target than their male counterparts. I read the numerous articles that have been written about the actions of such women and found that in the main they concentrated on asking—chiefly in terms of horror and outrage—"How could a woman do this?" The answer, if one was reading the popular press, seemed to be that they were all lesbians or, if not quite that, then feminists gone mad.

Look at the meal that was made of Astrid Proll's sexuality when she was arrested in London in 1978. The *Daily Mail*, among others, quoted one of her male roommates. "I loved her a lot, but [she] . . . was more interested in girls." A girlfriend of Proll's called Karen was referred to along with the fact that the couple "sometimes stayed the night in her room," and that they seemed "very happy together." The *Daily Express* was less coy: "People who worked with her in London said she was a woman's libber and had no boyfriends. In fact she was a self-confessed lesbian." The *Sunday Mirror*, in an article headed THE SEXY SECRETS OF A TERROR GIRL, revealed: "Friends told of her lesbian loves, and her delight at being a mechanic." The *Daily Telegraph* joined in: "When she first appeared in the area . . . it was thought she was a man."

Dr. Rose Dugdale received similar treatment when arrested for stealing oil paintings to fund the IRA. Newspapers described her masculine appearance, homing in on the fact that she wore no makeup and preferred men's clothing. The *Daily Mail* even asked, "Is Rose Dugdale a man?" Journalists were rather taken by surprise when she had a baby in prison.

So what, one may ask, if these women were lesbians? How does this shed any light on their decision to join groups that feel justified in the use of violence? The answer, given by the media, seems to be that because they were really lesbians they were not "proper" women at all. After all, normal women just did not do this sort of thing. This view was backed up by a German Interior Ministry official when he commented on the number of women in the Baader-Meinhof gang. He said there was "something irrational about the whole thing" and referred to the fact that "so many girls are involved." He cautiously suggested, "This could be one of the excesses of women's lib."

Other theories put forward by the media include the suggestions that these women are so very ugly that the only way they can catch men's attention is by becoming killers. Or alternatively, they are so pretty and gullible that they have been seduced into the web of terrorism by the sexual enchantment of men like Carlos. Even in articles that take a more serious stance, there is hardly more information: women who carried out acts of violence were rebels, and sometimes they proved more ruthless than men. No one seemed to go any further than that and ask why. It seemed enough to express incredulity, and to press home the point to the newspaper-reading public that these women were all either hideous misfits or cute little things who had fallen for the wrong guy.

Perhaps it is not surprising that women who engage in violence for political purposes should be treated in such a manner. The number of women who commit violent crime is tiny in proportion to the number of men. Statistics issued by the Home Office in Britain for 1989 show that 179 men were found guilty of murder, compared to 10 women; for attempted murder—60 men and 5 women; for threat or conspiracy to commit murder—482 men and 32 women; for the crime of manslaughter—232 men were convicted, 34 women. Of all the 55,600 people who committed "violent offenses against the person," just 4,400 were women. In nearly every category of serious crime, women were in a minority—the only exception to this being the crimes of infanticide (three women were found guilty of this, but no men) and of cruelty to or neglect of children—107 women compared to 105 men.

The numbers from the United States also show a huge gap between the number of crimes commited by women and the number commited by men. According to statistics released by the Federal Bureau of Investigation, 315,082 men were arrested for and charged with violent crimes in 1989, compared with 38,104 women. In that same year, of the total number of convicts sentenced to state and federal prison terms, 643,555 were men and 37,254 were women.

On average, criminologists estimate that of all the violent crimes committed just 6 percent are carried out by women. The majority of these women have harmed their own children, mostly those under the age of four. The number of women, therefore, who carry out violent crimes does seem to be small. Thus when one of them comes to the attention of the media—by being arrested, or shot, or appearing in court—everyone gets overexcited and there is mass coverage. So long as the woman's motives accord with the traditional view and can be described as "passionate" in some way or another, all is well. The one thing that is not deemed necessary, however, is to consider the possibility of political motives. It is much more interesting to question their sexuality, point out their ugliness or beauty, and discuss the disastrous relationship with a man that led them into trouble in the first place.

Beyond this, scant effort is made to understand why women should become violent. In the two areas where women outnumber men, infanticide and cruelty to children, there is often a certain amount of sympathy for the woman. We read that she is the victim of poverty, isolation, frustration, stuck at home with the child all day. Her anger boils over, and in most cases she is thoroughly horrified by what she has done to her child. But can there be any understanding or pity for a woman who takes her gun and shoots an industrialist in the head before escaping on her motorbike?

It seems that there are only a very limited number of instances in which society can understand a woman being violent. When a woman fights off an aggressor or a rapist, she is congratulated, usually in terms that suggest she is "a brave little woman." If her children are threatened she is more or less expected to fight back, along the lines of a lioness and her cubs. After years of being beaten by her husband, a woman may finally hit back, sometimes to the extent of killing him. There are also occasions when a woman suffering from either premenstrual tension or postnatal depression can be excused her violence on the grounds that her peculiarly female condition has rendered her insane.

In times of war, when the homeland is threatened, women are permitted to enter the arena of violence—up to a point. In the Second World War, Britain called up all single women between the ages of eighteen and thirty, though they were not required to fight at the front or drop bombs on Dresden. Of course, many thousands of women did kill as members of the European resistance movements, and they were honored for their actions. But as soon as the war was over they were glad, we are led to believe, to go back to their "natural" roles. It was a necessary evil, one Italian partisan fighter explained, done for the sake of the family. "They say that women have babies and so don't kill. . . . At that time it was clear that each Nazi I killed, each bomb I helped to explode, shortened the length of the war and saved the lives of all women and children." But men remain far from happy about them taking part in frontline action. In 1991, over 30,000 American women soldiers participated in the war against Iraq, but against the wishes of many of their menfolk. The Israeli Army, which once put women soldiers on the frontline, eventually had to reverse its policy partly because the men got so upset when a woman was injured or killed.

Many of the women interviewed in this book believe themselves to be at war, fighting for their homelands. The trouble is, though, that they are not on the winning side, at least not yet. Part of the price they therefore have to pay is being seen as monsters, or fools, or deviants—who lack even the justification of being male and therefore predisposed to the use of force to achieve their ends.

Although they may fail to evoke even basic understanding, women prepared to use violence and risk death for their ends do often arouse a degree of awe. The teenage girls who became suicide-bombers in Lebanon during the eighties are a case in point. Aged between seventeen and nineteen, many were filmed before setting out on their missions to blow themselves up along with their targets. On the videos that were released, they wore makeup and smiled for the cameras—and they sent shock waves into family living rooms around the world. In their Western clothes, they looked just like ordinary kids; and yet they were about to kill, and die themselves, in the most horrifying circumstances. Experts opined that they had been brainwashed or drugged; these suggestions were quickly taken up by the media. Anything rather than believe that these girls were sane, deeply committed, and acting of their own free will. Whatever the truth, the image of these pretty, smiling teenagers, intent on the kind of violence that few would even contemplate, was extraordinarily potent.

There is no doubt that a certain glamour surrounds the world of the freedom fighter, the revolutionary, the terrorist. There is something attractive about someone who scorns all the norms of society and risks her life in a seemingly hopeless cause because she believes so passionately in its justness. Such figures appeal to the rebel in all of us—just because they are dangerous, have stepped out of bounds. According to novels and films, the male revolutionary has great sexual appetites and powers, and women are irresistibly drawn to him. Is the same true of female revolutionaries? Do they enjoy a certain status that other women, perhaps secretly, long to achieve? Do men lust after them? Certainly, some of the most powerful photographs of revolutionaries are of women: Patty Hearst with her gun at a bank raid, standing resolute in front of the revolutionary flag; Leila Khaled, her head demurely covered, gripping the hard steel of her Kalashnikov; Ulrike Meinhof, hands clasped behind her head in a posture of openness and defiance—a picture made into a poster that adorned students' rooms throughout Europe in the seventies. "You must understand," Astrid Proll told me, "that then the most fantastic thing in the world was not to be a rock star but a revolutionary."

Such images certainly assisted in breaking down the view that women are weak creatures who need men to protect them from harm. The fact that they also seemed to contain a dangerous sexual element makes the threat to social taboos doubly disturbing. Not only do such women take on a masculine role—aggressive, predatory, political—they also appear to become more attractive as women by doing so. The idea that terrorists—rather than film stars—might thus become role models for teenage girls rocked society's view of women as well as of itself. This was the enemy storming the ramparts on the one hand and slipping in the back door on the other.

The glamorization of male revolutionaries is nothing new—from Robin Hood to Che Guevara, the process has proved unstoppable. In the case of their female counterparts, the phenomenon appears to be relatively new. So too is society's standard response: that such women have been seduced into committing acts of violence by their men. This idea conveniently serves all ends: the men are ultimately responsible for the violence; the women, victims of their own weakness, play a subordinate role; and the women's real motive is nothing more or less than passion—here associated with weakness rather than a strength: the women are seen as overly emotional rather than fiercely committed.

Some women, of course, have been duped into carrying out terrorist acts: Ann Murphy, the pregnant girlfriend of Hindawi, was entirely unaware that the suitcase she was carrying was jammed with explosives; Carlos is notorious for using his girlfriends in Paris as providers of safe houses and as messenger girls. But listening to the British Anti-Terrorist Squad officer I spoke to referring to a woman animal liberationist who had been jailed as "that poor little girl" who had been tricked into taking violent action by the male leader of the group, and hearing a Home Office psychiatrist whose clients are serving prison sentences for bombing and murder blithely stating, "Of course, most of them are there because of their men," I began to wonder if this could be so. It seemed too pat, too easy.

Going beyond the question of motivation, theories about the effect of women members on violent organizations seem also to support a traditional view of the female role. According to Professor J. K. Zawodny, women incite men to violence. In an article entitled "Internal Catalysts of Violence Within Terrorist Movements," he argues that because women are in the minority in most of these movements, the men will try to "outdo" each other as a way of gaining a woman's admiration. In the paper "Profile of a Terrorist," Charles A. Russell and Captain Bowman H. Miller suggest that the danger of "female terrorists" is that, "posing as wives and mothers," they can enter restricted areas without arousing suspicion and gather intelligence for their male comrades. Again, the woman is seen as a basically passive adjunct to a male-oriented organization.

Such theories are all interesting, and all probably contain elements of truth. But I felt that they were at best inadequate, at worst dangerously ignorant. What makes a woman step so dramatically outside her supposed role? And having taken this step, is it true that she becomes especially dangerous? I realized that the only way to find out was to talk to these women myself.

It has been an extraordinary learning experience, and one that has destroyed many preconceptions that I had. When I first started to read about these women, I wondered what I had got myself into. I came across an account of the careers of two leading women members of the French revolutionary group, Action Directe. They were considered to have been responsible for the brutal killing of a Renault factory manager outside his front door. They shot him at point-blank range. When he was lying on the ground, dying, one of the women administered the coup de grace—a bullet in his eye. "Is that it?" her companion asked. "Yes, for sure," she replied.

When one of them was arrested she was with her boyfriend. He gave in without a struggle. She pulled out two guns and blasted away at the police, screaming as she did so, "I am Action Directe!"

Soon after, I read about a woman known as The Red Queen of Terror, Fusako Shigenobu, the leader of the Japanese Red Army. She apparently believes that most revolutionary groups are not violent enough. She has a particularly unpleasant way of handling those army members who deviate from the revolutionary code: she is reputed to have had fourteen killed for, among other things, wearing makeup after she told them not to.

It was not really surprising, therefore, that I expected at least some of the women I talked to to be demonstrably evil. Surely I would feel the hairs (not many) on the back of my neck rising as I sat next to them? This did not happen. The vast majority of the people I met seemed to be extremely ordinary. They were married, or had boyfriends, or were gay; they loved their children; they were shy or gregarious, and on the whole welcoming. In all, they bore a remarkable similarity to the rest of the female species. They were not poring over the latest instructions for making a bomb, or uttering banshee shrieks of delight that they had just killed six at the supermarket. They sat quietly in bars, or relaxed at home with their children, or cooked me meals. After the first few interviews, I stopped looking for their horns. That is not to say that none of them appeared to be frightening or chilling, just that the majority were disturbingly normal.

I swiftly discovered that if you ask a person who is, or was, a member of a movement that endorses violence why they killed or terrorized, you get the obvious answer: "To get the Brits out"; "To establish our homeland"; "To bring about the revolution." I had therefore to attempt to separate the women from their wars by asking about their emotions, their feelings about violence. Did they think that they had greater commitment to their cause, were capable of being more ruthless and determined than men? Were they more likely to shoot an enemy than drop their weapon? I wanted to know how they saw themselves and how their male comrades viewed them. I wanted to find out why the less violent sex is regarded by anti-terrorist squads as the more lethal.

Shoot the Women First

Chapter 1

AMONG THE WOMEN OF ETA

"We have so much more to lose."

A labyrinth of passages and dark, cobbled alleyways makes up the old town of Bilbao. It is here, in neon-lighted bars and in the shadows of high and ancient buildings that the heart of ETA, Europe's most venerable urban guerrilla movement, beats strongest. Its lifeblood is the young people who throng the old quarter; its pulse is the drumbeat and the haunting flute of the three slow-stepping musicians, two men and a girl, on their march of the streets.

Red graffiti scars the walls of the fifteenth-century church: the letters of ETA, the proclamation CIVIL GUARD, MURDERERS!, with the promise of vengeance underneath. On one wall is scrawled the story of a woman called Maite, a comrade killed by the police; inside a nearby bar a rough pen-and-ink drawing hangs of another woman of the same name, similarly killed.

Standing in this desperately packed bar it is necessary to shout, but the women I am with are relaxed; they are among friends. Everyone is young, everyone has a friend who is involved in the struggle for the Basque homeland in one form or another, and the women I am speaking with have that special camaraderie born of joint suffering.

Alazne's was the saddest face I had ever seen. She could have been pretty, with startling blue-green eyes and fair hair, but she looked utterly caved in as if she were waiting for the next punch. It was not for several hours that her air of total defeat was explained. Amaia, big and bouncy, with a ready answer for any and all questions, was entirely different. She was the Basque answer to Roseanne Barr. With very little preamble, and with scant attention to the other customers, she launched into her story: "I was detained for being a member of an armed band—somebody else gave me away."

Both Alazne and Amaia had been arrested and tortured and had broken in the end. One swiftly learned that there was no blame attached to eventually blurting out information; indeed, it was entirely understandable: "With the methods they use, everyone breaks." Txikia, four feet eight inches tall, weighing ninety-one pounds, had been tied hand and foot to a beam and then beaten. She had hung like a monkey staring at the ceiling splattered with the blood of previous detainees.

Their torturers were members of the Spanish police force—a fact recorded in Amnesty International reports. The police and the Spanish Civil Guard are ETA's chief targets, and ETA commandos are taught at an early stage of their involvement the kinds of torture they should expect if caught. Several ETA personnel have died in detention; others, it is claimed, have been targets of GAL (the Anti-Terrorist Liberation Group). GAL is allegedly made up of mercenaries, soldiers, and police and has threatened to kill one Basque activist for every ETA victim.

In 1990 it was revealed that GAL has direct links with the Spanish Ministry of the Interior, and two police officers were charged with the attempted murder of five Basque refugees living in France. Numerous cases were cited by the ETA women of comrades—male and female—being found dead under mysterious circumstances, such as the couple whose bodies were found at the foot of a ravine in June 1990. A suicide pact, said the police. It only emerged later that the man, who had supposedly shot his girlfriend in the back of the head before jumping to his death, had died by drowning. Another man was found dead by the roadside—with burned feet. All were said to be the work of GAL or overzealous police interrogators. GAL also operates a policy of "determent"—a woman student activist had the letters ETA carved into her face.

ETA stands for Euskadi Ta Askatasuna ("Homeland and Freedom") and was set up in the late fifties to combat repression under Franco. The dictator had banned the Basque language and culture, partly to punish the Basques for fighting on the Republican side during the Civil War, and partly to enforce his dream of a united Spain. Hundreds of ETA personnel and their supporters were imprisoned and tortured, but its key leaders fled to southern France and set up training camps. From there ETA units were sent over the border to attack targets in the Basque country and in the rest of Spain. A degree of sympathy among the French authorities for a people who had fought fascism allowed the movement to flourish.

In 1975, when Franco died, the Basque population hoped that they would finally be allowed independence, but although their language and some cultural traditions were reinstated, the majority of the population felt that democracy had failed them. In 1979 the Basque country was granted a degree of autonomy, including a local parliament, but to ETA this was simply seen as a barrier to full independence from Spain.

Today, ETA continues to carry out dozens of actions a year. Although politicians, police, and the Civil Guard are its main targets, it has also expanded its actions into ecological and moral fields. Industries perceived as threatening the environment are attacked, cinemas showing sex films are bombed, and drug dealers are knee-capped or killed. Responsibility for the actions is claimed every month in ETA communiqués, which are then published in the Basque newspaper, *Egin*. The language of the communiqués is flowery and terribly polite; occasionally deeply remorseful. For example, on October 9, 1989, one reads: "We claim responsibility for the failed action against a member of the Spanish police in Basauri, following the placing of an explosive charge under his car.

"We very much deplore the accidental injuries involuntarily caused to his neighbor, Carmuelo Alonso Lopez, and we wish his prompt and complete recovery."

In the same month ETA killed two policemen; placed bombs in factories producing the French cars, Peugeot, Citröen, and Renault; and failed to assassinate the Spanish consul in Rotterdam, who was targeted because the Dutch had extradited four "Basque political refugees" to Spain.

They also bombed the offices of a company constructing a motorway through the Basque region and sent a letter bomb to the director of Public Works, who they claimed had ignored public feeling in going ahead with the project. There is a long polemic attached to this last action, urging the government and the construction company to take notice of public disquiet, including the statement that "ETA . . . expresses its fervent wish to avoid by all means any form of painful outcome." The missive ends more threateningly: "A negative response will, unfortunately, and very much to our regret, newly aggravate the situation created after the start of the works on the present project. We trust that prudence and good sense will prevail for the good of our people." "Otherwise," it might have added, "you will be dead."

In 1990 there was a spate of ETA letter bombs, but several were opened by postal workers or employees of the intended victims. When Pilar Fernandez opened a letter for a prison official and received serious injuries, ETA apologized to her, but added: "With the intention of avoiding a repetition of serious occurrences of this nature, we insist once more that no one open correspondence or parcels not addressed to them personally."

More baldly, another communiqué claims the responsibility for killing a woman judge: "Execution of the state prosecutor, Carmen Tagle, one of the most important representatives of the National Court, which had become the spearhead of direct repression of numerous patriots and revolutionaries from the Basque country as well as from the rest of Spain." ETA has also in the past conducted a campaign of bombing vacation resorts, although the explosives used were designed to frighten rather than kill.

The organization funds itself in a variety of ways: armed robbery, kidnapping, extortion, and donations from sympathizers, including a number of Basque priests, who have traditionally supported ETA's goals, although more recently many have come to deplore the escalating campaign of violence.

Over the years, ETA has evolved from a group seeking a social-democratic Basque homeland, into a Marxist-Leninist one. This change, and others including arguments over the use of violence, has resulted in much splitting and factionalizing, and now there is only one "armed spearhead," called ETA-m or "Milis." Their motto is allegedly "Actions unite; words divide." ETA is regarded by police forces throughout Europe as one of the most highly trained and organized terrorist groups.

Infiltration by the police has caused the organization to institute a system of "sleeping commandos." These men and women lead apparently normal lives, with regular jobs, but at the same time are being trained for specific actions. Often the commandos are unaware of each other's identities and receive their instructions in code from an unknown source. Once their action has been carried out the commandos immediately resume their everyday lives.

ETA, like the IRA and its political wing, Sinn Fein, has Herri Batasuna ("Popular Unity"), and during the most recent elections for the Basque parliament in October 1990 they retained their 1986 figure of thirteen seats out of seventy-five, coming in third out of the eight parties. These figures give the lie to some Spanish press reports that the Herri Batasuna party (which alone out of all the political parties in the Basque country refused to sign a pact condemning violence in 1988) was losing grass-roots support.

I witnessed the extent of local support not just for the political wing, but for ETA itself, shortly before the elections in 1990. The organizers had told me there would be a march of 10,000–15,000 people through the streets of Bilbao. It was estimated that the actual turnout was closer to 50,000, and the marchers ranged in age from toddlers to old ladies. It was like an outdoor mass; sparklers were lit as wave upon wave of demonstrators surged through the city center; elegant, middle-aged women rubbing shoulders with students, businessmen, and children, all chanting, "ETA, ETA, Liberty."

Initially, there was a great deal of nervousness and suspicion in granting me interviews with ETA women. The elections were coming up, and an ETA leader and ten commandos had just been arrested. A week before I arrived, 500 pounds of explosives, bomb-making equipment, and weapons were seized in a cave. I might have been an infiltrator or a police informer and no one in the movement wanted to accept the responsibility for trusting me. Eventually the problem was solved by a woman in Belfast I had met through Sinn Fein, who vouchsafed for me being a journalist.

My initial briefing was given by two sisters, Begona, a nurse, and Yolanda, an economist, both in their late twenties. Begona worked for Egizan (literally in Basque, "Act Woman!") a feminist movement affiliated with ETA's political wing; her younger sister worked for Herri Batasuna. They explained that Herri Batasuna, and an amnesty group seeking release for ETA prisoners, were legal organizations. Others, like Egizan, for example, were illegal because they demanded a homeland for Basques. ETA personnel may be members of any of these groups.

Yolanda was bright and bitter. "We are allowed to speak the Basque language, but we cannot study it at all levels. For instance, at university there are very few subjects you can study in Basque, very few university level books in the language, and hardly any teachers are taught their subjects in Basque. Besides, learning is not free; you must pay, so some people cannot learn it.

"We are told that the language is expanding rapidly because we are allowed to have our own Basque television station. This station has two channels, but one of them is in Spanish and the other one frequently advertises in Spanish.

"There are about two and a half million Basques here, yet we have three police forces—the Civil Guard, the national police, and the Ertzantza (Basque police). When they first set up Ertzantza, we were told it would replace the other forces, but that has not happened, so we have lots of police. We have four governments: the Basque government for three of the Basque provinces; the government of Navarre for the fourth; then there is the Spanish government, which is really the one in charge; and the French government for the quarter million Basques living there."

Although both sisters fully supported ETA's actions, they denied that they personally knew any active ETA women, which is not surprising as that knowledge could result in a prison sentence. Yolanda summed it up: "I don't know who is in ETA and I don't want to know."

Occasionally the sisters broke into a language that left the interpreter openmouthed. It was Basque, and bore no relation to Spanish or French. They discussed a question about the formation of ETA cells in their own language before returning to Spanish.

"They have had to get more and more complex. Occasionally a cell is formed where people live together, but at other times no one knows each other. They have taken a lot of care because of infiltrators and they have done very well.

"ETA decides everything by committee before taking an action. In summer they put the railway network under siege, by blowing up sections all over the state in order to get maximum attention. It is the only way—the Spanish government only understands the fighting language."

Begona was the first sister to have become politically active within the Basque separatist movement, but she laughed when it was suggested that she had influenced Yolanda to join. Her younger sister, she said, had a mind of her own. More seriously, she replied, that yes, their parents were very worried about them. "They have been afraid for a long time. They think what we are doing is very dangerous and they are frightened of the police."

She explained that although the Herri Batasuna party had four MPs who were entitled to sit in the Spanish parliament, all of them practiced abstentionism as a matter of principle. Even being a duly elected member of Parliament does not, it seems, protect one from the attentions of GAL. Begona spoke of one MP, who had been murdered on the way to Madrid to be sworn in—the only occasion when Herri Batasuna MPs will attend the Spanish parliament.

"At first it appeared that he had been murdered by two right-wing police officers, but at the trial it came out that one was not right wing at all. We believe he was murdered on the authority of the government. He was killed on the anniversary of the death of Franco, a very right-wing anniversary when something always happens."

Neither sister could even hazard a guess at how many ETA commandos were currently operating, or what percentage of them were women. However, women make up about 10 percent of imprisoned ETA members, so that would be a guide, they suggested. Although they both insisted, as did every Basque activist, that ETA was only one part of the national struggle for independence, it was obvious that they, and everyone else, regarded the armed group as an elite.

Nowhere was this clearer than in Begona's account of the setting up of Egizan, which had only occurred in 1988—late, one might think for the emergence of a feminist group in a revolutionary struggle. Begona explained that after years of various women experimenting, and failing, with a feminist movement in the Basque nationalist organization, it had been ETA which had taken decisive action.

"In 1980, there had been a women's movement, but it had failed due to political arguments. There were disagreements on how women's problems were viewed; some people thought that the very notion of women having their own problems was too bourgeois.

"It was ETA that insisted that there should be a women's organization set up because they saw that women did have special problems, not inside the movement, but in society—and it is they who have done most to make sure Egizan actually happened. ETA has a great ability for political analysis, and is very articulate—more than any of the other groups.

"Now we have five hundred members and we shall be going out into the villages with our message. All the women in Egizan have a very highly developed political awareness but I do not think any of them belong to ETA, although some could belong to both."

I asked why ETA had been able to sort out the confusion about how to deal with women's problems. Was it because there were so many women in leading roles within the organization? Begona, who has never been militant, did not know, but other former women commandos agreed that, yes, that was the reason.

It was surprising news—I had nearly omitted ETA from this book because of an article I had read by Robert P. Clark, entitled "Patterns in the Life of ETA Members." He stated that ETA strongly opposed women's participation because "their place is in the home" and "they talk too much, especially to their parish priests." I asked all the Basque separatist women I interviewed to comment on this quotation, and the responses were identical— fury, and denial. There have always been women commandos and operators in ETA, I was informed sharply. To prove the point, in the course of twenty-four hours I met four.

Alazne and Amaia had both been commandos; Alazne with an extreme anarchist offshoot of ETA called the Autonomous Anti-Capitalist Commando and Amaia with ETA-m. The sad Alazne had been imprisoned for four years, and the gregarious Amaia for five. Each had been convicted of membership in terrorist groups; there had been no evidence extracted from them, even under torture, to charge them with anything else. Yet, within the first hour of meeting, sitting in a crowded café in central Bilbao, they talked freely about the sort of actions they had been involved in. They only asked that their names should be changed, a request I complied with. It showed an enormous degree of trust, and I felt almost protective toward them.

Both had been "sleeping commandos": Amaia working as an assistant in a bakery; Alazne for the tax department of a village council. Alazne, who was thirty-three but looked far older, spoke quietly with her eyes down.

"I come from a village near San Sebastian that is ninety percent Basque-speaking, but that was not the reason that I joined the commando unit. The village was hardly a center of political knowledge or activity, and my parents certainly did not have any influence on what I eventually did. I became aware of injustices and the repression of the Basque people when I was a teenager, but it was not until I was twenty-four or twenty-five that I joined the movement. I got involved because a man I knew was a member."

This appeared to lend credence to the most commonly held view that women get "mixed up" in such movements through relationships with men, usually their boyfriends. I asked if many ETA women had become involved in armed action via this route. The response was immediate and explosive.

Alazne laughed and shook her head; Amaia launched into a diatribe for several minutes until the interpreter held up her hand. Roughly, and without the expletives: "absolute rubbish," she translated.

Alazne went on. "The man I referred to was just a friend. He participated in an action that I approved of and because I knew him, I was able to get into the group." Yes, she had carried out numerous actions, "as a result of which people had been killed," she admitted carefully. No, she did not believe that women in armed groups felt they had to prove anything to men. Amaia, who was still simmering, joined in: "If women decide to do an action, they will do it for themselves! They don't have to prove anything to men."

Amaia took over the conversation, something she was apt to do: "ETA is the vanguard of our revolution. If the revolution plans to change society, it means that the vanguard has to change its own attitudes towards women in the first place. You can hardly change society without changing the very macho attitudes that men have, and even women too. Women can be equally 'machista' in supporting the supremacy of men. In that way they pass on the violence towards women that is at the heart of macho men. The revolution, if you like, starts at home."

But she also showed some sympathy toward women who were dependent on men. "Here, for instance, a lot of women depend on men economically and so there must be cases where women are drawn into the armed struggle through their men. But certainly that was not what happened with us.

"There are fewer military women in ETA because women are only just beginning to come out into the street. It is part of the emancipation process. Men are used to being seen as strong and macho and women are expected to follow them—both men and women are still indoctrinated. In ordinary life, in work, women perhaps have to be much better than men just to show they are equal to them. But in revolutionary groups, the basic understanding is that we are equal."

One wondered whether some of the anger and frustration that had led Amaia to strike out violently against authority was rooted in her society's acceptance of macho violence against women—with the women themselves passing on this acceptance from one generation to the next. She had seemed extremely angry at the notion that ETA men could influence their female comrades in any way at all—either in drawing them into the group, or in making the women guerrillas feel they had to prove themselves to the men. ETA is, after all, like many armed sections of nationalist movements, viewed as the elite; and if men held the reins of power at such a level, the group would simply be reflecting the society they are fighting against. In such a society where women seem powerless to break the chain of violence against themselves, being a commando is certainly one way of being pretty powerful.

Amaia was eighteen when she joined the cell of ETA-m; before that she had participated in Basque demonstrations. "I was born in Bilbao and grew up here, so I became aware of the movement when I was very young. When I was around fourteen years old I began to meet new friends and we went to demos and events. We all wanted to do something more than just accept the treatment we got.

"When I became a commando, I lived a sort of double life. I lived here with friends and worked in the bakery as an assistant. But at the same time I was a member of ETA-m and carried out five or six actions over three years. My targets were mainly the police, the Civil Guard, and I also took part in bank raids to obtain funds for the group.

"Usually you don't go and live with others in a house to prepare an action. You would just maintain contact with someone who would occasionally tell you that you were needed to do something. Every now and again a supporter would give up a house for a set period of time for a group to live together. But mainly it worked this way: a message would come in that I was needed for an action. If it happened during working hours, I would say that I had to rush off to the doctor. Afterwards I would bring in a medical certificate."

I imagined Amaia, rather a portly figure, about to pop her tray of scones into the oven when the message arrived. It seemed comical, and yet the message would presumably have ordered her involvement in an act of murder or robbery.

"Anyway, even though I worked, I had the evenings free—I was available from seven P.M. till one A.M.—and of course there were the weekends as well. And between each action there would be big gaps of several months. I did everything from gathering information on targets, to carrying a gun, doing armed robbery, and planting bombs . . ."

She was blasé as she recounted the depth of her involvement, as if she were reeling off items on a shopping list. So, she was responsible for killing people? Oh no, she insisted, she had never directly killed anyone. I did a double take and asked her about the bombs she had just mentioned. How did she feel when she heard that her bombs had been "successful"?

"Satisfaction," she shot straight back. "The bastards, they deserved it. Yes, I planted bombs that killed people." I wondered whether she was as confused as I was by her two different answers in so short a space of time. She appeared to be proud of killing, and she had no remorse. Was she as hardened a killer as she appeared? I felt that she was blocking the truth out, almost playing the part of the merciless guerrilla. I asked whether she had ever looked into the terrified eyes of one of her targets.

Amaia's response was much slower than her normal, quick-fire delivery. "No, I have never looked someone in the face then shot them. I imagine if you had to go up to someone and shoot them dead, that would be difficult, that would be much harder than just leaving a bomb." She trailed off, then regained some of her revolutionary poise: "If you are a commando you accept that it might happen—that you will be asked to kill. There is satisfaction in belonging to such a group. It must happen, the violence is necessary for the struggle, and you feel you are doing something."

She had skated away from the thin ice, but she was still disturbed. How did she feel about killing people with that bomb? The question appeared to pierce the defenses she had put up around her emotions; it was almost as if, extraordinary as it may seem, she had never before addressed herself to the consequences of her actions. Her mood suddenly swung from one of bravado to despondency. She buried her head in her arms. For a few seconds there was silence, then she looked up, almost beseechingly.

"Oh, God, this is getting hard," she groaned. "Look, we hadn't prepared ourselves for this interview; we didn't know what sort of questions were going to be asked." They had to go now, she added, the demonstration was about to begin, but they would come back later.

I almost did not expect to see Amaia and Alazne again, but out of the night and the throng of demonstrators they appeared, smiling and waving. A third woman, Gloria, who had been found by Egizan in the intervening hours, joined us. We walked through the labyrinth to a "quiet" bar—one where you had to keep your voice only at a raised pitch, rather than a shout. On the way, Gloria explained that she had not been a commando, but she had been sentenced to fourteen months in prison for working for ETA's radio station. She had met Alazne and Amaia while serving her sentence and between all three of them was that special bond of former prisoners. Gloria was thirty-three and seemed sensible and thoughtful; she was also, as was to be demonstrated, extremely tough.

Alazne and Amaia seemed fortified and ready for whatever questions I might throw at them, but they could not get a word in. How, I asked, did they cope with feelings of guilt for their actions?

The quiet Gloria erupted: "There is no need for anyone to feel guilt when they participate in revolutionary action—no need at all. It is not a personal thing. There is no personal guilt; there is no place for individual guilt in revolutionary violence. Violence is necessary for the struggle, and if anyone feels guilt, it is for themselves to deal with. The responsibility for killing is the movement's."

These were hard words. In the struggle for a Basque homeland, violence is justifiable and no one who kills need bother about it. It was interesting that Amaia and Alazne, who had killed, now seemed prepared to explain how they coped with their emotions while Gloria, who had not, had all the propaganda off pat. More than that, she was doing her best to stop the other two from talking. Even Amaia had grown silent and was nodding respectfully at the rhetoric, as if it provided all the answers to questions that confused her. It became obvious that unless the intransigent Gloria gave the word, precious few would be uttered by the commandos.

Throwing caution to the wind, I quoted Mr. Clark and his belief, based on an interview with an ETA man, that women talked too much to have any useful role in ETA. Amaia appeared to be suffering from an apopletic fit; Alazne's dead eyes blazed and Gloria gawped. When the storm died down, the interpreter translated: "They are fucking furious at the idea and want to know who said it. They say it must have been a male chauvinist, or someone playing a joke on the author." Gloria seemed to have decided that rather than let me continue under any misapprehension, Amaia and Alazne should speak.

Alazne's story was horrifying and the reasons for her immense sadness became all too clear. After two years with her commando unit, during which time she had been responsible for some killings ("But I did not shoot anyone face to face"), she was arrested: "I was parking the car when the police got me. It wasn't that someone had given me away; it was the car. It had been traced to the organization. The two policemen asked for my ID, then told me to get out of the car. I was taken to the police station where they tied me to a table, so that my back was hanging over the edge. Every time I tried to lift myself up—lying in that position is extremely painful—they hit me.

"They brought in a vat of water and pushed my head into it so that I nearly drowned. They did it again and again; they wanted names, names of my comrades. After three days of torture, of incredible pain, they forced me to telephone my home and tell my friends I was well and staying with someone, so that they would not worry and would not alert anyone that I had disappeared. They also made me phone work and tell them I was fine, and make up an excuse about my absence. I knew then that nobody knew where I was, and no one would suspect anything, which was very frightening. It was as if I had disappeared, and the interrogators kept telling me that they could make me disappear—they had done it before to many comrades and they could do it again.

"They put a plastic bag over my head to the point of suffocation. And they threatened my family. The things they said and did were really unbelievable.

"I had to break, and I did. The police knew that I had comrades who were hiding in France and who were due to come into Spain to carry out operations. They were aware that I knew they were coming so they made me call them and say it was OK to come. They came by boat, and when they were near the shore, the police ambushed them. They put on searchlights and killed all of them.

"There were five people in the boat, all men. Two died instantly and three jumped overboard. Two more died in the water, but the third survived and is now in prison. The fact that I set up the ambush is the most difficult thing for me to live with."

She took a deep breath before continuing: "I did more than set it up; the police took me with them to the ambush because I had to give the signal to the men in the boat; otherwise they would not have approached the beach. My hands and feet were tied by a piece of rope and a policeman held the end of it. As soon as I had given the signal, he pulled me down. I had only known one of the men. I had worked with him before, but the others were all my comrades. I lay on the ground and I heard the shots. I have to live with that."

She had told her story unemotionally, but in the dim light of the bar her face shone with tears. "I was charged with collaboration with an armed band and was sentenced to six years. At my trial I tried to talk about the torture and how I had been forced to participate in the ambush, but the court refused to let me speak. The police maintained that my comrades had been killed when they opened fire; it had been an armed confrontation and the police acted in self-defense. They said there had been no witnesses.

"It is quite customary for them to say such things; or sometimes they pretend that commandos they kill have committed suicide. I believe the legal system is in the hands of the government. If a body is found with the feet burned, there may be suspicion, but there is no evidence that the person was tortured. The police suppress information, and in my case, it was my word against theirs, and who is going to believe me?"

Why had she not told her story to the press? She just shrugged: "Basically, the newspapers take the government's press releases and police statements as read. That is why it is so important we have our own newspaper.

"I spent four years and three months in prison. The amnesty section worked on my behalf and I did maintenance work while I was in prison. That was why I was released early, for working in the prison, not because of good behavior. I got out two years and five months ago in May 1988." (She said it without calculating, as if she would always know the number of days she had been free).

"I started work for the amnesty movement. My group had folded in 1986 because it was very small and it had no grass-roots support. It had always shared the same aims as ETA, so it was not a question of me changing my views. Now I could not take part in any armed action, because of my prison record."

She had stayed composed even when crying and she was someone I felt had been terribly, almost mortally hurt in both a spiritual and physical sense. My sympathy warred with the fact that she had killed. She left the table, and Gloria said that when she had first met Alazne in prison, she had looked utterly "caved in." I told her that had been my impression of Alazne too. Gloria was surprised:

"Oh, but she is so much better now. Then she looked utterly destroyed."

Alazne briefly resumed: "My arrest and imprisonment were very hard on my family. They were terribly upset when I was arrested, but they were always there at the prison to visit me whenever they could. It was very tough on them because they couldn't entirely understand what I had done, yet they kept supporting me. We are a much closer family now and they pay me far more attention than they used to."

When Alazne was jailed in 1984 the authorities had a policy of placing all ETA prisoners together which resulted in a community of self-help. It was undoubtedly the support of her comrades that helped her to retain her sanity. Recently, however, the Spanish government has introduced a new system of splitting ETA prisoners up so that the mutual support no longer exists.

All three women attributed their relatively stable psychological state to that closely knit prison community. None of them, even the wounded Alazne, has sought psychiatric care, although they admitted that some ETA prisoners have needed it.

Amaia explained: "In the prison with other women who had experienced the same torture, we were among friends, and there was a process of normalization, which only those who had suffered in the same way could bring about. In our experience, after the torture, we all had a form of amnesia. We couldn't remember little things, like the names of some friends, of streets. It was very disturbing. When a new prisoner was brought into the wing, we would talk to her about that loss of memory and assure her that she was not mad, that she would remember those things in time. Now the prisoners are all isolated, and only allowed visits from their families, not their friends. They are in a much worse state than we were."

When it came to torture, Amaia went on, the police seemed to be harder on ETA women than men. Many criminologists believe such treatment can be explained by the way society regards violent women: that they are "doubly deviant." They have not only committed a crime, but in doing so have threatened the traditional image of women as gentle, law-abiding creatures.

"It is almost as if they wanted to punish us more for daring to be involved in the armed struggle. They cannot accept that women can do these things. They shout at you, laugh, abuse you verbally, physically, and sexually, and they treat you as if you were unnatural deviants. They particularly torment women who have children with the fear of what will happen to them. Because of this there are only a very few mothers who are commandos; mostly they play supporting roles.

"Of course the police use the fact that we are afraid of rape and threaten us with it. Unfortunately it is not simply a threat; women have been raped during torture, even raped with a truncheon. When the interrogators tell you that is what they are going to do, you know it is no idle threat. They say, 'Remember what happened to so and so . . .' "

Torturers were barbaric, Amaia concluded. They were mad, and there was "something wrong with them." The maddest and most barbaric of all were the women. Women police officers often took part in the torture of ETA women. All three women remembered that there had been a woman present during their torture. Alazne said rather dully that it had not made much difference to her, although she added, "The woman was sometimes far more brutal to me than the men." Amaia recalled that it had made her feel very uncomfortable that a woman was present, hurling obscenities at her broken body; the woman was an "added psychological torture." Gloria, who had escaped physical torture but had been subjected to psychological terror and verbal abuse for seven days, had been most shocked by the woman interrogator: "I remember thinking, How can you take part in this torture against another woman? How can you stand there and let these men do these things. How can you? The worst thing for me was that I had my period and I had to ask for towels [sanitary napkins], and they all laughed at me. It made me feel so vulnerable."

It was a fascinating perspective on how women who have chosen to participate in violence viewed other women who had made the same decision—but on the other side. It is a generally held view that those who commit terrorist acts are either mad or bad, particularly women who are expected to nurture life, not to destroy it. These three women justified violence as part of their revolutionary struggle; yet they used the same terms of condemnation against women interrogators as are generally applied to themselves and expressed the same bewilderment at how women could be torturers. That is not to say that torture is not the most heinous of crimes; but then how many victims of bombings and shootings do not die but spend their lives being tortured by their deformities?

It was shocking to be told that women in the Spanish police force participate in torture—"I cannot comprehend how they can live with themselves," said Amaia. Yet if part of the reason that there are Basque women in ETA is due to a natural progression of emancipation (Amaia's own words), why should it be surprising that women participating in the destruction of the commandos should have graduated to using the foulest of means at their disposal?

"They can do it and live with themselves," continued Amaia, "because they are supported by a structure; they are given official sanction to torture us. Their job is to dehumanize us, but it is themselves they end up dehumanizing." One thinks of how many times the same thing has been said about revolutionary groups who have committed acts of terror—the perpetrators are referred to as "mad dogs," "beasts," "depraved killers," and their deeds as "inhuman." Possibly, if one were to meet a woman torturer outside office hours, one would find she was as warm, friendly, thought provoking—as human—as these three women.

Amaia moved on to her own story of arrest and torture. She seemed to want to play down the details as if in deference to Alazne's appalling account.

"I was arrested in Bilbao in 1983; I think because someone gave my name under torture. I was in the street, shopping, when four policemen surrounded me. They asked for my ID, then said, 'Come with us, there are just some questions we want to ask you.' I was put in one police car, with another one driving behind. I remember I still had my shopping bag with me.

"In the police station I had the same kinds of torture as Alazne and I was also given electric shocks. They do that because it leaves no marks—it is the same with putting the plastic bag over your head—and without scars it is very difficult to prove they used torture. Then there was the more acceptable form of interrogation: the good and bad questioner, but they changed roles so you never knew who the good one was.

"The police went to my house and arrested the boy and girl who lived there; they were not part of the organization at all and didn't know anything. They were released after a few days, but the police told them, 'Don't say anything to anyone about her arrest or else we will arrest you again.' For three days no one knew where I had gone and anything could have happened to me during that time. After that my family found out, and my mother and sister—my father had left us some time before—were very supportive.

"I was held in the Commissariat for ten days being tortured

before I was put on trial. Like Alazne, I tried to tell them about the torture, but the judge said no one was interested in my allegations. I was only charged with membership in an ETA gang because there was no proof of any actions I had been involved in."

Not unnaturally the police interrogators are chief targets for assassination by ETA commandos and are apparently moved every three months to a different police station to avoid being identified. Amaia added: "Now the interrogators wear balaclavas so that we cannot identify them. When I was arrested, they had not started doing that, but they kept shouting at me not to look at them, to keep my head down.

"They are prime targets not only because of what they do to ETA people, but because of the way they are protected from justice by the government. There are a lot of them, and they are very highly trained. We have passed on information to Amnesty International and there has certainly been contact between AI and the Spanish anti-terrorist squad, but the torture goes on. The French government has asked questions about the treatment of prisoners, but mostly there is very little proof."

The women considered that the sentences metered out to ETA supporters and those in contact with ETA gangs were particularly harsh. It seems that the Spanish police have the power to arrest and detain on suspicion, and that young people who take part in demonstrations are automatically suspect. All three claimed that they knew people currently serving lengthy prison sentences whose only crime was that they were friends of commandos.

In the last ten years, they said, the authorities have realized that ETA could not exist without its infrastructure of support from many people in the community. Consequently, equal seriousness is now attached to those giving succor to ETA cells—gathering information, supplying the occasional safe house, carrying information—and that generally means women. Gloria paid tribute to these essential back-room workers: "Without their support, direct action could not take place, and so the police view any work for ETA as nearly the same as an actual commando. Ten years ago people charged with supporting ETA would have received small sentences; now they serve considerable time in prison."

She was a case in point. Her ex-boyfriend, an ETA suspect, was being hunted by the police. Arriving home one day, Gloria found a gun at her head. "I had gone out with friends and didn't get home until eight o'clock in the morning. I found the lock had been broken and the door was ajar.

"I was a bit frightened, thinking there had been a break-in and wondering if the burglar was still inside. I went in cautiously and suddenly there was a pistol at my head. There were five policemen and one policewoman. They had arrived at two A.M., broken in and then waited for me. They were looking for an old boyfriend of mine, and they thought I might know where he was.

"They wanted him because another young man they had arrested had referred to him. All the prisoner could remember about my ex-boyfriend was that he had gone out with a girl called Gloria. He had met me because at one time my old boyfriend and I had gone traveling with him and another girl. He knew the other girl's name was Arantza and that she knew me and where I lived. He could only remember that Arantza worked at a particular factory.

"The funny thing is that Arantza is a very common name, but that did not stop the police from going to the factory and arresting every girl with that name. There were a lot of arrests! Eventually they found the right one and she told them my address. Apparently before they tracked me down, the police had arrested two other girls who had gone out with my ex. We had only split up a year previously and he had had two more relationships! These other girls had not been able to tell the police where he was, so they came after me.

"Unfortunately, while they were waiting for me to return, the police searched my flat and found papers that proved I was working for ETA radio, which is illegal because they say it incites armed action. They arrested me and interrogated me for seven days. Apart from one blow in the stomach right at the beginning they did not torture me physically, only psychologically. They tried to implicate me in ETA actions and they interrogated me in a very strange way. They sat me in a chair and then stood around me—sometimes six or seven of them, sometimes just two. They questioned me constantly—'Do you know so and so from university?' 'When did you last see X?' They shouted all the questions; it was very intimidating.

"Because they had been in my flat for six hours—it is their habit to arrest in the middle of the night—they had had time to read all my letters and papers, and so they knew everything about me. They had read letters from people I had not seen for years, but I did not realize this. It seemed very strange that they knew so much about me, even about old friends, and it was very unnerving. Another game they played was to say that my lawyer had arrived. A man came into the room and I thought, 'He is here to protect me.' I soon realized, though, that he was a policeman, and in the end I couldn't trust any of them or anything they said.

"Luckily, one of my neighbors had seen the police arrive at my flat and had notified my friends and family. Although I was unaware of it, the very next morning news of my arrest was on the radio and in the press, so it was public knowledge. Even though everyone knew where I was, the police still held me for ten days, and the interrogation without the torture was bad enough. Then they sent me to Madrid.

"During the interrogation I had become so frightened that I signed a statement saying I had done all sorts of things I had not. When I got to Madrid headquarters I told the police there that I had only signed because I was afraid of torture, so I was just charged with working for ETA radio."

Gloria was at pains to point out that although ETA men on the whole expect women to play supporting roles, once a woman is part of a commando unit, she is accepted as an equal comrade. She laughed: "Do not imagine, though, that all men in ETA are women's libbers—many of them are still bound by social prejudices and traditions; they have to be educated too."

There are ways, all three agreed, that woman can achieve more than male commandos by the simple expedient of their sex, although as women commandos become more commonplace it is not as easy as it once was.

"In the past the very macho system worked in our favor," recalled Amaia. "If the police caught a woman's husband or boyfriend, they assumed the woman was innocent. In that way women got away with a lot because the police simply could not imagine women playing an active role in the armed struggle. We used to use their macho ideas to our advantage. If you were caught, even if you did not have a boyfriend, you said you did, and that you had no idea what he had been doing or got you involved in. Or if you had done something, you cried. 'He made me do it.' "

Even today, they claimed, the police are still unable to accept that "certain kinds" of women could be members of an ETA cell embarking on an action. The secret, apparently, is to dress very elegantly and to wear lots of makeup in order to appear middle class and respectable. "Several actions have been carried out by very elegant women," Gloria said.

I asked Alazne and Amaia, neither of whom looked as if they relished cosmetics and elegant clothing, if they had ever disguised themselves in such a manner. Amaia chuckled: "No, but once I was with a male commando in a bar when the police came in. I pretended to be, well, terribly involved with him, when in fact we were doing something very different indeed." Planting a bomb? She just laughed.

Another woman was mentioned, Belen Gonzales. Ms. Gonzales is apparently the most wanted ETA woman on the police computer and according to the authorities was personally present at every shooting and bombing in Madrid. A couple of years ago she was trapped in a police cordon in the city. She strolled over to where a young couple were standing and asked if she could "borrow" the boy for a few minutes. She embraced the bemused youth, then in a loving clinch, they walked straight through the police barrier.

Amaia roared with laughter: "All the police could see was a pair of lovers. Afterwards, when they realized that she had escaped, they were absolutely fucking furious, much angrier than if it had been a man who had got away. There was a strong element of hurt male pride that they could not catch this bloody woman and that she had slipped through their net. She was a real thorn in their side." Ms. Gonzales was now believed to be living safely in South America.

Everyone appeared to be in a relaxed mood now, so I posed the question I had been rather anxious about asking—the use by ETA of what they called "revolutionary tax," but what others would probably call extortion. This method of fund-raising relies upon the fact that ETA has a policy of kidnapping wealthy and prominent businessmen and killing them if the ransom is not paid. Revolutionary tax does away with the messy business of kidnap. They simply use the threat of its well-established existence to extract large sums of money from businesses in the Basque country. Some businessmen have resisted the tax demand and paid dearly; most of the business community, including banks, have paid up quietly while publicly condemning ETA. It is believed that some members of GAL are mercenaries hired by businessmen who are fed up with paying the revolutionary tax.

My tentative inquiry only brought broad grins from around the table. Yes, they all nodded, the tax brought in valuable funds to the movement. It was clear they saw no moral dilemma in the practice: "It is obviously the big companies that we target because we wouldn't want to ruin the smaller ones. We address our demands to the owners or top people in companies and banks who have a lot of capital and are exploiting people. The money we get in tax is used to pay the workers back, to liberate them." Was the threat of kidnapping necessary? This brought a jeer: "They wouldn't give the money voluntarily, would they?"

It all seemed dreadfully reasonable, as long as one accepted the revolutionary reasoning, saw businesses as legitimate targets, and ignored the fact that they were subjecting human beings to terror.

Then I asked how they justified killing innocent people by mistake. In 1987, for example, an ETA bomb exploded in the living quarters of the Civil Guard; eleven people were killed, including four young children.

Alazne, who had been silent for some time, spoke out: "Obviously nobody likes that, or wants it, and it hurts us all. We do not do it deliberately, but such things happen in a war."

Amaia chimed in: "The press uses such tragedies against us. If women or children are killed as a result of an action then they say we do not care a damn, we are ruthless killers of innocents. That is not true. It is very painful for us, but it happens by accident and we consider it is inevitable.

"At the same time, it often happens that the police and Civil Guard abandon children when they take their parents away for interrogation. The children are just left in the bakery or with neighbors, not knowing what has happened. That is cruelty to children. Tragically, people who have nothing to do with the armed struggle get caught in the middle."

Gloria, who had grown increasingly human and agreeable as the evening had worn on, wrecked it: "In the cases of the Civil Guard living quarters and other bomb attacks—these organizations cannot hide behind their women and children. The women and children have no business living there; but if they do, they are part of the organization, part of the repression against our people, and as such they are a legitimate target."

One did not know whether Gloria sounded so ruthless simply because she had never killed or injured anyone, or whether if she had not been captured for operating ETA radio she would have gone on to blow up kindergartens full of Civil Guard offspring without turning a hair. I had never met anyone who could even say such things—and Gloria said it with such conviction.

She did, however, refer to the bombing of a department store in Barcelona in 1987 as a mistake by ETA, and one for which the movement apologized: "The store was part of a big chain and the bombing took place when ETA was targeting chain stores that had a state interest. Normally the bombs would be timed to explode when there was no one in the stores; but in this case, the bomb went off without warning and between fifteen and eighteen people were killed.

"There was an enormous amount of self-criticism inside ETA for that action, and from outside, too, obviously. People in the organization were shocked because it is never intended that innocent people should die. We do not want indiscriminate killing, and it was something we should not have done. We deplored it." This was more understandable; Gloria appeared to be genuinely sorrowful— but she had to go on: "There was criticism of the action, too, because we had counted on the police to pass on the warning that there was a bomb in the department store. ETA generally notify the police of a bomb, but in this case the authorities deliberately decided not to pass on the warning. It was for propaganda purposes—they wanted there to be an enormous public outcry against ETA."

Alazne engendered sympathy and respect for her suffering and her gentleness and Amaia was a sort of likable and honest rogue. Both had suffered for their actions, and their rhetoric was tempered by experience. Their accounts of torture had been deeply moving, so much so that one had to force oneself to remember why they had been arrested in the first place. Gloria's words, however, made me shudder. It was difficult to reconcile the two sides of her personality: the woman who had felt so humiliated and vulnerable when she had asked her interrogators for sanitary napkins and the revolutionary theorist who ruled violence was OK and that the children of her enemy had better watch out.

The young woman's pseudonym, Txikia ("the small one") could not have been more appropriate. It was difficult not to think of this tiny creature as a child. Any such thoughts were, however, quickly dispersed when Txikia began to speak. She was deeply frustrated that after serving an eighteen-month prison sentence she could not rejoin an ETA-m unit and become what she had wanted to be—a frontline woman guerrilla. Then there was her experience of torture and the lasting sense of guilt that she had in the end broken down and given information. Finally, she firmly believed that violence, including murder, got things done far more quickly and effectively than words.

Txikia had been in an ETA-m unit for only a few months when she was arrested. As a new member she had been involved at a fairly low level—gathering information on targets for the movement—but freely admitted that she would have gone on to higher things if her career had not been cut short. She refused to say how she had performed her duties, but one imagined that she would have made a good intelligence officer; no one would have suspected that the minuscule figure with the sweet face was carefully noting when the police officers were changing shifts or where they went for a drink after work.

Her information would have resulted in the deaths of those she observed, but she was entirely unrepentant. She derived satisfaction from her role, and enjoyed the sense of camaraderie in the group. Although the majority of its members were men, and included her live-in boyfriend, there were also some women commandos, whom Txikia admired and resolved to join. She was not, after all, just a woman in a repressive society; she might be a tiny woman, but even a tiny woman is a force to be reckoned with if she is carrying a gun that she knows how to use.

The decision to become a guerrilla was not, she explained, one that a woman took lightly; she had so much more to lose than men. It was clearly a subject she had given much thought to: "Women face far more difficulties in going underground and becoming fully operational. Undoubtedly it has a lot to do with the traditionally strict attitudes in our society toward women—that they should stay at home and have children. That sort of thinking is changing but we are all still conditioned to want security, and in joining a commando cell there is the very strong possibility that you will lose your family, your home, and, of course, all security.

"For men it is easier. Traditionally they are expected to be away from home, earning the money. They know that whatever happens to them, their wives will still look after the children. But if a woman does the same thing, she must cut all those ties and abandon those feelings.

"For me there were not so many problems. The boy I was living with was just a boyfriend, and besides, we were both doing the same thing."

She emphasized that her boyfriend had not influenced her in any way about her decision to become "fully operational." "I cannot remember which of us joined first, but it was through the group that we met. I don't know of any ETA women commandos who have been driven to frontline action by their men. Though in the case of general support I think it may be true that women get involved through their men—doing such things as providing safe houses, financial support, that sort of thing.

"But women who actually become commandos do so on their own and are seen as equals to men in decision taking. The people who get to the level of armed struggle are far more committed to the revolution than anyone else. Politically they are more advanced and that means the men are more aware of women's rights."

In Txikia's unit, everyone from the newest recruit to the most experienced fighter was taught what to expect if captured: "Torture. We had psychological preparation and were told about the different types of torture and how to recognize what was coming next. If you know what is coming it is easier to brace yourself for it."

The tuition stood her in good stead when she was arrested and detained, first in Bilbao police station and then at Madrid police headquarters.

It was 2 A.M. when the police broke down the door of the flat where Txikia lived with her boyfriend. "There were about twenty police, all armed to the teeth, and they grabbed everything—books, photographs, anything they saw. They were shouting abuse at us, particularly me, calling me a slut's daughter, a whore; meaningless swearing. They arrested both of us and I was taken to the police station in Bilbao.

"Straightaway they began beating me. I remember they were all big men standing around hitting me. They had tied me up by my wrists and ankles to a beam of wood so that I was swinging like a monkey between two tables. I felt my back was breaking.

"Their method is first to break you down physically and then to apply psychological torture. They taunt you with the fact that you know about other comrades who have died under interrogation. They threatened that they would arrest my mother and father. That was a terrible thought, knowing that they could do that and perhaps torture my parents as well.

"I was tortured for seven days, the first three in Bilbao, and then I was taken to Madrid headquarters for the next four days. Being taken to Madrid is the worst thing that can happen to anybody. The interrogation rooms are underground and the ceilings are vaulted, painted green. The blood of the prisoners is spattered on the ceiling—it is like a medieval torture chamber."

She confessed that the memory of her failure, when she broke down and talked, still haunted her. Hesitantly, and with downcast eyes, she continued: "I feel very guilty about it. It is so very difficult not to say anything at all when you are being tortured like that. I had to speak in the end, even though it was very much against my will. It is hard for me to admit that I talked and it has left me with a feeling of guilt ever since." Did she betray her comrades? "Yes," she whispered, "but I did not give enough information for anyone to be arrested."

Nine years later, she still suffers back problems caused by her treatment under interrogation. She referred to her transferal to Madrid prison where she served eighteen months as a "liberation" after her time spent with the police. They had threatened her with six years imprisonment, so there was an added feeling of release at the relatively short jail sentence.

On her admission to the prison, she was given a medical examination by the prison doctor. According to Txikia, he looked at the extensive bruising, the battered hands, and dismissed her in perfect health. "He said, 'Oh, that's nothing. Today your bruises are purple, tomorrow they will be yellow.' He did not even check my hands to see if any bones were broken."

It was 1981 when she was imprisoned and her cell mates were other ETA women. Apart from giving each other support and encouragement, they also shared everything they had—food parcels from home were particularly important as the prison meals were "disgusting." However, she remembered the time bitterly: the women warders, she said, continually harassed the prisoners, opening and slamming cell doors in the middle of the night and subjecting them to verbal abuse.

In spite of the treatment, Txikia was far from broken: "My experience in prison convinced me that the armed struggle was the only way to get these people to change. When I came out I desperately wanted to continue with the commandos, but of course my face was known to the authorities, and it was too easy to check up on my movements. Some ex-prisoners get telephone calls in the middle of the night from the police and are followed everywhere. For security reasons, I could not join another ETA unit.

"When I got out, the movement held a huge celebration party for me and within two months I was working for the amnesty group." It had been through working with this group four years before that Txikia had first decided to join ETA. It was a route to violence that was fairly common among the women I interviewed. First, the supporter of prisoners, then, perhaps out of a sense of frustration that the prisoners were still being mistreated, the realization that the only way to stop the injustice was to personally strike back. Women seemed to become far more emotionally involved than men with the suffering of prisoners, and when they made the transition from supporter to guerrilla, appeared to carry their deeper sense of commitment with them into battle.

"I was in constant contact with men and women who had been tortured and were serving long jail sentences. I was working on their behalf and I realized that I should fight too. It was not a sudden decision; it was a natural progression for me, becoming politically more aware and feeling I had to do something to fight back.

"From as far back as I remember I had felt angry about the oppression of the Basque people. I came from a working-class suburb of Bilbao, where Basque was spoken in the streets. But at home, although my parents were Basque, they could not speak the language because Franco had banned it when they were children. It always seemed so wrong to me that they could not speak their own language. My grandfather had fought on the Republican side during the Civil War, and my parents were still afraid. In the streets outside I learned to speak Basque and became aware of the Basque struggle for a homeland.

"From an early age I was angry at the injustices done to us by Franco. At school the teachers were fascists; they were all 'Viva Franco' people. The Basque language was forbidden; it was looked down upon as something backward. If you spoke it you were made to feel bad as if the Basques had absolutely no cultural heritage.

"My mother had only two children, me, and my sister, who is seven years older. She was in a dilemma: on one hand she wanted us to do well at school, go to university, get a good job and be independent women; on the other she was afraid for us and very protective. As I grew up and started to seek my own identity I felt it was very strongly interwoven with the Basque movement. I wanted to be a Basque woman."

In November 1975, when Txikia was fifteen years old, Franco died. By then she had already joined the Basque Patriotic Youth Movement and had been attending meetings and Basque cultural activities arranged by a group of left-wing Basque priests in her neighborhood.

"I remember the sense of elation when Franco died. Everyone thought things would change. Not overnight, and not that things would all be wonderful, but we believed that things would improve. But gradually it became evident that, after all, Spain was still ruled by a very strong state structure. Our dreams of self-determination did not materialize and there was still oppression.

"I left school and went to teacher training college, but at the same time I joined the amnesty movement. I was twenty-one when I joined ETA."

In 1988 Txikia became one of the first members of Egizan and now channels her undoubted fighting spirit into campaigning for better conditions for Basque women, both in the home and in society. Yes, she said, the work was demanding, given that she also had a full-time job as a Basque translator, but it was satisfying. Not, however, she suddenly shot out with a sparkle in her eyes, as satisfying as being a gun-bearing ETA woman.

She sighed for what might have been: "Working as I do now, day to day, you put a hell of a lot of effort into it for sometimes very little visible result.

"I think that with arms you can cut through all this work, and get the results very quickly. It is true what the revolutionary writers say, the daily struggle is the hardest. Violence is certainly necessary for our struggle."

She illustrated her point: in 1981, ETA kidnapped the chief engineer of a nuclear power station that was under construction in Lemoniz, near Bilbao. They demanded that, in return for the man's life, the semi-built power plant should be demolished, starting in one week's time. The construction company refused to negotiate and a week later the man was found dead. ETA also bombed the station and killed two employees—after that work at the site was stopped.

Little Txikia enthused: "It was a victory for ETA. For years the local people had protested about the nuclear station, held demonstrations, sent petitions. They had been ignored; the construction company went ahead. Then after ETA acted, like a spearhead, what everyone wanted was achieved. It showed that violence was the only thing the authorities understood.

"In that situation, ETA and the people worked together: ETA would not have killed without the support of the people and the people would not have got what they wanted without ETA."

Her words betrayed no remorse for the dead engineer, a thirty-nine-year-old father of five, who had been a modest and popular figure in his local community. Nor did she refer to a demonstration by some 10,000 people through Bilbao demanding the man's release. The killing, in fact, led to serious criticism inside ETA and caused intense disgust throughout the Basque region and Spain.

Having given her example, Txikia moved on to deny that women are in any sense more ruthless than men. "I think it is a police view because they think that women should be the ones who care for others, not fight them. The women I knew, once they became committed, were very determined fighters. They felt that they were doing what was right, and they followed an action through unhesitatingly. But I couldn't say if they were more committed than men.

"The only way in which I think that women fighters are stronger than men is that they are more used to pain than men are. Perhaps, because of that, men give out more information under torture than women." This observation was one that came up in several conversations with women from different groups: because we are women we are better at suffering; we have to endure it in our everyday lives, and therefore we are stronger than men.

We left the drab office that was Egizan's headquarters and went to a bar in the old quarter. Again, there was a picture of Maite (whose name means "love" in Basque) above the bottles, and Txikia told me the story of her death at the hands of GAL. Matter-of-factly, she commented: "We know any of us can be killed at any moment and perhaps our bodies will never be found.

"Oh, my parents worry about me. The fact that I was tortured was very difficult for them; it reminded them of the Civil War. At first, you know, they couldn't believe that I had been involved with ETA; they were sure it was all a mistake. But the overwhelming thing was their determination to protect me, that was their first thought."

She does not see her father much now, she added, but when she does he always buys her a meal and gives her money. She wondered aloud why it was that she alone in the current generation of her family had decided on the armed struggle. "It is odd that I should be the one," she mused. "My sister has married and settled down and has nothing to do with the movement. For myself, I keep putting off having children. I think, I am young, I can wait a bit longer. Having children would change my life so much.

"It is strange that it is me alone who has carried on the role of the fighter from my grandfather."

Chapter 2

❧ *KIM HYON HUI*

"All I had to do was drop the bomb."

It was the middle of the night and most of the passengers on board Korean Air Flight 858 were asleep for the three-hour journey between Baghdad and Abu Dhabi. Only two could not sleep, although they pretended to do so: one was a strikingly beautiful woman in her twenties, a Japanese according to her passport, and the other was a seventy-year-old man who appeared to be her father. Both had their eyes closed and were trying to breathe slowly and deeply, but it required every ounce of their training and energy to maintain the act.

Just above their seats in the overhead compartment was a plastic bag. It contained a Panasonic radio packed with a 350-gram bomb and a bottle of what looked like whisky but was in fact liquid explosive. The radio bomb was due to detonate in nine hours' time, but the woman and the man did not know, in spite of all their careful preparations, how reliable the timing mechanism would be. They did not speak either to each other or to anyone else; in their nervous state they feared making a mistake in their speech and revealing their true nationalities.

They were North Korean agents on what they believed to be a holy mission. The woman had trained for these moments for seven years. She tried to block out the sounds around her; the talk of two South Korean men sitting behind her, the attempt by a French woman passenger in the window seat next to her to strike up a conversation. She had not noticed if there were any children on board, but it would not have mattered if there had been an entire school party, for all who had booked on the eventual flight to Seoul were to be sacrificed. The woman had no room for pity; she knew too that her life might be forfeited, her guidance officer had told her that if it became necessary she would have to stay on the plane. To be captured and forced to talk was out of the question; a cyanide capsule hidden in the filter of a Marlboro cigarette in her handbag ensured that.

Nothing went wrong. The plane landed at Abu Dhabi at 2:44 A.M. and fifteen passengers prepared to disembark. The Japanese woman and her father took two overnight bags from the overhead locker and calmly left the plane. No one noticed that they had left their duty-free bag behind.

Korean Air Flight 858 sat on the runway for just under an hour being refueled and taking on board some extra passengers. It left for the next leg of its journey to Bangkok and was on time to land at Seoul, capital of South Korea and home for most of those on board. Five hours later, at 2:05 P.M. Korean time, the plane exploded over the waters of the Andaman Sea. There were no survivors.

The two agents by then were in their room at the Regency Intercontinental Hotel in Bahrain, where they had flown after leaving the plane.

A child film star turned terrorist; a brainwashed beauty, victim of an Orwellian regime; a fragile princess who is loved from afar; a china doll killer. Kim Hyon Hui fits all these descriptions and more. The Far East is fascinated by her—how could a woman so beautiful, so delicate, kill so ruthlessly? The question has been answered by Kim herself, for she was captured and failed to crunch up her cyanide capsule properly.

Her explanation for her involvement in what is the most horrifying act of violence described in this book makes Miss Kim—as she is called by her captors—a unique case. She had been coerced all her life and there was not an ounce of the rebel in her, just the opposite in fact; she was the most conservative of women. She was not interested in feminism; she was not driven by a sense of injustice; nor did she want to overthrow the society in which she lived. She was, quite simply, obeying orders when she and her fellow agent placed the bomb on board the aircraft. Miss Kim, unlike some of the women interviewed, had no hesitation and displayed no confusion in accounting for her ruthless behavior; it was as if, she said, she was a bomber pilot. When given her orders, she was overwhelmed, certainly—but only at the wonderful importance of the mission she had been selected for.

It was difficult to attribute many human emotions to Miss Kim, for she was really so robotlike. However, a characteristic that does seem to run through her life is ambition; she was an ambitious child and an ambitious agent. She expressed glee that as a relatively junior agent she had been picked for the mission, while many of her older comrades were still waiting to go into combat. She strove for perfection always, and she was bitterly angry with herself when she botched her suicide attempt.

The justification for her action was that she was brainwashed, and this naturally leads one to consider the other famous brainwashed revolutionary, Patty Hearst. Miss Hearst, however, did not kill anyone; moreover, if one is to believe her story, she did not really adopt the revolutionary life that her kidnappers demanded; she acted as a revolutionary to save herself from death. Miss Kim, on the other hand, was fully committed to her country and prepared to die by her own hand to safeguard the secrets that had been entrusted to her.

Bound and gagged, she was extradited to South Korea, the country she feared the most, where the relatives of her victims were screaming for her blood. The team of interrogators who escorted her from Bahrain were amazed at the first sight of the terrorist; they described her as a "toothless tiger." Kim was shaking and weeping, convinced that she was to be tortured horribly before facing a brutal death. But the South Korean CIA had different plans for her; they wanted a full confession, and they wanted her alive and coherent to demonstrate to the world the evils of North Korea.

It took eight days for Kim to break, days in which she clung to a variety of disguises and refused to eat. She was a Japanese girl, adopted by an elderly man who had taken her on vacation; she was Chinese and recited Chinese poetry. On December 23, 1987, at around five in the afternoon, Kim suddenly laid her hand on the arm of a woman interrogator. In Korean she whispered, "Forgive me. I'm sorry."

Kim Hyon Hui had been born in Pyongyang, capital of North Korea, in 1962, the eldest daughter of a diplomat. At six years old, her beauty and family background led her to be elected for work in propaganda films, and she was taken from her parents for a year. At eighteen, while at university studying Japanese, she was chosen again—this time to become a spy. After seven years training Kim was told to blow up the South Korean plane. The aim was to frighten countries from sending athletes to the Olympics to be held in Seoul the following year. She obeyed unquestioningly.

In 1988 Kim was put on trial, and the Olympics went ahead. She watched them on the television set in her room at a government safe house and wept for what she had done and the futility of it all. She repeatedly expressed the wish that she should be killed one hundred times for her crime, and in 1989 it seemed that that wish would be fulfilled; she was sentenced to death. But a year later the government granted her a special pardon saying that she had been brainwashed and was not responsible for her actions.

Kim was then technically free in the country where her victims' relatives sought her death, but the freedom has made little difference to her circumstances.

Today she lives in another safe house, surrounded by bodyguards and with the twenty-four hour attendance of interrogators from the National Security Planning Agency, the Korean equivalent of the CIA. She is on the death list of North Korea, as a supreme agent turned traitor. Her best friends are her interrogators; she calls the four women among them her *onni*—meaning big sister. An *onni* or two, all selected for their beauty so that Kim's own attributes pale into insignificance, always accompany her when she goes shopping. A film has been made about her in South Korea, called *The Virgin Terrorist*, but she has never seen it, preferring instead *The Sound of Music* and *Ben Hur*.

She has appeared several times on television: weeping with her head bowed while she made her confession; in court where victims' relatives threw their shoes at her; in church, after her pardon, at a Witness ceremony, whispering that she had become a Christian. According to Korean newspapers, each appearance has merited record-breaking numbers of viewers, with men rhapsodizing over Miss Kim's delicate beauty—she has received hundreds of marriage proposals from Korean and Japanese men. Even the chief interrogator, a gray-haired man in his forties, seems to have fallen under her spell; he brings her presents and admits he would like to be more friendly with her. His professional status, however, prevents that.

There is certainly a glamour surrounding his captive. She is probably the supreme example of the fascination such women have for men. She has become a sex symbol to the men of the Far East; perhaps they feel they can tame her or reeducate her. She presents a challenge. They would also be assured that Miss Kim, in spite of her notoriety as a mass killer, would not kill them, because she has renounced her past. She would not really be a threat; she would probably be eternally grateful, a poor little thing who has been led astray and needs protection.

Of course, Miss Kim has beauty in her favor—one doubts if she would be the object of such adoration if this were not the case. Her beauty also poses problems for those experts who believe that women who turn to violence are generally ugly, and that their only hope of attracting male attention is at the point of a sword. Miss Kim is aware of her beauty and equally aware that it has got her plenty of attention in the past.

To understand her, it is necessary to know about the country where she was born. Its leader, Kim Il Sung, came to power in 1948 and has imposed a totalitarian, Communist regime ever since. In 1950 he launched the invasion of the South. The armistice ending the Korean War was signed in 1953, but tremendous enmity still exists between the two Koreas. Each side is deeply suspicious of the other and Kim Il Sung is still determined to "free" the South for Communism. North Koreans are taught to regard Southerners as puppets of American capitalists, and Americans themselves are nothing short of the devil incarnate. Kim Il Sung has rewritten history, including his own birth; he was not born of woman, but created as a star which then became incarnate as a man. His son experienced a similar creation. North Koreans fear and worship the Kim family as gods; to slander the president or his son results in a particular type of execution—being hit on the head with an iron bar.

Orphans are the most privileged class because it is held that they cannot be corrupted by parental influence. They are raised in Orphanage Schools for Revolutionary Offspring and are given gifts by the president. At the other end of the social spectrum are the president's enemies: those who have dared to step outside the Workers' Party line. For them and their families there are concentration camps or the firing squad.

It is a society that is riddled with paranoia. The population lives in small housing units, and in every group of five families there will be one family who are informers. Children are encouraged to replace filial loyalty with loyalty to the state, including reporting on their parents. The indoctrination starts early. All North Korean women must work, and at two months old their babies are sent to a nursery where, as Kim explained, they are taught their first words: "Thank you, Great Leader Kim Il Sung." At school, textbooks inculcate a deep hatred and violence toward Americans. A mathematics problem for example: "The Korean People's Army has killed two American Yankee bastards and captured four. How many American Yankee bastards is that?" In every household there is a picture of the Great Leader, along with a special cloth, which is only used for dusting it. The family bows to the picture each morning.

This is the regime that formed Kim Hyon Hui. Initially she was trained as a spy with the intention of infiltrating Japanese society and gathering intelligence. She was sent on her first mission in 1984—to accompany another North Korean agent on a tour of Europe so that they could both learn to adapt themselves to capitalist societies. The pair excelled themselves as Japanese tourists, the twenty-two-year-old woman posing as the daughter of the sixty-seven-year-old man. When the president's son hatched the plot to stop the Olympics being held in Seoul in 1988, the Party's research department submitted the names of Miss Kim and her "father" as outstanding candidates for the mission.

"I had never dreamed I would be expected to kill anyone. For seven years and eight months I had been trained to become a foreign agent operating in Japan. Then on October seventh, 1987, I was told of the mission by the deputy director of the Party. When the order came through that I and Kim Sung Il [the seventy-year-old agent] were to blow up the South Korean plane, I was overwhelmed with gratitude to the Party. It was such an enormous mission, and I was very, very proud of the trust shown in me; it was a sign of honor that the Party had endowed upon me. On the other hand, I was terrified at the idea of carrying out the order. I felt it might be too big for me. I thought, Can I do it? Will I be able to perform it properly? But there it was—the order had been given, and it came from Kim Jung Il, the president's own son.

"It was impressed upon me how important it was, that on no account were we to fail. If there was any question of having to stay on the aircraft to detonate the bombs, then we were to do it. Our personal lives were to be sacrificed on the altar of reunification of the fatherland. I was prepared to die; I saw myself as a bomber pilot who was on a combat mission in the enemy's zone. If the pilot is ordered to drop the bombs over a certain area, then he automatically drops the bombs. He doesn't have the leeway to think about the lives of the people which are going to be blown away by the bomb. That is how I thought of it; all I had to do was drop the bomb."

On first sight it is difficult to imagine Miss Kim, a dainty and very pretty woman who giggles coyly and bows shyly when introduced, as a ruthless bomber pilot. In the words of the chief interrogator, who was interviewed separately: "She is very obedient, conservative, and self-effacing toward me. She is subservient to men, and although she is not too coquettish, she has quite a good manner with men."

She was demurely dressed, in a knee-length black skirt, long-sleeved, high-necked, mustard linen jacket with black and pink embroidery on the front. Her long hair was held back by a pearl ornament and her makeup was minimal and carefully applied. The interview took place in a villa on the grounds of a hotel overlooking the River Han in Seoul, which had been rented for the day. Just inside the front door was a room containing bodyguards; in the main area Miss Kim had risen to greet her visitor. She bowed and the interrogators, representatives of the Counter-Terrorism Squad, interpreters, and a man whose card proclaimed he was a "special agent" bowed back. They were all there as witnesses and all wrote feverishly for five hours. An *onni* provided drinks and Miss Kim waited composedly for the interview to begin. Although the temperature was about 100 degrees and the humidity around 90 percent, Miss Kim, alone among the room's occupants, did not appear to feel the heat; she remained upright and cool throughout.

The effect of "dropping the bomb," she explained, would demonstrate that the choice of Seoul as the Olympic venue was "a manifest manipulation of Korea by an imperialist power and an attempt to perpetrate the division of the Korean peninsula." By stopping the Olympics through fear of terrorism, a blow of paramount importance would be struck for reunification.

The prospect of blowing up 115 people did not affect Miss Kim at the time. "Of course, momentarily I thought about the people who would die as a result of my acts, but again my first and foremost task was to carry out the mission, and I thought that for the sake of the fatherland, it was unavoidable for these people to be sacrificed.

"We boarded the aircraft at Baghdad and Mr. Kim put the two bombs, one in a radio and one in a bottle of whisky, in the compartment above our heads. I sat in the middle seat and Mr. Kim beside me next to the aisle. We were very nervous; we did not know if the bombs would explode at the proper time, which was nine hours later. The plane took off at eleven thirty-five P.M. and most of the passengers were asleep. Mr. Kim, my fellow agent, and I both decided that it would be a good idea to feign sleep because we might make a mistake in our speech and reveal ourselves to be North Korean. I did not have the time and was not in the state of mind to think about other people. I was under such pressure to carry out the mission, to do well and to escape, that I had no feelings for anyone else." She did not attempt to apologize for her lack of emotion.

"It was not until we got off the plane at Abu Dhabi that I remembered a few things: a French woman who had been sitting in the window seat next to mine. Just after some drinks and dinner had been served, I got up to visit the washroom, and so did this woman. I started to go toward the first-class washroom, and the woman told me I should go to the one at the back, so we went together. I did not speak to her. The only other thing I remember is hearing two South Korean men talking to each other in the seats behind."

As it happened, the French woman must have disembarked at Abu Dhabi too, for she was not on the casualty list. Stewardesses and the wife of the Korean consul in Iraq were the only women victims; the vast majority of the rest were young South Korean men engaged in engineering projects in the Middle East. It is thought that the flight, which was en route to Seoul via Bangkok, was deliberately chosen as it was unlikely that there would be foreigners traveling on it, and North Korea did not want to risk world condemnation.

Would it have made any difference to Miss Kim had there been a school party on board or, indeed, any children? She was unequivocal in her reply: "I could not have afforded that sort of feeling; it would not have altered anything." This dedication and ruthlessness, coupled with ambition to become an elite agent and considerable intellectual capacity, were qualities that made Miss Kim a superb prospect for an agent.

Miss Kim was a bright and beautiful child. Her earliest memories are of the time she spent with her family in Cuba where her father had been posted as a diplomat. She remembered at the age of three her father standing with her on the seashore and pointing toward the United States, warning her of the foreign devils who lived there. She had an excellent memory, even recalling the Spanish word for ice cream, because every day at noon her mother would give her money to run to the ice-cream peddler as he passed outside their house.

"My family was very close-knit. There was myself, a younger sister, and brother. Because of my father's position in society we went abroad, which for many North Koreans is a lifelong dream. When we returned to North Korea we had more toys than other children, and at home we had a fridge. We were considered to be a member of the 'core' class, the most trusted group, whose loyalty to the Party was unquestioned. But there is not much difference between the rich and poor in North Korea; I can remember at home there were times when we did not have enough to eat, just rice made from corn, and how we children would fight over it. But like many other people I think my childhood, with the love of my parents surrounding me, was the happiest time in my life."

As with all Korean families, Kim's mother, who was a schoolteacher, had to work to help support her family. Kim was placed in a nursery at the regulation age of two months, not simply to free her mother to return to her job, but to ensure that the child was raised as far as possible by the state. So the infant would have lain in her cot along with dozens of other babies, and she would have been taught to speak her first words of gratitude to Kim Il Sung.

"Even when our parents gave us a present, we thanked the Great Leader first for the gift, and for allowing our parents to buy it for us," recalled Kim. "From the age of two months you are cared for by a long line of other people. From the nursery you go to kindergarten, then elementary school. The first thing you learn is to thank the Great Leader; then you are taught other ways of saying greetings or showing your loyalty to the Party. Even when you eat a meal you are made to express gratitude to the Party and to the Great Leader.

"All you learn in the nursery is about Kim Il Sung. You have the picture of the Great Leader hung on the wall, then you learn such expressions as, 'It is great to be able to see the picture of the Great Leader every day.' Almost all the expressions you pick up at the nursery are related to the Great Leader, even baby songs and fairy tales."

Her mother was a good Party member, but she was determined to give more time than was normally allowed to the upbringing of her family. The Party told mothers that they would provide everything necessary for the offspring; they were not to worry too much about lavishing attention at home. The system wanted to produce good, hardworking, and dedicated revolutionaries and was designed to prevent parental interference. Lengthy working hours meant that most mothers had no time to spend time with their children; waiting in line for food took up any free time, and from primary-school age onward children were members of a variety of youth movements, which they had to attend after school. But Mrs. Kim, according to her daughter, squeezed extra time out of the day to be with her children for half an hour before packing them off to the state nurseries and schools. She instilled in them "home education," a Korean expression meaning good manners and kindness to others.

Her family did well, both academically and in their outside-school Party activities; they were the envy of their housing unit. Then came the day when Kim's school was visited by the Party's film unit and she was elected to appear in a film.

In North Korea, only the healthiest, prettiest people from elite families are chosen to be actors, so it was quite a privilege for the Kim parents. Their daughter was to play a little girl who is brought up in poverty and misery in South Korea. When she grows up the child flees to the "beautiful workers' paradise of North Korea" and the last scene of the film is her weeping for her mother left behind in the South and crying for the reunification of the Korean peninsula.

The making of the film had a great effect on six-year-old Kim; she was taken away from school and her family for about a year to be filmed on location in the countryside. When she returned, Kim admitted that she had become rather spoiled and swollen-headed with the compliments heaped on her by film producers, her teachers, and school friends. She got a swift crash course in home education from her mother, who repeatedly informed her daughter that she was "just an ordinary little girl, like anybody else." Miss Kim, it seems, took the lesson well; there was no seed of rebellion in her; she was the perfect daughter.

"It was a great honor for me to have been chosen for the film, which was the first in Technicolor. I was spoiled by the attention, but at the same time, being the eldest daughter of the family, I had to carry out my duties: cleaning, washing, and working in the kitchen. I dutifully performed all these tasks and listened to my mother when she insisted I had to be nice to other people. She was very strict on these points."

Mrs. Kim took the family to see the film, and some of her daughter's pride evaporated when she saw that she had accidentally shown her knickers in one scene. "That distracted me and I was embarrassed, but I remember the last scene; it was so sad. I wept for the mother in the film, who was in South Korea." Another film role followed, then Kim returned to Hashin People's School.

She was taught the Party line on South Korea and hatred for capitalism, particularly in the South, America, and Japan: in the South, children were so hungry that they strapped old tins to their waists and went begging for food; at night they slept under bridges and died from starvation and disease; South Korean society was so permeated with American and Western influence that the cultural heritage had been corrupted and decayed; in capitalist societies the rich deliberately kept the poor starving and invaded other countries to bolster their economies. One song learned at school was "Get Out of Here, You Bastard Yankees," another was "Hack to Death the Capitalist Dogs."

"We were taught to call the U.S. imperialist bastards 'two legged dogs,' and were told that at the thought of the U.S. bastards even the mountains and rivers thunder and shake and tremble, and the animals blush, so great are the atrocities of the U.S. imperialists. Even in classes of drawing and painting you are told to draw the Korean People's Army shooting the Yankee bastards or running them over with tanks or the army trampling them with their feet."

Apart from these lessons, the children were encouraged to play violent games: "When you are playing with your friends, you draw an image of a Yankee bastard on the ground, with a skull for the head. Then you all pick up clubs and take turns in pulverizing the skull to show your hatred. We are taught to hate the bastards so much that to spend a day with one of them is unimaginable."

Kim began to describe a slogan that told the people what to do if they came across a Yankee bastard strolling through downtown Pyongyang. With her nails she clawed the air, but she could not quite get across the degree of violence she wanted to demonstrate. The chief interrogator came to her aid, going to the fridge in the room and pulling out a tray of ice cubes. He ripped them out one by one with an ice pick. Kim giggled behind her hand and explained: " 'Yes,' the slogan says, 'let us tear every piece of flesh away from the bone, drag it out.' "

Kim was a good student and ambitious to be the top of the class, which she frequently was. She joined the Party Youth League, as all North Korean children did, and at ten years old another honor was bestowed upon her: she was chosen to present a bouquet of flowers to a South Korean diplomat visiting the North on a mission of greater understanding.

At this early age Kim and her classmates were only too well aware of what happened to people who stepped outside the Party line; they and their relatives just disappeared. "One day there would be gaps in the classroom because the children had been taken away with their parents to a concentration camp. The children always said, 'Let's not talk about it.' " But when Kim was thirteen, her best friend vanished. "She was my bosom friend, from elementary school days. Rumor had it that her father had uttered a wrong statement, or her brother was a South Korean agent—something like that. So all of a sudden the family vanished; even the married sister was divorced because of the shame. We heard that her parents had been put in front of a firing squad and she and her brothers and sisters had been sent away to Yang Kang province to the concentration camp.

"I don't know how it managed to reach me, but one day a letter arrived for me from this girl telling me about the hardships she faced.

"Disappearances happened so frequently that you were aware from very young that if you put a foot wrong, then that is what would happen to you. We lived in an atmosphere of fear and intimidation. Not only do you have agents from National Security watching you, but in each of the housing units one family out of the five will be informers. This family must report everything, so they watch and monitor you at all times, therefore you have to behave very carefully at all times.

"When I came here I was told that wives worry about their husbands' drinking because of concern about their health. But in North Korea the wives are more afraid that a husband who is drunk will say something that violates the Party line and will endanger the whole family."

In high school, North Korean students must donate one month of labor a year to the Party and 150 days throughout the year as volunteers for rice transplanting, harvesting, or construction works. The children are formed into units called "Speed Battle Youth Shock Brigades" and have built railroads, a museum, an apartment complex, and a children's amusement center. Kim was sent to work in the paddy fields, where her ambition kept her at the backbreaking task. "It was very hard labor for children, always bending down, but I was determined not to take a rest to show that I was better than the others."

When she was around fourteen, she expressed the wish to become a biologist—simply because Kim Il Sung had recently honored a woman biologist. Then she toyed with the idea of becoming a musician, specializing in Korean music. But her parents were anxious for their beautiful and talented daughter to marry well when the time came. Her father urged her to study languages, particularly Japanese, in the hope that she might become a diplomat, be posted to Tokyo, and make a good marriage.

She enrolled at Kim Il Sung University and did outstandingly well in the Japanese language course. In her second year she was summoned to the office of her department head; her progress and dedication to the Party had attracted some attention. In the room were some Party officials from headquarters, and three other female students. The girls were all asked about their family background, and their attitude toward serving the Great Leader. Kim remembered that it was just a general discussion. Some days later she received a letter ordering her attendance at Party headquarters. She found that of the four students originally interviewed there was just herself and a younger girl left. They were both questioned again, then informed that they were to meet some guidance officers from the research department, the North Korean equivalent of a secret service. The guidance officers quizzed them on their political ideology, ability to memorize facts, and observation skills. Kim was further tested in her proficiency in Japanese; then they were both dismissed.

Three days later came another order to attend headquarters, when Kim was introduced to the director of the research department and more Party officials. She was instructed to have a full medical checkup and after that was photographed. She had passed all the tests. A week later a Party official arrived on her doorstep: she was to return her library books, pay her outstanding university fees, and make the most of one last night at home.

"I was very excited," recalled Kim. "Any personal order that comes from Central Party headquarters is a supreme honor and is accepted unconditionally. My father, being a diplomat, probably knew what such an order from such a department meant, and he might have felt a sense of distress, but all he said to me was, 'Just go and do well.'" With full parental approval and pride, then, Miss Kim set out on her career as an agent.

It was the last time Kim would see her family for two years; the last time she would ever be able to talk to them about her life. Her family ties were to be snipped and her ideological training intensified. The Party was prepared to invest a lot of time, effort, and funds in making the eighteen-year-old girl a finely tuned, emotionless, and obedient robot.

She was driven away in a government car to Kimsong Political Military College, where she was to stay for a year of basic training. She lived in student accommodations with another young woman, who was also undergoing training and who was assigned as her partner.

They had each been given new identities, and in order to maintain total security they had to wear dark glasses when they were together. Whenever they went out they had to cover their heads with umbrellas. Kim's sense of isolation was complete. The pair did not initially trust each other, suspecting the other was an informer. "I felt loneliness in my bones," she said. They were forbidden any contact with the outside world and any discussion of their past or families.

The course was hard and the hours long, with intensive daily sessions on political ideology, small-arms fire, codes, languages, and instruction on operating communications equipment. Kim found that in addition to Japanese she also had to learn Chinese. Although the two young women attended lectures at the college, they saw no other students because the classrooms were partitioned into cubicles, surrounded by screens. But worst of all for Kim was the physical training: "You know, we had just been taken straight from college life into this world of student-agents. You have left your home and you do not know when you will see it again. Then the very hard physical training began, and I suffered greatly from the stress and strain on my body.

"For the first time in my life I had to run several miles at one stretch; at times I felt like I was going to drop dead. But every time

I reached the limit of my strength I told myself that I had to push further so that I could become an able revolutionary; so I gritted my teeth and went on. At the end of my training I could swim two kilometers and run forty kilometers over rough ground at night."

After the first year she was warmly commended by her guidance officer on her progress and told she was much better than her partner. Miss Kim's hunger for approval had been satisfied; after that the relationship between the two women grew more friendly, with Kim helping her partner over difficult tasks.

They were dispatched for more skilled training into the mountain range that covers most of North Korea and leads to the border with China. Within the mountains are located ten guerrilla camps where in the last twenty years over 10,000 foreign trainees have received instruction in kidnapping, assassination, ambush, marksmanship, bombing, and agitation.

Their home for the next six years was to be a government "guest house" in the mountains, near to one of these camps. In spite of the proximity of hundreds of other student guerrillas, the two young women met no one. The research department had decided to concentrate on perfecting Kim's Japanese to the point where she could be placed in that country to gather intelligence.

Kim was taken to a separate house, where she met a Japanese woman, Li Eun Hye. Li was in a state of shock: she had just been kidnapped from a beach in Japan by North Korean agents. She was a married woman with two children aged two and five. At first she refused to eat and sat weeping; but eventually she seemed to give up and accepted Kim as her first pupil.

A typical day of becoming Japanese started at 6:30 A.M. with ninety minutes' intensive exercise. Breakfast was at 8 A.M., followed by prayers to Kim Il Sung for thirty minutes. Lessons in Japanese lasted for four hours, followed by lunch, more Japanese, supper at 7 P.M., then watching Japanese documentaries and reading Japanese newspapers until 11 P.M. Each morning for twenty minutes Kim was questioned on the previous day's work and was taught about Japanese food, dietary habits, housewives' daily lives, geography, how to use trains and buses in Japan. On Saturdays there was a general examination to evaluate what she had learned that week.

Miss Kim was initially cold and disapproving of her Japanese teacher, noting with disapproval that "she frequently drank, and smoked a packet of cigarettes a day." The excuse for such unlady-like behavior, she surmized, was that the woman "had loved her children very much." Eventually, however, a crack in Miss Kim's emotional and ideological armor appeared:

"At first I was not sympathetic to her at all because Japan had occupied our country for thirty-six years and the Japanese had committed terrible atrocities against our people. I felt that the Japanese had moral obligations to help us in our efforts for reunification. So this woman was only doing what was required to pay for the past wrongdoings of her people.

"But as I got to know her—we lived together for a year and a half—I began to feel sorry for her, and in the end we became close friends. I had to be 'Japanized,' so I had to learn their customs and habits. Her job was to educate me as swiftly as possible, so we talked Japanese all the time—in the end I became very convincing."

The abduction of Li Eun Hye may sound farfetched, but there have been newspaper reports of similar cases. The kidnapped Japanese apparently enjoy a privileged lifestyle for teaching North Korean agents their language and customs. It is unlikely that they would ever be allowed to return home.

After two full years' training, Kim was told she was being allowed home for two nights and three days—the occasion was Kim Il Sung's birthday on April 15. There were several conditions: she was not to talk about her training or hint at what she was doing; she was not to meet up with any old friends; she was not to go out. Surprisingly Kim broke one rule: she invited some of her best friends to her parents' apartment. It was a strange reunion: "My parents and relatives were of course very happy and elated that I was visiting because they thought that I might not come home at all. Although they did not know exactly what I was doing, they knew it was something to do with the Central Party and they suspected it might have something to do with reunification. They might have guessed at more but everyone understood that it was not a matter to be openly discussed.

"My mother did show some distress. It is known in North Korea that working for reunification is very dangerous and can involve risking one's life. So although my mother was delighted that I looked in good shape, and was hale and hearty, she couldn't entirely hide her feelings of concern."

Back in the mountains, Kim underwent advanced training in professional espionage, including military training, driving cars, photography, and a course in clandestine telecommunications. Then, in July 1984, after four years' training, she was given her first mission.

Her new partner was introduced to her, a sixty-seven-year-old man called Kim Sung Il. He was an expert in electronics; proficient in Japanese, Chinese, English, and Russian; and he had been a "supreme" agent for many years. Kim's first impression of him was that he was old and weak; she was right—he was suffering from a stomach growth, which was causing him much pain.

The two agents were told that they were to pose as a Japanese father-and-daughter team, and their first assignment was to visit Europe to acclimate themselves to capitalist cultures and to test their cover and effectiveness as Japanese tourists. Again, Kim recalls that she was "overwhelmed at the trust the Party put in me" in allowing her to travel overseas.

A month later they traveled to Vienna, Copenhagen, Frankfurt, Geneva, and Paris. They were provided with false passports and instructions: on their return they were expected to write a critical report on conditions of poverty; they were not to write a travelogue. With such a command ringing in her ears, Kim remembered little of the tourist attractions on the way. She liked the streets of Paris and was awestruck by the mountains of Switzerland. She was fascinated by the fast-food establishments and yearned to go into a pizza parlor and eat, but she was afraid that it would be too expensive. "I did not know that it was relatively cheap food, and although I was in charge of the money, ten thousand dollars, we were expected to be frugal."

She and Mr. Kim got on well, and the young woman revered the elderly man because of his vast experience. They always shared a room together, but their relationship never became sexual. "That was out of the question. I looked up to him and respected him and he respected me," she said firmly.

They were not there to enjoy themselves, so Miss Kim dutifully recorded every beggar she saw, every poor family. She had been entrusted with the physical care of Mr. Kim, and had to make sure he took his medicine on time. They were frightened to be among Japanese tourists in case they made a mistake, and for much of the time they stayed in their room, blaming the cold weather for their seclusion.

There was an unusual amount of trust between the pair. On their return to North Korea, they had to write three reports: one of conditions in Europe, and then two other critical reports, one of themselves, and the other of their fellow agent. In Vienna they had an argument that, if they had reported it, would have caused severe difficulties for both of them. In a department store they lost sight of each other. Kim went back to the hotel to find her "father" waiting for her and they quarreled because their instructions were to go nowhere alone. "We agreed not to include this lapse in our reports," she said.

She returned to Pyongyang laden with clothes and gifts for her family, guidance officer, and section chief. There was cloth for four men's suits and dresses for women, a Parker fountain pen, ten luxury lighters, and ten boxes of ballpoint pens. Kim had also bought several outfits for herself, but these were considered to be essential equipment for her future role as an espionage agent. "It had been difficult for me to find clothes that fit," said Kim, who is small framed and five feet three inches tall. "The only ones I could find had been made in South Korea, so I could not buy them."

I asked her if the experience of seeing so many people who were obviously not starving or dying of disease and shops full of consumer goods in capitalist European cities had not made her question Party teachings? No, she had been like a tank moving through enemy terrain; nothing could dent her. "When I saw the wonderful affluence, I didn't admire it. I thought that we would have all this one day in North Korea, and the only reason we do not have it now is that we are fighting against capitalist forces, so our money has to go for defense. Seeing the much better standard of life in Europe made me want reunification more, and then our own people would enjoy the luxuries I saw."

The mission completed, Kim wrote a glowing account of her fellow agent's conduct, and of her own she included just a small piece of self-criticism—that she had wanted to buy some cosmetics and went off on her own. Not to have criticized herself would have led to questions being asked.

The research department was delighted with the two Kims; the Party officers thought they made a perfect Japanese traveling couple. "They felt we were fail-proof, I think. The only problem was that sometimes I looked more like his granddaughter than his daughter but that was not important. We camouflaged each other very well."

For the next three years, Kim underwent further intensive training in languages. She was sent to Canton in China to acquire an authentic Chinese accent and to Macao for eighteen months. All her training was reinforcing her belief that one day she would be sent to Tokyo as a spy. She had no idea that her next mission would make her a mass murderer and change her life forever.

On October 7, 1987, she was summoned to the research department in Pyongyang, where she found Mr. Kim waiting. They were to be paired again as father and daughter, he told her, for a very special mission. The young woman was shocked at Mr. Kim's appearance; he was seventy now, but he looked extremely ill. There was no time for further conversation; the pair was shown into the office of the director.

On his desk were some extremely important orders, the director told them. They came directly from Kim Jung Il, son of the Great Leader and commonly known as "The Dear Leader."

"The Party has decided to bomb a Korean Air plane with the aim of blocking South Korea's attempts to perpetuate the two Koreas and also to host the 1988 Olympics on its own.

"This project, to be carried out at a crucial juncture in time, will pour cold water on the desire of all nations of the world to participate in the Olympics and will deal the South Korean puppet regime a fatal blow.

"This project must be accomplished without fail and must be kept in absolute secrecy."

Those were the orders, and it had been decided that the excellent Japanese father-and-daughter team was to carry them out. Miss Kim was staggered at the enormity of the task before her, but delighted to have been chosen. If she succeeded in her mission, honors would be heaped upon her. To refuse would be out of the question, she explained: "I could not have disobeyed the order, even if I had wanted to—if I had done so I would have been put straight in front of a firing squad, and perhaps my family too. Once you are an agent, you go all the way. Once a mission is given, there is no question of an individual even thinking about it because to do that would be to suggest that the Party could do wrong, and that is not possible.

"Although I was overcome by the enormity of it, I was determined to accomplish it. Besides, I had been waiting and waiting for that final day, for an important mission. The previous trip to Europe now looked like nothing, just a dress rehearsal. I had trained for seven years and eight months for this and it was a great honor. Many other agents had waited for much longer than me to be given a mission, and then nothing like the one I had."

The director impressed on the two agents that this mission had to work. "In the case of any emergency, he told us we were to stay on the plane with the bomb and go all the way. He said that we were fighting at the vanguard for reunification and that we would be honored as such.

"I felt tremendous determination to succeed, even at the sacrifice of my own life. As agents, we had been told time and time again that if necessary we had to lay our lives down for the Great Leader. Also we should be ready and willing to die to keep the secrets entrusted to us."

The agents were sent to another guest house where they underwent extensive training in explosives for a month. Then Miss Kim was given special permission to visit her family, an exceptional privilege for, like all other agents, she had been allowed home only five times in the last seven years.

The question "Did your parents have any idea about the mission?" brought a swift and bitter response.

"There was no way they would have known about it. I had become a member of the Party's family. The Party had the only say in my future. My future was nothing for my parents to poke their noses into; I was the Party's daughter. I was allowed to see my parents because of my past ties with them."

Her eyes wandered from the table around which we sat, catching those of the *onni,* who was sitting with her back to us but watching Kim closely through the reflection in a mirror on the wall. It is beyond doubt that Kim's parents are, at least, in a concentration camp; at worst, executed long ago. On the last visit with her family she was told by her grieving mother that her younger brother had died earlier in the year of skin cancer. Her parents had tried to notify her, but the research department had forbidden it because it might have disturbed her training.

It was a terrible blow for Miss Kim, but the prospect of her forthcoming mission had left her emotionally numb.

On her return to the safe house, she was given little time to think. She and Mr. Kim were to fly from Pyongyang on November 12 on an inaugural flight from North Korea to East Berlin via Moscow. They were to be accompanied for the first part of the journey by their section chief and guidance officer, then they were to travel alone from Moscow to Vienna, where they would be supplied with explosives. After planting the bombs, they were to disembark at Abu Dhabi and fly back to Vienna, where their section chief and guidance officer would be waiting to escort them back to Pyong-yang.

Miss Kim was to prepare and set the time bombs, and they were both ordered to kill themselves by swallowing cyanide if they were caught.

At 6 A.M. on November 12, the Kims were formally handed the written order, personally penned by Kim Jung Il, to bomb Korean Air Flight 858. Then they were taken up to a lounge in the government guest house and placed in front of a picture of Kim Jung Il.

In a steady voice, Miss Kim repeated: "At this juncture, when the whole nation is undergoing the grand construction of socialism at the pace of the 1980s, the revolution in the South [student riots] is at a high pitch, and the enemies' attempt to perpetuate the two Koreas in getting increasingly malicious, I, having been assigned to a combat mission behind the frontlines, will keep in mind the Party's trust and consideration, will abide by the Three Revolutionary Codes (for organization, mission, and life) and will truthfully carry out my mission in close cooperation with my partner. I will fight to the death for the lofty authority and prestige of the beloved leader."

After the oath-taking ceremony, they had breakfast and at 7 A.M. left the guest house to be driven to the airport. Miss Kim remembered being given a variety of gifts by the air stewardesses on board the plane—playing cards, key holders, and wallets as mementos of the maiden flight. "It has stuck in my mind because I was not used to receiving gifts," she explained simply. A North Korean agent based at the embassy in Moscow met them on their arrival and informed them that they had six hours before catching a flight to Budapest. He took them out to dinner and then saw them off on the next stage of their journey.

They arrived at 4 A.M., were collected by another North Korean agent, and taken to his home. For five days they acted like tourists, visiting Budapest Square, the Lion Bridge, and the Palace of Buda, or at least Miss Kim did. Mr. Kim seemed too ill to do much and confided in the young woman that he had just had several operations on his stomach. The doctors had declared him seriously ill, but the Party was determined that he should carry on with the mission. He refused to tell her the nature of his illness, but she guessed it was cancer. She was concerned for her fellow agent because if he became too ill she would have to go on with the bombing herself; also she felt genuine fondness for the old man.

"He could not eat properly, and no rich food at all. I had to make sure he took painkillers at the right time and always had his drugs on him. He did not help himself because he insisted on drinking six cups of coffee a day, but whenever I protested, saying it would inflame his stomach, he would say, 'I have lived long enough, and I like coffee.' "

Miss Kim went shopping for clothes and jewelry. It was not, she insisted, that she liked shopping, or being photographed beside the Lion Bridge just days before planting bombs. "I had to look like a tourist, and the new clothes were necessary because I should not be seen to be wearing North Korean garments."

The Budapest-based agent drove the Kims to Vienna in his car and left them at a hotel. The next day Miss Kim walked into an Austrian Airlines office to buy tickets to Belgrade, then Vienna and on to Baghdad, where they would board the plane that they would destroy—Korean Air Flight 858 to Seoul. There were ten days to go before the bombing of the aircraft.

They spent the time sight-seeing, taking pictures of each other, and buying more "equipment"—clothing and shoes. They flew to Belgrade and booked into another hotel. At 7 P.M. on November 27, there was a knock at their door; their station chief and guidance officer from Pyongyang had arrived with the explosives, already packed in the radio and whisky bottle.

November 28 was D day for the agents. By nightfall they would have placed the bags on board the aircraft. By the early hours they would have disembarked—as long as nothing went wrong; otherwise they would probably be dead. On the morning of the twenty-eighth, the Kims tried to rest, but found it impossible; neither of them had slept much for the past sixteen days. At 2:35 P.M. they flew from Belgrade to Baghdad, arriving at seven o'clock in the evening. They had a four-and-a-half hour wait before boarding KAL 858.

They had a tense moment before boarding when a woman airport official searched Miss Kim and her personal belongings. The official took the radio out of the plastic bag and tossed away the batteries, which were needed to trigger the explosion. Unfortunately for the other passengers, Mr. Kim saved the day by swift presence of mind. In a loud voice he complained that no other airport official had ever treated his daughter like that, and picking up the batteries, replaced them and switched the radio on. The official shrugged and let the Kims pass.

Twenty minutes before boarding they set the alarm of the radio clock for nine hours later. Miss Kim claimed that she cannot remember looking at the other passengers when they began to embark. "We were so uptight and tense that I have no recollection of feelings of any kind," she said. She placed the bag in the overhead rack and then leaned back to count the minutes to Abu Dhabi.

It was just before 3 A.M. that the Kims walked into the terminal at Abu Dhabi. If they had believed in a God they would have been praying to him, but all they could do was trust that the bombs would work. The most crucial task now before them was to escape, and suddenly things started to go wrong.

They had intended to wait at the airport for a few hours before flying to Rome. But immigration officials demanded to see their visas for Abu Dhabi, and they had none. The officials then asked for their tickets, and they had to show them, revealing that Bahrain was their next destination. The Bahrain destination was only a decoy, but they were forced to board the flight by the airport staff, who thought they were being helpful. The Kims became afraid that they would be sitting targets in Bahrain if any Korean Air official checked on them.

They still hoped to be able to fly to Rome as soon as they arrived at Bahrain, but found that all flights were booked for the next two days. They checked into a hotel in the city and prepared to sit it out.

Meanwhile, Flight 858 had disappeared after its last communication with Rangoon control tower. Immediately the Korean government suspected sabotage, probably by North Korean agents. Korean Air started to scan the list of all passengers, particularly those who had disembarked at Abu Dhabi. The Korean Air branch chief in Abu Dhabi thought that two Japanese were suspicious: Mayumi Hachiya, a twenty-seven-year-old woman, and her father Shinichi, aged sixty-nine.

When he checked their previous itinerary on the computer he found that they had visited well-known haunts of North Korean agents, Belgrade and Vienna. Although they were on a long trip they had checked no baggage, and also they had not used their family name for their tickets, giving instead their first names—and Japanese never did that. Stranger still, they had used Korean Air Flight 858 passing through Baghdad and Abu Dhabi and endured three- to six-hour waits in transit lounges, when they could have reached their destination, Bahrain, by a direct route from Belgrade. The Korean Air office in Bahrain was asked to try to locate the mysterious Hachiyas.

An official there began phoning around hotels and discovered that the suspects had booked into the Regency Intercontinental. He obtained their passport numbers from Bahrain immigration control and passed them onto the Japanese Embassy.

Startling information came back. The young woman's passport number belonged to a man; she was using a false passport.

The Kims had spent November 30 getting tickets for a flight to Rome the next morning and sight-seeing in Bahrain city. They returned to their hotel room in the early evening to find their telephone ringing: it was the manager asking for their names, dates of birth, and passport numbers. The phone rang again, the Japanese embassy asking the same questions, and then a third time, a South Korean diplomat from the embassy saying that he would be calling on them soon.

The diplomat arrived to find Miss Kim apparently asleep on the bed; he was greeted cordially by her "father," who expressed bewilderment at the intrusion. In a mixture of Japanese and English the diplomat explained that the plane they had left at Abu Dhabi had crashed. Lying on her bed, Miss Kim breathed a sigh of relief; mission accomplished.

Their visitor did not stay long. Although he suspected that the couple was involved in the jet's disappearance, he was not sure that they were not Japanese, and if that was the case, the Japanese would want to take over any investigation.

Left on their own, the Kims were jubilant, but fearful. "We had to get away, that was our chief worry," recalled Miss Kim. Her fellow agent assured her that all would be well; they would be off to Rome at eight-thirty in the morning.

They overslept and awoke at 7 A.M. While hastily packing their few belongings, Mr. Kim reminded his partner about the cyanide capsule in her handbag. They both knew that death by their own hands was becoming a strong possibility.

As they left for the airport in a taxi, a Japanese diplomat arrived to question them, and finding the Hachiyas had just checked out, sped after them. He spotted the pair going through passport control and asked Bahrain officials to arrest them.

Miss Kim recalled: "They took us into a room, and the Japanese man told us our passports were false. We would be sent to Japan for questioning.

"We were left alone, and Mr. Kim said that we were finished. If we were sent to Japan they would torture us and get the truth somehow; we had to take the poison right away.

"At that moment, the Bahrain policemen came in and took us to separate rooms to search us and our belongings. It was a thorough body search, but they did not check my packet of cigarettes. Then they put us back together, but with a police guard.

"Mr. Kim whispered to me as he lit a cigarette: 'I have lived my life, but you, my beautiful young lady, that you should have to die, I am sorry.' I took out my packet of Marlboros and prepared to bite into the filter. I thought, this is it, this is how I shall die, and my mother's face appeared to me. But I said, it is better this way; no one shall know our secrets.

"The policewoman saw the cigarette in my mouth, and suddenly made a grab for it. I bit into the filter and lost consciousness."

The cigarette fell from her mouth and she did not inhale enough of the cyanide to die. She awoke in a Bahrain hospital under heavy guard and was overcome with self-disgust at her failed suicide attempt. She was told that her partner had died instantly, and felt only envy for him: "He had succeeded and I had failed. I felt full of revulsion for myself that I was still alive. Now, I thought, I will be dragged to South Korean and tortured. I felt a great sense of nihilism, of groping in the dark. My own self was repulsive to me and rebelled at life."

She was so terrified of the South Korean CIA interrogators when she was taken on board the plane bound for Seoul that she did not look at them. "I thought it was the end of the world, so I closed my eyes and did not open them." In a further desperate bid at suicide, she began biting her tongue, so a gag was placed in her mouth.

Thus, gagged and shaking, she was half carried down the aircraft's steps when it arrived in Seoul. The *onni*, a young woman only a few years older than her captive, was dumbfounded: "I had expected a very tough, well-trained terrorist. This girl was pathetic, so weak. I did not feel sorry for her; I was just very surprised."

Miss Kim was taken to a safe house and put to bed. She was filmed and taped secretly, and the first shot shows her lying on what appears to be a hospital bed, clad in white silk pajamas. She is extremely listless as a doctor examines her left leg, which was hurt when she collapsed after biting into the capsule. Carefully, he lifts it, holding it up, bending it. In the next frame, a day or so later, Kim is sitting beside a table with an IV in her arm because she is refusing food.

Then the interrogation begins. Miss Kim is wearing trousers and a jerkin and pretending to be Japanese. An *onni* sits beside her, and there are several men in the room, one sitting opposite and firing questions at her. The *onni*, speaking Korean, has a plate of food in her lap, which she is encouraging the prisoner to eat. Miss Kim responds in Japanese, disdaining the Korean national favorite of dried seaweed. "What is that, burned paper?" she demands.

Soon she appears more relaxed, wearing the clothes of the *onni*. At one point on the video, she reveals in Chinese that she is an orphan and the *onni* puts her arms around her, as if in sympathy. The interrogator talks to her in Chinese, Korean, Japanese, and Miss Kim appears nervous, plucking at the sleeve of her sweater. She recites Chinese poetry.

Slowly her story begins to fall apart. She is asked in Japanese if she has a television at home. Yes, she replies. What make? asks the interrogator. Azalea, says Miss Kim. It is quite an error. Azalea is the name of the only TV set sold in North Korea. She is asked the name of a former prime minister of Japan; she gets it wrong. What is the driver's side in Japan? Left, she says—wrong again.

On the eighth day she breaks. Laughing, throwing her hair back, she writes her real name and address on a piece of paper. To me, it seems odd that she is laughing as she confesses that she bombed a plane—more like a ten-year-old caught scribbling rude words on a blackboard—but the interrogators explained that laughter is the Korean way of showing great embarrassment and regret. Strange, but true; a Western friend living in South Korea told me how he had been in the process of explaining to a Korean colleague that his young daughter had been seriously injured in a road accident, when the man burst into peals of laughter.

The interrogators began to drive Miss Kim around Seoul so that she could witness for herself people walking freely in the street and see the goods in the shops. They made her watch television to see the news programs, and gradually a change came over their prisoner. She became confused, then finally angry, when the television news showed a photograph of her at ten years old and presenting flowers to a South Korean diplomat. The North had issued a statement saying that Kim Hyon Hui was a fictitious name; she had never been a resident in their country, and, moreover, a North Korean woman living in Japan had claimed the photograph was of herself.

"That is when she finally started to trust us," said the *onni*. "She felt betrayed and came to see that the North told lies."

The chief interrogator added: "When she first came here she was shocked when we talked of Kim Il Sung without first using an epithet like Great Leader. Now she shouts and swears when he appears on television."

He has grown fond of Miss Kim. On her desk in the safe house is a small rock that he had given her. When I asked why, he became rather defensive: "Because I like giving her presents," he said. He beams upon his captive rather in the manner of Professor Higgins with Eliza, and he has good cause to.

Since her confession, Miss Kim has made a complete about-face on the teachings of her childhood and training as an agent. "I am now dedicated to eliminating terrorism around the world and to exposing the evils of North Korea," she announced, adding rather naively, "I wish terrorists would go away."

She sighed: "In my case, I thought I was on a holy combat mission, but eventually I ended up becoming one of them, a terrorist. I understand why it happened to me, but it is very hard for me to understand the acts of terrorism in free societies. They are people who, in the first place, live in open worlds, where they can see everything with their own eyes, hear everything with their own ears, where they can make their own decisions based on what they know.

"I cannot comprehend how it is possible for them to do terrorist acts while living under such tolerable conditions. It is a very piteous thing they do, a very dreadful thing, and I think they should disappear from this world. I think they must be people who have lost their judgment, these people who choose to commit terrorism of their own volition, without being driven to it." Miss Kim, then, would be of the school that considers political revolutionaries to be mad. She had a special word to say on the subject of women who might become involved in such movements:

"As for women choosing terrorism, I do not think that in this area they need to compete with men. It is OK for women to try to be equal to men for the good of society, but not to its detriment."

The notion that women may feel so angry and frustrated at being repressed that they want to hit out violently at the system was utterly alien to her. She did, however, believe that she had been chosen for her mission because no one would suspect a Korean woman of bombing an aircraft. Her beauty and demure appearance had been used most calculatingly by her masters. It was in the same league as women being used to carry "baby bombs." Who would suspect an obviously pregnant woman of concealing anything but her unborn child beneath her smock? Miss Kim's ambition to succeed, her desire for Party approval, and deep sense of commitment had also been used; her masters had been in no doubt that if the occasion merited it, she would have become a suicide bomber, obedient to the last.

"In Korean society, women are thought to be afraid to walk about on their own, so it would be unthinkable for a woman to put a bomb on an airplane. Also, I was not a gloomy person; I was quite vivacious and I had a good record in my training. I know that Mr. Kim wanted me for his partner because we got on well."

She had shown no emotion, beyond envy, on being told of Mr. Kim's death, but the interrogators do not consider that as unusual. The *onni* commented: "I have known her for two years now, and she has never shown any emotion—neither to me, nor to anyone else." Any emotion that Miss Kim did have was systematically erased during her training. One remembered her response when asked if she thought her parents had any inkling of what she was about to do when she visited them for that last time. She had snapped, "My future was nothing for my parents to poke their noses into. I was the Party's daughter." Also, I had at first found it difficult to understand how Miss Kim, knowing that she had left a bomb on an airplane, could have gone sight-seeing in Bahrain, or shopping for clothes immediately before the mission. She had explained that such activities were essential to maintain her cover as an innocent tourist. After meeting her I understood that it was not fair to expect her to feel as other people would. She was no longer an individual, she was a machine, and it seems that whatever had been done to her emotions was permanent.

The *onni* was not critical of Miss Kim; she felt pity for her. "I do not think she is a malicious woman, just that her training has made her that way. I can remember once there was a cockroach in her room and she would not kill it. She has been made the way that she is, cold emotionally."

The interrogators rejected the idea that Miss Kim needs any outside counseling or psychological help. The chief interrogator insisted: "We are all that she needs." However, a few months after her confession, and just before her trial, he admitted that their captive began to show signs of deep depression. He presented her with a Bible and some Buddhist writings, which she eagerly read, then she asked to see a priest. Under heavy security one was brought to her. Shortly afterward she declared that she had converted to Christianity.

Her new faith, she claimed, has helped her enormously. "Before I began to believe in Christ, I deplored my fate to kill so many people. I lamented the twisted path of my life and I suffered deeply. I simply wanted to die and to die a hundred times for what I had done. But since I came to believe in God, I feel I have been given the gift of life. I read the Bible where it says that our sins are washed away and that we are born again.

"If it was up to me, I would live a life of remorse and reflection. It is only now that I am in a free society that I can feel remorse for what I have done. When I left the bomb on board, I did not have even a sliver of remorse. Oh, what a fool I was. Now, again and again I think of the people I killed and how that nothing I do can condone that action. The only thing is for me to talk of the evils of North Korea and fight terrorism, and that is what I will do, rather than live as I would wish, in seclusion."

There is little chance that Miss Kim will be allowed to pursue a life locked away from the world, although she is technically now a free woman. South Korea has given her life, but there are strings attached. Whenever the students riot and call for Communism, she will be wheeled out to rail against such mad behavior. Whenever the CIA, the Japanese intelligence unit, or any other power friendly to the South wants to see her, she will be on show.

If it had been left up to her, Miss Kim would never have granted this interview. She is shocked, she says, at the way in which she is looked upon as a sort of star. "It is a freakish idea. I deserve to be punished, not to have films made about me. I am a criminal and I deserve to be pointed out as one for the rest of my life." There is only one thing that frightens her—the prospect of being cast adrift from her interrogators. "They are my closest friends, to whom I have bared my soul. I feel deeply sorry for the way I acted toward them at first, pretending I was Japanese or Chinese." Most tellingly, she added, "They are going to take care of me and make an entirely new person out of me."

The interrogators take their role in re-creating Miss Kim very seriously. She is seldom allowed to be on her own, apart from a brief spell in the morning when she reads the Bible. Every few days they take her for a walk in the city, "to acclimatize for freedom," but as in the days of her espionage training, Miss Kim is always in disguise. When she began to get fat after months of inactivity in the safe house, it was the interrogators who put her on a strict diet.

She finds it difficult to think for herself: when an interrogator asked her why she was not keeping a diary, Miss Kim replied nervously, "Because no one told me to."

One ends by feeling a degree of sympathy for Miss Kim, for the way in which, if she is to be believed, she was turned into a machine to carry out the whim of a dictator. She appears to have retained her sanity, now that she has switched sides, by loading all the blame of her bombing of the aircraft onto her upbringing and manipulation by evil masters. Not only is she now in the hands of the righteous, but she has got a new life through religion, a religion that blots out the past. When asked about accepting any degree of responsibility for her past actions, she clucked her tongue with impatience. "I think that is an approach only possible in capitalist societies where one has free choice. It was not possible for me in North Korea."

Now that she is living in a free society, she continued, she is learning to make her own decisions. One questions how free she really is. If she was molded into becoming a terrorist, she is equally being molded now into a mouthpiece for the South. She was most reluctant to pose for photographs, but she really had no choice; she was told by the interrogators that she was to be photographed. Perhaps, I suggested, she should think of becoming an interrogator herself? Her eyes lit up, then caught those of the *onni* and she lowered her head. "I have not yet thought about that," she said softly.

Chapter 3

✿ THE WOMEN OF THE

WEST BANK

"The Intifada is my son."

It is just past midnight and the woman in black is there again, standing alone in the outskirts of the village. As she starts to hurl stones at the soldiers' jeep, flashlights break the night sky and there is a warning burst of gunfire. The woman vanishes. Ten minutes later, when all is in darkness, she reappears and the stones fly again. She keeps it up for two hours. It is the second night she has performed her solitary demonstration. No one in the village knows who she is or where she comes from.

The blue sky seems to be filled with flying objects—stones and rocks, some catapulted by an expert eleven-year-old, others thrown a few feeble feet by a toddler. Tires are set alight, their acrid fumes burning the eyes and nose. The soldiers retaliate in a rush of gunfire and tear gas. Now everyone is running, but a boy, perhaps ten years old, is caught. His screams rend the air as a soldier's wooden truncheon smashes into his back and legs. From nowhere a crowd of women appear running like the Furies at the soldier who has the boy. They surround the pair, and the soldier, frightened, ceases beating. He tries to ward off the women who are all screaming that this is their son. In the confusion one grabs the boy and hurries him away.

There is gunfire and shouting in the camp—the soldiers are here. The mother kicks her eight-year-old son, sitting absorbed in the exchange between his sister and the interpreter. The boy jumps up, red faced, and runs out. The interpreter explains: "She said, 'Shame, get out and fight with your brothers and sisters.' "

This is the Intifada, the uprising by Palestinians begun in October 1987 against Israeli military occupation of the West Bank and the Gaza Strip. One might be forgiven for thinking that the stones and lumps of rock, which constitute the main arsenal of the fighters, would not qualify as weapons of terror—especially against a well-armed and trained army. The Israeli authorities, however, have decreed that anyone who throws a stone at an Israeli soldier is threatening state security.

The Intifada was temporarily suspended at the outbreak of the war against Iraq, when Palestinians living in the occupied territories were placed under almost continuous curfew. At the end of the war, however, the Intifada was reborn with a vengeance.

When I visited in the summer of 1989, it had been in full swing: everyone appeared to be involved, from stone-throwing toddlers to eighty-year-olds, but none more so than the women. "They are worth ten men," said a camp commander with a rueful grin.

Young girls constituted at least half of the *shebab*—the army of young people that hurled missiles at the soldiers. They were experts in the tactics of street warfare and were treated as equals by the boys. In the Gaza Strip, where the unrest began and where the pure white sand was blackened by fire, girls and boys, eight years old and upward, erected roadblocks of burned-out cars, oil drums, and debris from the camps before a demonstration began. Many were dressed from top to toe in black, their eyes gleaming through slits in their hoods. Their weapons were sticks and stones, sling-shots and bicycle chains. These small black figures called themselves the "Ninja."

On general strike days, which occurred at least twice a week, the girls joined the boys in stoning anyone driving a car or attempting to work. The *shebab* was a fearful force, the girls possessing as deadly an aim with the stone or Molotov as their brothers.

Fatin, a blond, blue-eyed ten-year-old from Al Jalazoun camp near Ramallah on the West Bank mimed a hand-to-hand struggle she had had with a soldier the previous day. Her family had been given ten minutes to evacuate their home before it was demolished as a "terrorist stronghold." Her struggle was over a pane of glass that her father was just about to install. Fatin fought bravely, her parents said, but the soldier smashed the glass anyway. Beside Fatin stood her twenty-year-old sister, holding up X rays, which showed two bullets lodged in her chest—the result of being outside during a demonstration.

The older women of the Intifada perform a variety of tasks. Some stand at the front of demonstrations, believing that the soldiers are less likely to shoot them. They also organize the riots, acting as lookouts during the fighting and warning the *shebab*, by prearranged signals, of a hidden soldier or the arrival of more troops. They descend on soldiers in droves to rescue the captured.

Women of all ages operate a highly effective intelligence network. Their voluminous traditional clothing hides a wide range of armor. They carry the weapons of the Intifada—stones, Molotov cocktails, and the illegal Palestinian flag—and march boldly through groups of soldiers. The Israelis are well aware that women are the chief weapon carriers, and although some women are stopped and searched, there is still an apparent reluctance in the army ranks to manhandle women. When it does happen, the soldiers have to be prepared to fight off an angry mob of Palestinian Muslim men, outraged at their women being physically violated by a male infidel hand.

Relying on the soldiers' fear, the women have grown bolder and smuggle money from the Palestinian Liberation Organization into the occupied territories. Other women operate safe houses for men and women on the run, moving their charges at night and carrying messages to their relatives.

One group of women with nursing or first-aid experience specializes in caring for those injured in the riots and in ferrying them to trusted doctors. Many Palestinians refuse to go to a hospital because of frequent raids by soldiers into the wards. Dr. Jurgen Rosendale, director of Ahli Arab Hospital in Gaza, said that arrest squads were frequent visitors. Staff were beaten up if they tried to intervene as soldiers dragged injured suspects from their beds.

Women are particularly active during curfew when it is forbidden to even appear at a window and the penalty is to be shot on sight. They form a network of food distribution and sneak out at night to take provisions to homes that run out. At Nablus, an Arab town on the West Bank, which was under military curfew for over a month, women rode out on donkeys at night to neighboring villages to get food. Some were caught and allegedly left tied up all day in the sun as punishment.

Other women run a different sort of Intifada—economic war against Israel. This is in response to a call from the underground PLO Unified Leadership—made up of the four main factions: Fateh, the Popular and Democratic Fronts for the Liberation of Palestine, and the Communist Party. The Leadership, which issues commands through Intifada leaflets, has appealed to all 1.5 million Palestinians to boycott Israeli goods and to create their own economy.

Four women's committees, each one representing a political faction, have accepted the challenge with a vengeance. They offer a series of training programs from sewing skills and yogurt-making to metalworking, with the finished goods going on sale to the local population. The committees also run health-care programs, kindergartens, and supply their own "popular" teaching for children in the West Bank, where schools have been closed down by the military authorities as "hotbeds of sedition."

More traditional women run charities, which offer the same sort of programs, but are largely based in towns. Neither these women nor those active on the committees, however, are looked on as philanthropic organizations by the military. Many of the women claim that they have been beaten and imprisoned for their work, materials and literature have been confiscated, their buildings closed down. It is illegal to give donations to the charities, as they are seen as centers for inciting the Intifada.

Palestinian women are well aware that they are on the frontline in every aspect of the Intifada. As the insurrection developed and tens of thousands of men were detained by the military, women took over the fight. With their men gone, there was no one else to do it, but it was more than that. The women became aware of their importance, and they were no longer prepared to be bystanders or widows. Participation was all.

They recognized, even as they fought, the similarity between themselves and the Algerian women in the war against French colonial rule in 1958–1964. Then, Muslim women also carried weaponry under their clothing and sacrificed their freedom and lives for the cause. After independence was won, however, the men made sure they went back into the home and the traditional role of

Muslim wife—even to the extent of being forced to wear the veil once more.

Palestinian women are thoroughly determined that they will not meet the same fate once the battle is won and an independent Palestinian state exists. They have the Algerian example, and they know their men. They are not prepared to be soldiers now and second-class citizens later. Their battle for independence as women has to be fought along with the Intifada, while they are in a position of power.

It is a lesson that women guerrillas from other societies are learning too. One thinks of ETA women and their determination to destroy the machismo that is so deeply ingrained in their men. The IRA women, too, have realized that the struggle for women's rights has to go hand in hand with their fight to evict the British presence from Ireland.

The Palestinian women have taken the lead in this war on two fronts. To prevent an outcome similar to that of the Algerian women, a small group formed the Women's Higher United Council. By June 1989 they had already drafted an Equal Rights for Women bill and placed it before the Unified Leadership. The men of the movement, relying as heavily as they do on the women's crucial roles, agreed, albeit reluctantly, to the bill. "Of course, there is no way that we would stop our activities, but we wanted the men to know that we have teeth too," said one of the women from the Higher United Council.

Israeli soldiers have been ordered not to open fire on women, but in the heat of battle and because of the way in which bullets are fired indiscriminately into crowds of rioters, inevitably women are killed. During the war with Iraq, when Palestinians were confined to their homes under the military curfew, a young mother from Nablus was shot dead by the Israeli Army. She had broken the curfew by standing on the balcony of her home.

By January 1991, ninety-seven females (12 percent of those killed) had been shot dead. Many had been killed in demonstrations either as participants or as innocent bystanders, after being hit by rubber bullets or live ammunition.

Thousands more women were injured, some crippled or maimed for life, by beatings. It is women who form the largest group of those requiring hospital treatment after beatings. They are attacked as they try to protect children and are particularly targeted when soldiers break into their homes searching for suspects. There is evidence that soldiers deliberately try to terrify entire families by showing brutality to women.

Soldiers have apparently been given detailed training in how to beat rioters and those who protect them. In their first three days of training, they are taught to administer "dry blows," which break bones swiftly, without blood being spilled. Doctors have noticed a pattern of injuries consistent with systematic beating. The orders come from the very top. The defense minister has decreed that rioters should be "left with scars. It is not enough for them to know they risk imprisonment." Bones are deliberately broken so that the victim is too incapacitated to participate in further rioting. Latest figures (1991) show that 105,000 people have been seriously injured through beatings in the uprising.

Women are also more susceptible to the effect of tear gas, which is apparently fired directly into houses. Many women—an unknown number—have suffered miscarriages or even died due to its effects.

Anyone who throws a stone is considered to be a terrorist. "A five-year-old child who throws a stone at a soldier is threatening the security of the state of Israel." Homes of suspected terrorists are demolished and the families are forbidden to rebuild them. Houses are also sealed, forcing the occupants to live outdoors. At least 1,790 homes have been demolished or sealed.

It is an offense to be a member of, or show support for, the PLO. It is a proscribed terrorist organization in Israel, although all Palestinians, with the exception of the fundamentalist group, Hammas, proclaim the PLO as their government and Yasser Arafat as their president.

The activities of the women are well known to the military authorities and viewed with alarm by the Israeli Security Service. Particularly worrying is the hold of the women's committees on Palestinian society and their success in waging economic war. Terry Boulata, one of those interviewed below, was considered to be "one of the most dangerous leaders of the Intifada"—not only for her own activities but because she won international recognition for her plight. She is revered by the next generation of fighters.

Nadia and Aida were middle-class women in their thirties living in the suburbs of Ramallah. Both were extremely active on the underground Intifada Committee, organizing demonstrations and relaying an intelligence network throughout the occupied territories. Neither had been caught, although the extent of their activities suggested their freedom would be short-lived. Both were mothers, Aida of three boys—two already in prison—and a four-year-old girl. Nadia felt that her involvement was enough for any family—she kept her ten- and thirteen-year-old sons out of any activities.

At the first meeting, in a hotel in Jerusalem, both women were extremely nervous, insisting on sitting in the middle of the sun terrace away from bedroom windows and doors. They spoke so quietly it was difficult to hear the words; later they became so impassioned they were shouting. Gradually, after several meetings, they revealed more of their clandestine lives and the risks they were taking.

Nadia had been intelligence gathering and came back laughing. "Today I learned something wonderful that will save many children. I was watching a demonstration—the children had been as usual very brave and thrown many missiles. The soldiers were chasing them with their batons raised for the beatings, and I was directing the escapes.

"Standing not far from me were two small boys eating ice cream. The soldiers ran up to them, saw by how much they had eaten that they could not just have been engaged in throwing stones, and ran on.

"Now that we know children eating ice cream are safe the sale of ice cream is going to rocket. We shall buy dozens of ice creams before the battle and tell the children of the strike forces where to find us when they have to run. We will take a couple of bites out of the ice creams before handing them over so it looks as if the children, like the boys today, had nothing to do with the fighting."

Nadia was speaking in a room full of trusted women comrades. By nightfall her piece of information would be all around the territories. Small, with a white face and dark-rimmed sleepless eyes, Nadia was positively sparkling. But her mood changed swiftly and her face saddened as she considered the effects of the street war upon the child soldiers.

"Often I wonder what we are doing to our children. We have made them into fighters at the age of three years old. We do not treat them like children, and they do not act like them. In many ways they are our superiors because they are most vulnerable on the frontline. By three they have lost their childhood and no one can give it back. I worry what it will be like when they have grown up. I know that they will be full of hatred and bitterness if we do not win."

I remembered the small black-clad children I had seen on the Gaza Strip, the Ninja. They had not looked like children at all and I had found them genuinely threatening. As I spoke to the adults of the Intifada I gained the impression that they were beginning to be frightened by the generation they had created.

Nadia was also worried about the psychological effect her necessary and sometimes prolonged absence had upon her children. She was clearly torn between her love for them and a love for the thousands of other Palestinian children whom she felt responsible for. At least, she reassured me and perhaps herself, her own children had clothes and food; so many others had none. She knew, however, that material things were not enough: "I think perhaps my sons will hate me because I neglect them for the other children. I cannot give them the attention and love that they need. Before the Intifada it was I who took them swimming and collected them from school—now a hired man takes them everywhere."

Nadia also felt guilty of depriving the boys of their childhood, although it was necessary owing to the sensitive nature of her work: "They hear and see everything, even take part in discussions on our tactics—but are forbidden to utter a word to their friends. Every Palestinian child—but mine more than most—knows how to keep secrets. My boys hear details of everything—even the most dangerous missions—and store it all up, but never repeat a word. I wonder what it does to them. When they were very small and ran to me with their childish secrets, even then I was teaching them. I would not be interested in whatever they said if they began by saying it was a secret. I would be cold and say—do not tell me. They were hurt but I knew I had to prepare them for now. Now they have been so well trained they are safe.

"My sons blame me and their father for what is happening to them now. They ask why we did not have the Intifada before they were born. I reply that we, the Palestinians, have almost left it too late. So now all our efforts, all our sacrifices must be for it.

"But it is not just the boys. Look at me. Do I look as if I enjoy life? Do I look healthy? I have no rest, only a few hours sleep when I must rest or else collapse. I no longer enjoy food; I eat because my body requires it and my body is necessary to continue the fight. Do you know that before the Intifada my husband and I had so much to talk about; we were interested in so many topics. The whole world was interesting. Now is it only the Intifada, the planning, the next demonstration, how to move the hunted from one safe house to the next, how to dodge the curfew, and how to avoid capture."

She sighed. "It does affect everyone. My three-year-old nephew was visiting from America recently and he had been here only one week when he came up to me to ask how to make a submachine gun. He said he would use it to kill the soldiers and began to sing one of the songs: 'With our blood, with our souls, we will defend Palestine.' Another child who has lost his innocence."

Nadia took a deep breath and seemed to pull herself together. Her own life, even those of her relatives, she went on, could all be sacrificed. The important thing was that the Intifada should not die. In this mood, and uttering these words, she was inspiring, and one could clearly see how such a forceful woman could fill others with courage. The Intifada had enabled her and thousands of others like her to have power.

"Our lives, you must understand, are individually worth nothing. You can blow them away. But others will always rise up to take our place. It is as if we were in a big prison, and the only thing we really have to lose is that. Imagine what it is like to be me, a proud, well-educated woman who has traveled to many countries. Then see what it is like to be an insect, for that is what the soldiers call us—cockroaches, dogs, insects. Imagine yourself, full of dignity and confidence, and then a seventeen-year-old soldier approaches you in the street. Do this, he orders—and you, bright with shame, do it. That is what it was like before the Intifada. The soldier crushed us under his boot like insects. Then we said enough; we cannot take this any more, we are human beings. Our Intifada was born and we will not be crushed again."

Many of the women I spoke to referred to the uprising in these terms. It was as if they had transferred their maternal feelings to the fight. Some Israeli women I spoke to, several of whom were full of admiration for the courageous way Palestinian women were fighting for equality, were nonetheless puzzled at the way in which these same women could send their children out to fight. One Israeli mother whose teenage son had been killed in a Palestinian attack, summed it up: "To me and to other Israeli mothers, our children must be protected at all costs. The Palestinian mothers are prepared to let them be killed. I cannot understand this." It is a paradox: how the Palestinian women who undoubtedly adore their children can send them out, armed only with sticks and stones, against the military might of Israel. Perhaps it is because, as Nadia said, the most precious child is the Intifada.

This transferal of the maternal emotions was something that cropped up in other interviews with women from different groups and ideologies. The IRA women were equally determined that their fight should result in a better future for their children, but they did not send them on to the frontline. Susanna Ronconi, who founded an Italian revolutionary group, had greater loyalty to it than to her lover; she could not be critical of the movement even when others abandoned it. To her it was her son.

Nadia, in not allowing her own children to participate in the street battles, was an unusual mother. She could not bear for them to be harmed and was willing to sacrifice herself through her clandestine work. Her next words were slightly wistful, admitting that she lacked the courage for hand-to-hand combat: "Sometimes I wish I was brave enough to throw stones like the children or some of the women, but I am afraid of the pain of a beating or being shot. I know what I do is dangerous, but then just being a Palestinian is dangerous. You might as well do what you are best at. The Intifada needs everyone, especially women. They are the center of everything."

What of the men, I asked her. After all, there were thousands who had not been detained. She chuckled, "Men, I am afraid to say, by about thirty-five are out of it: They get scared and they have responsibilities. They like to talk politics, but they are bad at action." Other Palestinian women said the same thing; that men liked to sit and talk and think they ruled the roost, but in these days it was the women who acted.

Nadia gave me examples of the women's bravery. One old woman went out with the *shebab* on every demonstration carrying a big basket full of stones, which she handed out to the children. Another old woman from Dehaisha camp near Bethlehem had had her home demolished because she sat on the roof hurling slabs at the soldiers. Then there was the tale of a woman in the same camp who saved a four-year-old boy as he fled from the soldiers. The child ran into her house, and she gathered him under her dress. When the soldiers burst in to search for the boy, all they found was a woman sitting on the floor.

"You see, everyone does what he or she can. It is our way of life, and until we have won there is nothing else that is important."

Aida was a less fiery, more gentle woman than Nadia, and her eyes filled with tears when discussing the suffering of the Palestinian people. Her husband had been repeatedly imprisoned, her middle son, aged fifteen, had been sentenced to one year and one day in prison for stone-throwing just three days before our first meeting. During the previous year he had been kidnapped and tortured by the Shin Bet, the Israeli secret police. Her four-year-old daughter hated the Israelis with a vengeance.

Aida picked up a glass of water and cupped it in her hands. "Enough is enough, we sometimes think when another loved one is taken away. But we are so strong. Even when the glass is full we can still take more." The power of her words was emphasized by the simplicity and artlessness of her action.

She had seen her son for just a few minutes after he was sentenced. "I was trying to be brave but he could see I was upset and called me over to the cage he was in with the other men. 'Mummy,' he said. 'Be strong. Remember I am your son.' "

She smiled as she recalled his words; they had made her feel brave again. She knew that she had prepared him well for his ordeal, and that he would never confess. It was, she assured me, only what any Palestinian mother would have done for her child.

"When I heard that the soldiers had come to the house looking for him, I went quickly to his school and got him out. For the next five days I took him from one safe house to another to teach him how to deal with the interrogators and how to avoid their traps. I warned him that because it was his first time the Shin Bet would probably be very cruel to him and beat him badly. After the beatings, he would be left in a cell, and one man with a kind face would come into the room and put his arms around him. He would say, 'Don't cry anymore, those were bad men, but I am your friend. Tell me everything.' I told my son that he is the one you must be careful of. Maybe he will bring you cigarettes and food to eat. Be very careful of him.

"Then I told him that they would put him in a cell and maybe he would hear someone crying and sounds of a man being beaten. But it would be a tape recording, and the man would be saying, 'Please don't cut off my ear, please don't pull out my fingernails.' 'Ignore it,' I told my son, 'and ignore the boy of your own age who is put into your cell and who boasts of throwing Molotovs and his bravery. He will be a spy sent to loosen your tongue.'

"Then, when I had taught my son everything, I took him home and he was arrested. When I saw him, he said, 'Mummy, you were right. They did everything you said. At first I was so scared, but then I heard your voice.' When he said these words to me, I was so proud, I knew I had done everything right and I had brought my son up well. I taught him the best rule for life—to be psychologically stronger than anyone. 'Remember,' I told him, 'if you are weak the interrogator feels strong, but if you are strong, the interrogator becomes confused and then weak.' "

Aida did not look like the sort of woman who could instruct children in the rules of psychological warfare and then hand them over to the enemy to be put to the test. Nor did she appear to have the iron nerve required for her underground work. On the surface she was just a kindly shop owner who sold toys from her village store. Her experience, and those of her family, had taught her what she knew.

"My family has suffered so much, especially my children. When this son was thirteen he was kidnapped. He was playing with his younger brother in the road when a car stopped and an Israeli man got out, asked him his name, then flung him in the back and drove off. My younger son, who was eleven, took a note of the number [license] plate and then ran to me. I notified all the Arab press agencies immediately, then went to the police station. They seemed to know all about it and said my son had been taken by a settler. They told me to go home, sleep, and my son would be home in the morning. I demanded that they go and get my son back and refused to go home.

"After three hours, the police said that he was there in the police station and I should go home to wait for him. I went home and my son was there—in a state of shock. He had been beaten in the stomach and throat—we had to get the doctor, and for a day he couldn't speak. A Jewish journalist friend traced the car number; it had been hired by the Shin Bet."

When her son was able to talk he told her how he had been driven around for hours by two Israeli men, who took turns in beating him. They held him down on the floor while they kicked him. When his captors ordered the boy to say in Hebrew, "I love Israel," he could not because they had stuffed his feet in his mouth.

Aida insisted that she did not hate Jews, only Israelis who were capable of such acts. She was also angry at the rest of the world, she said, because they appeared to be blind to the suffering of her people.

Her four-year-old daughter was showing clear signs of disturbance, although Aida was trying to make sure that she did not become anti-Semitic. It was proving an uphill task, and Aida wondered what the effect had been on the child when she had been intimately searched by an Israeli soldier: "My daughter was just nine months old when I took her with me to visit relatives in Jordan. The Israelis searched me first, then opened her legs and looked inside for hidden messages.

"When she was two, she began throwing stones, but she was confused and threw them at any car. She had to be taught the right targets. She says, 'There is a Jew,' and I say, 'No, that is an Israeli; we do not hate because of a religion.'

"When we were waiting outside the military court for her father to be sentenced, she marched up to an Israeli soldier and kicked him. He asked her why she had done that, and she said, 'Because you took my daddy away.' He tried to explain that he had not arrested her father, but she insisted 'Yes, you all arrested my daddy.'

"Now my husband is out of prison, but if he is an hour late she becomes hysterical, thinking he has been taken again. All she talks of is guns. She is like all the children; even their games are the Intifada. They play a game of how to overcome interrogation. They test each other by attacking one to see how he or she will cope with the interrogators. Another game is lining up against a wall. One will be a soldier with a wooden gun and he will pretend to beat the others. When I first saw them playing, I asked the little boy why he was beating his friends. He said, 'I am preparing them.' I thought I was going to blow up inside when I heard that."

She gave a helpless shrug. Women, she said slowly, suffered the most and were the most active in the fight, perhaps because they had their children to protect and so were constantly on guard.

Aida bent over as if suddenly exhausted. But when she raised her face again, it was transformed with love as she spoke of her favorite child: "You see, the Intifada is my son. I would drown without it. Nothing else matters—without it we would die."

When the curtains were securely drawn and a child stationed on the front steps of the house as a lookout, the video was switched on.

Sitting on the floor were children of all ages, arguing over tactics but listening obediently when Nadia or Aida made a point. One boy was constructing an imitation machine gun—it was made of cast iron and looked very realistic. He was told to put it away; this was a teach-in session. The video had been filmed, in cooperation with the *shebab* and the strike force, by a woman who lived in their village on the West Bank. Occasionally the film's soundtrack was interrupted by her small daughter asking to be allowed to go and throw stones.

The woman had filmed in secret from a semi-demolished house. The film began with the *shebab* arming themselves (great admiration from the children on construction of slingshots). The camera scanned outward to show the advancing soldiers. A woman covered in traditional clothing was at the forefront of the demonstrators; she gave a signal and the children surged forward hurling their missiles. The woman urged them on, directing them away from the soldiers' fire, but near enough to hit the targets. She communicated by signals, sometimes a cry. Yet whenever she was in sight of the soldiers, she looked just like any old woman trying to cross the road and they ignored her. The age-old deception that a woman is by her sex innocent had come to her aid.

The purpose of the film, Nadia explained, was twofold. To encourage the children to fight and be heroes, and to learn from mistakes. "You see how important it is to have your escape route planned. See that boy who got caught. And look at that one hiding; he has not seen the soldier behind him. Remember to look everywhere and to listen. Never trust an old escape route—the soldiers might have learned it."

Had the soldiers raided that house during this special film show, all adults and children over twelve would have been arrested and detained. When they returned, it would probably have been to a pile of rubble instead of a home.

Bana Bassam al-Sayih, aged fourteen, was under house arrest and was shortly to be sentenced to fourteen months imprisonment for throwing stones at an Israeli bus. Although she hotly denied that specific incident, she admitted to many similar ones and was looking forward to the next step in her political education—her internment with older women in the Palestinian Political Women's Prison.

She sat upright and serious in her parents' home in Beit Hanina accompanied by a couple of her school friends. Her grandfather, the general secretary to the Palestine National Council, puttered in the background. Her father, who had spent the first eight years of her life in prison for his political activities, was in another room. Opposite her pretty, jean-clad daughter was Bana's mother, a little tearful but proud.

"I am no longer a child," Bana announced as much to her mother as to me, and in a way she was right. She had taken on the role of an adult combatant, and she expected to be treated as one. "Before my arrest I saw and heard everything and participated in the demonstrations, but I did not really understand anything. Now I know what it is like to be a Palestinian and to suffer.

"Sometimes I am a little frightened of going to prison and leaving my mother and my friends, but I look on it as going to university. I have spent the last two months since I have been home reading all the political books I can find instead of doing the homework my teachers send me from school. It is much more important that I learn about Palestine so that I will understand everything the women in prison can teach me. After prison I want to train to be a lawyer and defend the children of Palestine."

Anger and frustration at their treatment by the Israelis were the reasons that this fourteen-year-old—I had to keep reminding myself that Bana was just this old—gave for the Palestinian uprising.

"I don't know why it is my generation that has started it. Everyone was angry, especially at school because there we learned that the whole world was free except us. We knew that it didn't matter how clever you were because even if you had a degree, the Israelis would only let you be a dishwasher."

Her friends agreed; many of their parents, they told me, were highly educated yet had to beg for work in Israel. To these children, death on the streets seemed preferable to such humiliation.

Bana went on to describe the importance of stone-throwing. She was well aware of what excellent propaganda it was—for the Palestinian cause to have children pitting their missiles against the might of the Israeli Army. She knew that the television pictures being shown around the world evoked sympathy, and she was prepared to milk that for all it was worth. Her teachers, she admitted with a reassuring fourteen-year-old grin, had come to expect less attention from her in the classroom: "We used to decide during lessons that we would have a demonstration the next day and then bring the stones into school in the morning and hide them under the stairs. Some of the teachers knew about it and some of them encouraged us, but it was our own decision. Not everyone in the class did it; in my group there were about seven of us.

"It was very important to be in a group of friends because then you can watch out for each other and rescue someone if a soldier gets her. We don't have time to look out for the younger kids. Each group must concentrate on itself. We have all been beaten by the soldiers, and of course it hurts very much, but it is much better not to cry. I have been kicked in the face and all over my body by the soldiers.

"We practice how to throw stones because then our aim is better. Each has her own method. Some use the slingshot, which is difficult to learn, but a stone goes twice as far and the aim is very good. Sometimes we burn tires in the memory of a martyr and throw Molotovs, and we put nails on the roads so the soldiers burst their tires in the jeeps." How did the boys of the *shebab* treat the girls? I asked. "Huh, them," Bana's expression said.

"There is a boy I know who is too frightened to join the demonstrations. I tell him, 'It is your duty to throw a stone and to become a martyr. It is your national duty.'

"Girls in the strike forces [stone-throwers] are just as good as the boys because we can run as fast as they can and throw stones as well. Soldiers are also stupid—they think it is more important to catch the boys, so we carry the flags and distribute the Intifada leaflets. They are a bit scared about searching us as well because the men would attack them."

Bana and her fellow stone-throwers spent a great deal of time working out escape routes before engaging the soldiers. The enemy, it seemed, had caught them in the past and beaten them. One had to be constantly alert, she informed me, and on the lookout for new routes. Shops were good places to go because the girls could pretend that they worked there, but one had to know one's shopkeeper. "One girl was caught by the soldiers when the shopkeeper told her to get out. So we talk to the shopkeepers to find out what they would do for us if we ran in. We pass their names out to all the *shebab*."

For all her mature ways, there was still something of the child left in Bana. She obviously enjoyed the excitement of battle and the glamour attached to being a member of the *shebab*. She was looked up to not just by younger children, but by adults too. Yes, she admitted, she missed taking part in the demonstrations and the thrill of the chase.

There was a sudden burst of giggles from her friends as she said sadly that, since her house arrest, she missed going out for walks. After a few minutes of whispered consultation with the other girls, Bana decided to let me in on the secret.

"I break house arrest. I go and visit my friends, hidden in the back of a car. I am going to prison anyway, so it doesn't matter even if they catch me. I am going to be in a cell for a long time and I want to get out as much as I can now."

Bana had been a pupil at the Rosary Sisters School in Beit Hanina at the time of her arrest. The school falls within the district of Jerusalem, so it had been allowed to remain open—unlike schools two miles away on the West Bank.

"I was with four friends and we had just come out of school. We were inside a shop looking for a birthday present, when we heard stones being thrown. We looked out and saw the *shebab* were stoning an Israeli bus. We saw armed Israelis jump out of the bus and fire into the air.

"They saw us watching and started to run over to us. We were scared and ran out but one of the other girls fell and we stopped to help her. The men caught us. They had truncheons and beat us and then made us sit on broken glass from the bus windows. The men were settlers, and they said that seven people had seen us throwing stones. We told them the truth, but they beat us and gave us to the police. We said that we were in a shop in front of the bus and it was the back window that was broken, so it couldn't have been us. But they didn't listen.

"The police took us to the Russian Compound prison and we were interrogated for four hours. They told us to confess, but we would not. Then they put us in a cell with fourteen prisoners. It was terrible because the other women were criminals and spat at us. We were very afraid of them. They grabbed all the food and gave us none and said they would beat us. We stayed in one corner of the cell and comforted each other."

After eight days the girls' case was heard before a judge who proposed placing them under house arrest in Nazareth, Acre, or West Jerusalem. The girls' families agreed that they should be placed in the Rosary Sisters convent in Jerusalem—the same order that ran the school.

"It was better there because the nuns were kind," said Bana. "But we couldn't get out, and there was only an elementary school in the convent. We had to do work sent to us from our own teachers. We were there for two months, and it was wonderful when we were allowed home."

Home, despite technically being her prison, had its good points. Like any schoolchild, she relished the freedom from school, and she had frequent visits from her friends. Unlike a child, however, Bana showed a shrewd perception of her own position: "My friends think I am a hero, but all I am is a fighter like them. I am no braver than them, I just know more now. I know that the Israelis can't kill all of us because they would lose more world sympathy and they need that to survive. They don't know what to do because they know they must be careful not to kill too many of us."

Back now in her role as guerrilla fighter, she spoke words I was to hear a year later from a woman twice her age—a volunteer in the Irish Republican Army. Coming from Bana, though, they sounded doubly sad: "I can remember how it was before. I used to go to parties and for walks in the parks. It was fun, but now nothing like that happens. It is better because we are fighting and we know what we want.

"The Intifada is more than a war. War lasts for days or months, but with us it is a way of life."

The four seventeen-year-old girls knew they could be arrested right now for what they were doing—holding textbooks. They attended a school on the West Bank, which had been closed since the start of the Intifada. Their teachers, a mix of Palestinians and foreigners, ignored the closure order, thus risking imprisonment. The pupils—ages six and upward—continued to go to school and had become adept at dodging military patrols en route. Any child over the age of twelve could be arrested for having textbooks in his or her possession, but to these girls it was a risk worth taking. They were known by their teachers as the "back row activists" because they sat at the back of the class and planned demonstration tactics.

Ramia, by far the quietest of the four, was very much her own woman, and she was fighting her own war, an intellectual one. She explained: "The Israelis want to make us into illiterate peasants by closing out schools and making it illegal for us to learn. So I am fighting them by learning.

"The Israelis have taken all our rights away; we even have to pay them taxes for what they do to us. They don't want to live with us; they want to take our land. They take it from us and then they call us terrorists when we fight.

"Since I was nine years old, I have seen soldiers shooting people. My friend used to cry and run away when she saw the soldiers. We had to stop that. When someone loses her brother, father, mother, she feels hatred and does not want peace anymore.

"We have to fight them on all levels. We throw stones and participate in the demonstrations, but a new state needs people with degrees—not simply boys and girls who throw stones. So we have to divide ourselves—both throwing stones and learning."

It was difficult to apply oneself to learning, Ramia admitted, because of the lure of battle. Their school was very close to where many of the demonstrations took place, and it was hard to concentrate on books when one could hear the soldiers firing. "You think, 'Should I be in here while my brothers and sisters are out there, prepared to die?' Sometimes the only thing is to go and join them."

Even though Ramia was dedicated to passing her exams and going on to university, the interrupted schooling made her worry that she might not know enough to get through. Her teachers had to split their time between teaching the older girls and the younger ones; on some days there would be no teachers for the exam girls. She tried to study at home, but there were problems in that too. On the strike days, some parents refused to allow their children to study; one girl Ramia knew studied in secret, in the bathroom.

The exams were just two weeks away, but none of the girls knew if they would even take place. "It is a public exam," Ramia explained. "The authorities might not let us sit for it because it would constitute a public gathering."

If Ramia managed to take the exam and pass it, she faced another problem. All Palestinian universities had been closed down, so she would have to go to Egypt to continue her studies. That would mean obtaining her father's permission, and although women's rights had made some incursion into the traditional way of life, she doubted if her father would allow her to live as a single woman in a foreign country. Ramia knew that she faced a fairly bleak future, and that possibly her only role in the next year or so of her life would be as a fighter. She was doggedly determined in spite of all the obstacles in her path: "I hope that in the end I will be a writer and get across the message of the Palestinian people that way. I will be a fighter, like everyone else, but it is not what I always want to do."

Ramia's words had sparked off one of the other girls. Ruba agreed that studying was vital, but she viewed fighting on the street as the most important role.

"A girl's first duty is to be on the streets, throwing stones," she insisted. "When you throw a stone you feel you are doing something. Look, we could be put in prison for studying, so why not fight as well? Everybody in the world has the right to study, except us. It is a war we must fight on both fronts."

She took Ramia's point that in some ways it was easier to be on the street than to study. "There is a lot of pressure from people of our age to be fighting, and it is difficult to sit at home with your books.

"It is easy to be brave on the street and not to scream when they beat you. I saw a soldier dragging a girl by her hair and hitting her on the ground with his big boots. She was very brave and did not cry. Then she got up and ran but the soldier followed her onto a roof. He started to beat her again and said he would throw her off. She told him to go on and he was so surprised that he stopped."

Girls, she went on, were just as brave as boys, and sometimes braver. She illustrated this with another story, one which her classmates had obviously heard before, for they interrupted her with their own version of events.

"Another girl was throwing stones when she saw a soldier taking aim at a boy. She threw her jacket over the boy and pulled him away, then the soldier started shooting at her. She ran onto a bus, but he followed her so she ran out the back into a building and onto a balcony. He was still behind her so she jumped off, onto a roof, and escaped."

Yes, she and the other girls agreed, it was child's play being brave in the heat of battle. What was absolutely dreadful, far worse than physical pain, was when the soldiers shouted "bad words" at you.

I thought at the time that this squeamishness over verbal abuse was simply due to the way in which these girls had been brought up. However, I came across it again—with women from the IRA, and also from the Italian woman revolutionary Susanna Ronconi. It was a surprising common thread. It seemed that it was one thing to be shot at, another matter entirely to be called bad names.

Ruba was far too embarrassed to repeat what the soldiers had called her; she would only say: "The words are so bad that they should never be spoken—it is a deep shame.

"We were walking in the street and saw a soldier beating a boy and we asked him why. He used terrible words to us—we were girls and it was in public. We were so embarrassed to be scorned. He chased us and dragged us by the hair to his jeep and hit us. We didn't mind that—it was the terrible words that hurt more."

The soldiers have obviously picked up on the fact that words can hurt the girls of the *shebab* far worse than truncheons: "Sometimes the soldiers use loudspeakers to shout bad words at us in the streets. Once we started crying, but a little boy said to us: 'Ignore the words, because we can never be as low as they are.' It is very hard to ignore them, though. We are from traditional families, and our parents insist we are chaperoned everywhere."

Of course, she agreed, the Intifada was changing that. Out of necessity, the girls in the *shebab* had to meet with boys, often secretly, to discuss battle plans. It was something that the girls' parents did not like, but despite their disapproval the girls continued to do it. It was the only hint they gave of teenage rebellion. After all, these girls were, in their frontline actions, only doing what their adult world admired them for. They were being utterly conformist in this respect, and if their involvement in the fighting meant that they had to speak to boys, it was a price their parents had to pay for the longed-for victory.

The girls, having caught a glimpse of a less restricted way of life, were as determined as the older women not to let it slip from their sight. Ruba admitted that the Intifada had changed her and her friends: "We had to write an essay at school on what we would like to be when we were our mothers' age. We all wrote that we would treat our sons and daughters as equals and not expect our daughters to do nothing but get married. There is a change in our personalities, and I think the Intifada is helping us to be independent."

Their independent attitude was also reflected in their younger brothers and sisters: "When I told my little sister that she should study at home, she said she was too busy. She was cutting out newspaper reports on the Intifada and sticking them into her exercise book. Also it is natural for the kids when they cannot go to school to want to go out to fight."

No mother, she went on, could deny her child that right. She saw nothing unusual in her words; I was the only one to look startled.

"When they do go to school they learn so quickly how not to be caught. We have to teach the little ones at first, but only for a day. Everyone goes to school in normal clothes, not in the uniform any more. Often there are soldiers just outside the gates and we go out in batches, never more than three, and at intervals of five minutes.

"Our teachers are very good. We always try to let them know if we are going to a demonstration, but sometimes we only make the decision a few minutes before a lesson. It must be difficult for the teachers not knowing if there is going to be an empty classroom."

For all her fieriness, Ruba had gone to considerable risks in breaking the ban on Palestinian education. Earlier in the year, she and her friends had been underground teachers, running little schools of their own in friends' houses. They had given up after being threatened. "One night I got a telephone call. A man said, 'We know what you are doing and it is very dangerous. You had better stop it.' So I did. There is a girl who lives near here who was teaching a little group of six-year-old children. Fourteen soldiers came and raided the house and arrested her. That is how dangerous it is."

In spite of their different personalities, and the different emphasis they put on the two battles they were fighting, the girls were united: "Palestine needs us to be educated and to fight. But when we have our new state, we will have to learn everything again. We learn the Jordanian way of education now, and there is not one mention of Palestine. The Israelis do not want us to know about ourselves. We know no history except what our parents remember. We hope that there is time for learning properly when we win. We don't know what tomorrow brings; we just hope we are going to live to see our own state and president, but we are not sure."

Terry Boulata has achieved heroine status among the younger women fighters because of the suffering she endured at the hands of the Shin Bet. She was viewed by the police as a highly dangerous woman, a leader of the Intifada, and at first when she became ill in prison they thought she was shamming. For three months she was denied hospital treatment, and when she was finally examined it was discovered that she had chronic active hepatitis. Even when her condition was diagnosed and she was allowed home, the Shin Bet still picked her up, detained and tortured her.

Sitting in the front room of a modern bungalow just outside Jerusalem, Terry looked like a haggard, middle-aged woman. She was actually twenty-three years old and had just been released from prison following an international amnesty campaign that had culminated in a personal plea from President Mitterrand of France. Her freedom was temporary: she was permitted to travel to Chicago for treatment on the understanding that she return to Israel to face the charges against her.

She was not sure, when I spoke to her in June 1989, of the various charges that she might face. She had been charged with membership in the Palestinian Liberation Organization, with distributing PLO leaflets, and with buying cloth for a Palestinian flag. There was, however, a secret file on her to which neither she, nor her lawyer, had been allowed access.

It was difficult to see this gaunt yet strangely dignified young woman as a threat to the security of Israel. She sat upright on a floral-patterned sofa, remembering every detail of her illness and her treatment at the hands of Shin Bet.

She became ill soon after she had been imprisoned as a security detainee. After the first two months, she noticed that her limbs were swollen, and she was suffering from fatigue, but she attributed her symptoms to the effects of prison life. When she was released her parents insisted that she should see a doctor.

"I was sent to a hospital and had two liver biopsies. No one really knew what was wrong—all I was told was that it was very serious. I had the second biopsy on November thirteenth, 1988, the day before the declaration of the independent state of Palestine. The results were going to take some time to come through, and I begged the doctors to allow me home so that I could be with my family and friends on Independence Day. They were reluctant, but agreed in the end, provided that I rested all the time.

"I got home to my parents' at noon and of course it was a very special day. I couldn't do much, though, but sleep. At midnight we heard the army jeeps arriving outside the house. There were dozens of soldiers and they surrounded it. A Shin Bet man that I knew from prison interrogations came into the room. He looked very cheerful. He said: 'We want to celebrate your Independence Day with you, Terry. You are coming with us to a party and we are going to have music and balloons.' My parents said I was too ill to be taken away, but he just laughed and talked about missing the party.

"I was taken out of the house and put in his car, beside him. For the next four hours we drove around all over the West Bank while he and the soldiers arrested more people. It was freezing cold and I was numb, but the Shin Bet man just kept laughing and talking about what a fun party we were all going to have."

Terry was delivered to the Russian Compound prison just after four o'clock in the morning. She was left in a cell for thirteen hours and then taken for interrogation. "The interrogator called me a donkey and said he was going to kick me like one until I confessed. He seemed to be very angry and kept saying, 'I don't know why they keep bringing you in here; you never confess to anything. You can go to hell.'

"Then the same Shin Bet man walked into the room, smiling. He treated me like an old friend. 'Hello Terry,' he called. 'We are going to have a little chat.' He didn't discuss any charges, but talked about politics. He wanted to know where it would all end, and what I thought the announcement of the independent Palestinian state meant. '*Mabrouk!* Congratulations, Terry. Here's to Palestine,' he said. He had brought me Hebrew newspapers, which I would not read, and he tried to get my views on the proposed Israeli elections on the West Bank."

She remembered that he also asked her about the Likud party and the settlers, what her opinion was on a number of sensitive political matters. "He went on and on. I was not feeling up for a discussion. I was having severe pain from the biopsy—the wound was still open. The room was humid and my legs had swollen up. After three quarters of an hour they took me to the coffin."

The "coffin" is a cell, 1.7 meters high by 80 by 60 centimeters. The walls are made of concrete and the door of iron panels. Prisoners detained in the coffin are not allowed to use the toilet so they urinate, defecate, and vomit over themselves.

"They knew about the biopsy, but they shoved me in there anyway. I had no watch; I can only estimate that I was inside for between one and a half and two hours. I started to feel dizzy and sick immediately. After one minute in there you can feel the heat of the previous occupant. She had only just been taken out. It was very hot and smelly. There was urine and mold everywhere. I couldn't take it and fainted. When I came round I started knocking on the door. The Shin Bet man came and opened it. He pushed me and asked what was the matter. I said I wanted to be sick. He laughed and asked, 'You don't want to die?' He took me to a cell where there were other women, and I was sick all night."

The next morning, as she had now been in prison for forty-eight hours, Terry was taken to court where the authorities asked for an extension of her detention. No charges were mentioned, but the prosecution made reference to the secret file. The court granted the extension, in spite of the medical reports that had been produced by her lawyer. She was taken back to the Russian Compound.

"Buy now I was half paralyzed; I could not move or eat and had severe pain in my limbs. The prison doctor examined me and said I should be taken to the government hospital. I stayed there in the emergency ward until four A.M. the next day. I felt very strange; water was filling my body. The doctor at the hospital said my condition was very rare and I should go back to my own hospital." However, a police car took her back to prison.

By the next morning, Terry recalled, she felt sure she was going to die. She was called for interrogation, but could not move. She was lying on the floor when the Shin Bet man who had become her tormentor marched into the room and called jovially, "What's this Terry, refusing interrogation?"

"He tried to move my legs and saw that I was paralyzed. He got frightened and said, 'OK Terry, don't die, don't die here. I will have you released in ten minutes.' "

Terry was released on bail and her family came to collect her. She was immediately admitted to a hospital where primary chronic active hepatitis was diagnosed. After emergency treatment, she was allowed home, but had to return to the hospital every week. Doctors agreed that she would have to go to Chicago to have any hope of a cure, but the military authorities refused at this point to countenance such an idea.

Within a month, she was back at the prison for more interrogation, but curiously she was told that the authorities were no longer interested in her. They appeared to be playing a game of cat and mouse: a few weeks later the army arrived at her home. "What seemed like hundreds of soldiers surrounded the house. A soldier marched through the front door and told me to collect my clothes. I told him I was still too sick to be in prison, but the soldier just said, 'So, maybe you will die.' " They had to carry her out of the house.

She was placed in solitary confinement, in a windowless cell, but she was grateful that at least there was a toilet. There were few other niceties in Cell Ten: a small, bug-infested mattress and holes in the ceiling, through which mice dropped. She claimed that when she stood up, mice would fall onto her head. The food she described simply as disgusting.

The next morning, at eleven o'clock, she was taken to the interrogation room but no one came to question her until a quarter to three in the afternoon. She claimed that every so often a Shin Bet man came into the room and said, "Ah, you are Terry Boulata," before leaving her alone again. Realizing that they were hoping to wear her down by such tactics, she remained calm and defiant: "When one of them came in, I asked for my prison allowance of four agoras, untipped cigarettes. He offered me his Kent cigarettes, 'No sir, I will take nothing from you, just my allowance.' "

Eventually the Shin Bet man she knew of old arrived. She asked him what the charges against her were. "He gave me a big smile and said, 'No charges, but we want to have you in prison. We missed seeing you, we like to have you here.' "

He went on to ask her to define the words terrorism, and terrorist, and then talked about the National Council of the Intifada. Terry remained resolutely silent on these topics, but remembering his fear when she had collapsed before, warned him that she might become paralyzed again.

"I told him it was not good for him to keep me in prison because the swelling would start again. I asked him not to put me back in solitary confinement, but to be with the other girls in the eight-bed cell." He laughed, perhaps admiring her courage, and did what she asked.

"It was much better in the cell with the others. There were showers and food came on a small tray. But after forty-eight hours I started having pains again. The girls used to feed me, wash me, comb my hair." She paused, blushing at a memory: "One night I was very ashamed; I could not move to get to the toilet and, frankly, I wet the bed.

"The next morning the doctor came and asked why I was lying on a wet sheet. He ordered that I be allowed a commode and a special diet from my mother. The food I had been given in prison was full of pepper."

Terry was detained for a further six weeks and was then taken to a military court in Lod. At this hearing, she was finally told of the charges against her: PLO membership, giving seventy shekels to someone to buy material for a Palestinian flag, and distributing Intifada leaflets. The Shin Bet file was again mentioned but its contents were not divulged. By this stage, she looked at death's door, and the judge ordered her released on bail.

She had just two weeks at home before, yet again, she was picked up. The date was March 8, 1989, International Women's Day. "They round up everyone they think is active on the day of any big demonstration," she explained. Then she gave a rare smile: "I think they pick me up so often because the house of the chief of police is only up the road, and it is handy for him."

She was brought before the courts again in March, and at this hearing the judge had no sympathy for her. He accepted the prosecution claim that her release on bail would endanger state security and ordered her to be detained until her trial on September 29. Her parents and friends, fearing that she would die in prison, launched an international public campaign, and in June 1989 she was released.

I was talking to her three weeks before she flew to Chicago for medical treatment. She was philosophical about her future. "I will have to be back for the trial, but as long as I am well I don't mind being in prison," she said.

Update: After treatment, Terry returned to Israel but was not summoned to appear in court. Her case is still technically open, but it is thought that the publicity that surrounded her has stopped the Israeli authorities from taking any further action. In November 1990 she was married, and on the night of her wedding her husband was arrested and detained for a week. She now works for the Palestinian Human Rights Information Center in Jerusalem, and is still receiving treatment for her condition.

Chapter 4

LEILA KHALED

"Do you expect me to speak about fashion?"

Leila Khaled achieved in a few hours what the lives and deaths of hundreds of other Palestinian fighters have failed to do either before or since: she grabbed the attention of the world's media and held it enthralled. The way in which she did it—hijacking an aircraft, evacuating the passengers, then blowing it up—made her both a supremely dangerous woman, but also paradoxically, romantic and brave at the same time. She had not killed anyone (rather by good luck than by design), and she had risked her own life. The fact that she was beautiful and young had a lot to do with the sensation she created.

She became a sex symbol for her violence; she shattered a million and one taboos overnight; and she revolutionized the thinking of hundreds of other angry young women around the world.

They all wanted to be a Leila Khaled, from the women of The Weathermen in the United States, to the founding members of the Baader-Meinhof group in Germany, to the Angry Brigade women in Britain. She had seized power, and they wanted to follow in her footsteps. Her picture adorned newspapers and magazines worldwide, showing her head demurely covered, her hands caressing her gun. She was credited with being the first woman hijacker; the fact that an Argentinian woman had actually beaten her to it three years earlier in an attempt to "invade" the Falkland Islands did not seem to matter. Scant attention was paid to Leila's fellow hijacker, a young man. She was the one who had seized the public's attention.

Like Miss Kim, men wrote to Leila proposing marriage; she declared herself insulted by such advances. She was a good Palestinian girl who did not accept even compliments from men. Nonetheless, a sexual frisson surrounded her. The press reported at the time that she had hidden weapons and plans for the hijack in her underwear. Here was a woman who might be beautiful, but she was unmistakably deadly and, because of that, deeply thrilling.

The glamorous side of the revolutionary life was certainly one that she enjoyed to the fullest: after the hijack she toured the Middle East with a retinue of bodyguards and was wined and dined at embassies. Leila loved it all, the attention, the adulation, but her popularity threatened what she craved most: the chance to do it again.

She had apparently derived such satisfaction, such a thrill in hijacking her first aircraft—thrusting the grenade under the pilot's nose and then removing the pin, feeling a sense of power that few Arab women are allowed—that she was prepared to undergo agony to repeat it. Her masters in the Popular Front for the Liberation of Palestine (PFLP), a Marxist group, wanted to use her again for a spectacular quadruple hijack the following year. However, they feared that Leila's face was far too well known; it would be better to use someone else. Leila was not having that. She conceded that her face might be a problem, so she decided to change it. Over the course of several months she had her face painfully altered by plastic surgery.

On September 6, 1970, she and a young male accomplice attempted to seize an El Al flight. They failed; her comrade was shot dead by Israeli sky marshals who, however, spared her life. She was literally thrown out of the aircraft when it made an emergency landing at Heathrow Airport. She was then imprisoned at Ealing police station in London.

Although her hijack had failed, three others carried out by PFLP teams at the same time had been more successful. Two of the aircraft had been flown to Dawson's Field, a PFLP-held airfield in Jordan, where the lives of the passengers were to be bartered for Palestinians held in Israeli jails. When Ms. Khaled was captured, the PFLP leadership decreed that a British passenger plane should be hijacked and flown to Dawson's Field too. The deal for the release of these passengers would be the freeing of Leila from her police cell in London. No sooner said than done: a British VC 10 was seized and its 300 passengers were deposited at the airfield three days later. The girl with the gun, as she was known, had become the center of an international crisis.

She spent three weeks at the police station, where, by her own account, she enjoyed baiting the superintendent who attempted to interrogate her. Then, to the fury of Israel, the British government capitulated to the PFLP demands, and she was released.

The Dawson's Field incident led to King Hussein of Jordan expelling the Palestinians from his country. It was a bloody conflict, resulting in the deaths of hundreds of Palestinians, and the Arab world was appalled at the war between brothers. It was referred to as the "Black September" and gave birth to one of the most extreme terrorist groups of all, which took the same name. In 1972, Black September was responsible for the Munich massacre in which eleven Israeli athletes were killed.

Leila, meanwhile, faded from public view. There was a price on her head, and the movement did not want to lose its leading star. In 1980, she surfaced in Copenhagen, leading a Palestinian Liberation Organization delegation to the United Nations Decade for Women conference. She had become an elder stateswoman, her days of combat over.

It took some time to track her down. I was told that she might be living in Lebanon or Iraq. One of Yasser Arafat's chief advisers informed me that she had grown fat, had had eight children, and that all she was now interested in was cooking. However, another route led me to a meeting in a London Hotel with a PFLP sympathizer. He passed on my request to headquarters in Syria, and then he gave me her telephone number. With a sense of unreality, I called her up. "Yes, this is Leila Khaled," she said in only slightly accented English. "When are you coming?"

Today she lives in Yarmouk refugee camp in Damascus. The camp is a town in its own right with the tents donated by the Red Cross forty years ago now replaced by houses, shops, schools, and offices. Just off Palestine Street in the center of the camp is the headquarters of the Palestinian Popular Women's Committees, the women's section of the PFLP. The organization has long since renounced terrorism, and the women's department devotes itself, in the main, to social welfare issues such as nursery education. Any young woman wanting to join the hit squad would be pointed in another direction.

The work of the Popular Committees is carried out in a drab suite of rooms on the ground floor of a house occupied by several families. At the back is the office of the first secretary of the movement, Leila Khaled.

It is a large square room, dingily furnished with brown cloth armchairs spaced out along the walls. One corner is taken up by a wooden desk, littered with paperwork, and next to it a battered filing cabinet. There is a window, but any natural light is excluded by heavy metal shutters closed against the heat. The electric light is switched on, and a Calor gas lamp stands on the desk in readiness for the frequent power failures in this area. The only sound in the room is the ceiling fan.

Leila had warned—accurately—that no taxi driver in Damascus would be able to find her office address and suggested a travel agency in the camp as a meeting place. She was sitting inside the agency, in front of a life-sized cardboard cutout of a smiling air stewardess holding an Air France airbus in her hands. She did not appear to see the irony of her position.

She was immediately recognizable as the young Leila, which was surprising because of all those facial surgery operations. She explained to me, however, that after her second hijack she had returned to the plastic surgeon and asked for her original face back. She suffered headaches from the operations, but this pain is something she has grown used to over the years. The headaches had started with the first operation to alter her nose, way back in 1969. Perhaps she was immediately identifiable because of her most noticeable feature, her large dark eyes that slant noticeably upwards. I asked if this was due to the surgery. "No, it is natural," she replied, obviously proud of them.

She had grown plumpish, but she was still attractive. Her hair was short and well cut, and her clothing was that of a conservative, yet modern, Arab woman: dark skirts and modest, brightly colored blouses. As we walked to her office, I asked her about the eight children. "No, I have only two, and that is enough," she laughed. How about cooking? "I hate it," she replied with venom.

As we settled down to the interview, she told me how tired she was, how overworked. She did not know, she said as she poured coffee, how much time she would be able to give me. Then I produced a copy of her autobiography written in 1973, and she brightened considerably. It was the first time that she had seen the book in a language that she could understand, she exclaimed. The only other copy she had been given was in Japanese. She turned the few pages of photographs lovingly, and pointed out the evidence of her surgery in some.

At first, as she began her story, her English was hesitant, but as soon as she came to her hijacking days, the words and, at times, laughter flowed; her face lit up and her eyes sparkled. That period was clearly the highlight of her life, however much she protested that her work today was of greater significance.

Her obvious enjoyment of those days was something that was echoed by several other women. The Italian revolutionary, Susanna Ronconi, nodded sympathetically when I told her of Leila's enthusiasm in recounting her past. "Yes," she agreed. "There was something exciting in what we did. There was a heroic dimension to our lives." One of the ETA women, too, compared the drudgery of legal political work to the effects of using a gun: "I think that with arms you can cut out all this work, get through it all, and get the results very quickly." Women, perhaps more than men, appear to appreciate the power of the weapon and the authority it gives them.

Leila was married to a physician, her second husband. For security reasons, she referred to him simply as "Baader." She is, however, still known by her maiden name in the camp, where people of her generation revere her.

Her first marriage was to a "comrade guerrilla," but it ended by mutual agreement after two years. "We never saw each other," she explained simply. Now she has two small sons aged seven and four. She did not intend to have them so late, she laughed, but she only met their father eight years ago.

Her life was busy: her work at the office started at 8 A.M.; at 2 P.M. there was a three-hour break so that she could go home to feed and see her children; then it was back to the office, sometimes until ten o'clock at night. She was no less dedicated now, as a middle-aged woman, than she was as a girl. Hijackings, she said with a wry smile, were a thing of the past: it was the Intifada that was the important thing. "My job is to mobilize women for the Intifada. It is difficult—more difficult than being a fighter. But the most difficult mission I have ever had is being a mother."

I think she meant it. She loved her children, but she had had them late, and they exhausted her. She was obviously torn between caring for them and her political work. She felt so guilty, she told me, at the number of hours she spent away from her sons, and admitted that to make up for it all, she spoiled them dreadfully.

It was only recently, she continued, that she had judged her elder son to be old enough to be told of her earlier life. "He was so excited; his eyes went round. He asked me if I was not afraid when

I hijacked planes. I said no, of course not. Then he said that in that case he wanted to be a hijacker too."

In her role as first secretary, Leila has to visit many countries to "mobilize" women. She is, however, restricted as to where she goes because, she claims, the Israelis are still determined that she should stand trial for the El Al hijack. She has been to Russia, where she attended university in the early 1980s, and to Libya, where she was respectfully received as an elder stateswoman. Although she has been asked to attend conferences elsewhere in the world, she has to be careful of extradition arrangements and the possibility of assassination. There have apparently been several such attempts on her life. A bomb was planted under her bed at her flat in Beirut, and it was only because she was hunting for her slippers that she found it in time. Her sister was not so lucky: on what was to have been her wedding day, Christmas Day 1976, she was shot dead at Leila's home in Tyre, probably by agents of Mossad, the Israeli secret service, who mistook her for Khaled. She was anxious about her children being photographed, just in case Mossad should wreak frustrated vengeance on her through them.

Leila Khaled certainly does not lack maternal feelings, and I noticed, as she talked about the Palestinian struggle, the same extension of maternal protectiveness that I had witnessed in her countrywomen of the Intifada: she felt herself to be mother to thousands of Palestinian children. It was that awareness, that desire that they should have a better future, that spurred her on when she saw the children on the plane she was about to hijack.

Leila Khaled was four years old when her mother made the decision to flee Palestine with her eight children; it was 1948 and the state of Israel had just been born. Haifa, where the family had lived a comfortable, middle-class life, was being shelled, and many Palestinians had already fled in terror to neighboring Lebanon and farther afield. Leila's father, a property owner and businessman, had joined the resistance fighters and vanished. Her mother battled on alone for several months in the war-torn city, herding her children into the cellar during the shooting and bombing.

Eventually, convinced that they would all die if they remained, she hired a car to evacuate the family to Tyre in southern Lebanon where her relatives lived. Leila remembered the time well: "I heard my mother telling a neighbor that a car was waiting to take us away. I ran into the kitchen because my father had left us some dates, and they were stored there in baskets. I hid between the baskets and wouldn't come out. I felt I had to protect the dates because if we left them the Jews would get them. Suddenly there was a big bang—the car had been hit by a shell and had blown up. I had stopped my family being in the car.

"I remember my mother saying to neighbors that maybe it was a sign, and so we stayed on a little longer. But the fighting got worse and my mother decided we must go. This time I ran and hid under the stairs when everyone else was getting into the car. The house was shelled and a man was killed in front of me. I was screaming and all the neighbors came out to deal with the dead man. My mother had to help, too, so again we didn't leave Haifa that day.

"But the third time my sister dragged me out from under the stairs by my hair. She said, 'Are you stupid? If you stay the Jews will kill you.' "

Leila cried all the way to Lebanon, she recalled, laughing now at the memory of how she had clutched a carton of talcum powder for her baby sister all the way. "I was very determined that the Jews would not have her powder; it was the only thing I remember taking with me."

The family went to stay with an uncle in Tyre. Although they were offered rooms in his home, Mrs. Khaled insisted that they live in the basement of his house. She made this decision partly in the hope that they would soon be returning to their own home and partly as a symbolic gesture: she told her children that because they had been forced out of Palestine, they did not have the right to live in other houses.

Leila has never forgotten that sense of exile: "My uncle's house was surrounded by a large garden with lots of orange trees. As children at home we had always picked our oranges when we were hungry. My mother slapped our hands and said, 'Those oranges are not yours and you are not allowed to eat them.' Since then, I haven't been able to eat oranges. It brings such a feeling of sadness to me to see them and to think that our orange trees are still there in Haifa, but now they belong to somebody else."

After nearly a year in Tyre, her father appeared. He had finally fled his homeland with a group of Palestinian fighters and had been placed in a refugee camp in Egypt. He had suffered a heart attack there and a doctor who had treated him had smuggled him out of Egypt into Lebanon. But he returned to his family a broken man, sick, according to his daughter, "with his spirit gone." He was unable to work and his family existed for many years on food rations and clothing from the United Nations Relief and Works Agency (UNRWA) until his older children were able to work.

The absence of a parent, either through death, imprisonment, or illness, was something that I noticed in several of the women. I wondered whether it had led them to be angrier and more determined to strike back at the system, which had robbed them of a mother or father.

For the next sixteen years the Khaled family, which grew to number fourteen children, lived in a two-room house. Leila attended the only school for Palestinian refugee children, a large tent pitched in the road. She spoke bitterly of the conditions: over a hundred pupils of all ages sat on the ground, and four classes were conducted at once; in the summer the heat was intense and in winter the children froze. But any complaints to her mother fell on deaf ears; all their misfortunes had been caused by the Jews. "My mother blamed everything on the fact that we were no longer in Palestine. The only way to make everything better was to go back, and we had no means to do that. Everything, she told us, was in Palestine, and as we were not there we had no right to object or to complain about what happened to us in Lebanon. Only when we returned to Palestine would we have any rights, and only then could we live normally.

"I asked why did we leave—why are we here? My mother said: 'Because the Jews took Palestine. They were armed and we were not strong enough to fight.' " Leila admitted that from that moment on, "a great hatred of the Jews began in my heart." It was, she said, the beginning of her political awareness.

From the age of ten, Leila and her sisters joined other Palestinian children demonstrating on the streets of Tyre on national Palestinian holidays. At first her mother approved of such activities, but as her daughters got older and more involved, she grew afraid for their reputations and tried to stop them. Tyre was a very conservative city, and young girls were not supposed to go to political meetings where men were present. But her husband, whose own health had been wrecked for the cause, disagreed: "They want their homeland: they should fight for it."

It was a fairly revolutionary statement for an Arab father to make. With it ringing in her ears, Leila was able to rebel against her mother's and her society's teachings, and yet be a dutiful daughter in her father's eyes.

Mrs. Khaled tried to reason with her husband. Their son, who was studying at a university, could be involved in the fight if he wanted; her daughters, while they lived at home, had to consider their single status and the likelihood of their retaining it if they started to flout tradition. Her arguments fell on deaf ears, so she resorted to locking up her unruly daughter.

"One night I was so desperate to go to a meeting, but my mother had taken away my clothes. I got up and crept out of the house dressed only in my nightdress. I went right across the city in it. When I got to the meeting, I was criticized by my comrades because I was wearing unsuitable clothing. Then when I got home my mother slapped me for going out in a nightdress." She laughed at the memory, but it showed how determined she had been to be part of the action.

A year later, in 1958, when she was fourteen years old, violence flared in the streets of Tyre between the Lebanese army and the National Arab Movement to which Leila's older brothers and sisters belonged. Although deemed too young to fight, she was given the task of carrying food through the battle zone to the Palestinian fighters. She recalled the terror she had felt as she and other children walked through the gunfire with pots of food balanced on their heads.

"There was shelling going on around us as we walked, and I was afraid, but I felt I had to do it and I was happy that I was helping." When she found her brothers and sisters she begged to be allowed to join them. Abruptly they told her that her job was to bring them food; her time to fight would come when she was older. Leila bit back her frustration, continued her dangerous task, and was rewarded at the end of the fighting by being made a member of the National Arab Movement.

She took her role with the utmost seriousness. One of her duties was to distribute the movement's leaflets to sympathizers, a dangerous mission when the city was under curfew. She was nearly caught, but she used her appearance as a respectable Arab girl to full effect: "It was wintertime, about seven P.M., when no one was supposed to be outside their homes. I put the leaflets in my jacket pocket and went out.

"I had not got very far when a soldier stopped me and demanded to know where I was going. I knew I was facing arrest, but quickly I said that I had to get the midwife. He asked where she lived, and I pointed in some direction. Then I appealed to him, 'I'm afraid of walking about in the curfew, so will you wait for me here?' " The deception worked beautifully; the soldier waited as Leila went from house to house calling for the fictitious midwife and sliding leaflets under all the doors. In the end, she told me triumphantly, she distributed all the leaflets and then the soldier saw her home. "The movement was very pleased with me. It was seen as a test that I had passed very well."

As with Miss Kim, Leila loved the praise of her elders; such incidents as this have remained with her in detail. Her youth was no longer seen as a problem. In the company of her comrades, she visited the West Bank—"what was left of Palestine"—and attended more meetings.

At the same time, she was proving herself a bright pupil academically. At the age of sixteen, she won a scholarship to a boarding school in Sidon. From there, with another scholarship, she went in 1962 to the American University in Beirut. She wanted to be a pharmacist, but the money ran out and she had to leave after a year. It was, she reflected, one of the biggest disappointments of her life. One wonders if the world would have ever heard of Leila Khaled if she had been able to complete her studies.

As it was, she went to live in Kuwait, where she earned her living as an English teacher sending some of her salary back home to her parents. She did not find her job very stimulating, and she soon became immersed in Palestinian politics. In 1966, she joined the PFLP, an illegal organization in Kuwait, and started recruiting members for the movement. Then, a year later, there was the humiliation of the Six Day War and the occupation of the West Bank by Israel. Leila became convinced that her future was as a guerrilla fighter, and she begged the PFLP leadership to send her for training at one of their military bases in Jordan.

She was told to be patient, something she was not good at; to wait a year, and if she could recruit ten new members, she could go. Her determination and energy was phenomenal; in ten months she recruited twenty people.

In the summer of 1969 she went home and announced to her mother (her father had died) that she was going to be a guerrilla. Not surprisingly, Mrs. Khaled was none too pleased at the news, but Leila was now an independent young woman of twenty-five and her mind was made up. To her mother's plea, "Let your brothers go be fighters, you should return to Kuwait," she retorted, "I will either come back dead or as a trained fighter." Off she went, utterly of her own volition, but taking her two younger brothers to the camp as well. So much for women being dragged in by men.

It was the beginning of the happiest period in her life: "The camp was in the mountains and the training was hard—outside in the open air. It was very cold, even in the summertime, and we were living in tents spread over the mountainside. I did not notice the hardships; I was so happy that at last my dream to become a fighter had come true. Now, finally, I was doing something to stop the occupation of our country that had lasted for fifteen years. I was so happy that for the first three days and nights I could not sleep.

"There were girls in the camp, but more boys. Although most of the training was separate, and the girls and boys slept in different parts of the camp, we used to train together for some things. We were shown how to use guns, hand grenades, lectured on the tactics of war and hand-to-hand fighting."

All the various Palestinian political factions were represented at the guerrilla camps, as well as representatives from European revolutionary groups including the Baader-Meinhof gang. Just a month after Leila arrived at the camp, it was bombed by the Israelis, but no one was killed. The guerrillas moved, the Israelis found them again; this pattern continued all summer. At the end of it, Leila's brothers went home—she stayed.

It had taken her only a few weeks to decide that she should go into action: "When the training was finished I kept saying I wanted to go to fight the Israelis. The chief told me, 'Wait, your time will come.'

"One night I was called and asked to leave the camp for a mission. I didn't believe it. I thought my mother had sent for me and it was a trick to get me back to her. I said that I didn't want to go but the chief insisted. Even though he gave me the weapons to take to Beirut, I didn't believe I was being sent on a mission until I arrived there."

When she presented herself to the chief in Beirut he said, "OK, get your things. Are you ready to die?" Her response was that of the perfect guerrilla, "Yes, of course. I am a member of the PFLP."

He then asked her if she was prepared to do a hijack, and Leila nearly blew it by getting a fit of the giggles. She explained her mirth: "I had this picture in my mind of me carrying a plane on my back and everyone running up to me and trying to take it off." The chief wanted to know what was so funny; hijacking, he informed her angrily, was no joke. Leila saw her mission being snatched away from her. "I made an effort and stopped laughing in case he changed his mind. Then he told me, 'OK, you will be taken to a place to begin training for this mission.'"

In a sort of daze, Leila was taught, step by step, the mechanics of the aircraft she would seize. She had to absorb all the operational details of the Boeing 707 until in the end she could have flown it. It was not difficult for her, she said, because she was good at physics, math, and chemistry. The dazed state she felt was not due to the problems of the undertaking, rather to the enormity of it and the thrill of being chosen.

Here, she very much reminded me of Miss Kim and her delight in being selected "for such a big mission." Like that Korean woman, Leila had been singled out for glory from among older and more experienced comrades, and like her, she was determined that she should achieve her mission perfectly.

"I was happy that I should be doing something so big. I just thought about my happiness, not about any danger." And not about the passengers she was going to terrify and possibly kill.

When she asked her masters, "Why me?" they told her because she had been good at training and was so insistent on fighting. They had wanted a woman to show to the world that women were involved in the "revolution."

One does not know whether they predicted the effect a beautiful young woman hijacker would have on the world. Even if they had, they could not have foreseen the tremendous publicity she would attract; the mission could, after all, have gone terribly wrong.

Leila was dispatched to her mother's house to pick up her passport, and to tell her that she was going back to Kuwait to study. She did not mention her forthcoming mission, knowing that her mother would do everything in her power to stop her going. What did her mother think when she heard about the hijack, I asked.

"She first knew about it when she heard the news on the radio. It was before my name came out and the pilot was describing me—beautiful, charming, intelligent. My brothers and sisters said, 'It's Leila.' But my mother did not believe it. She said, 'My daughter is not so beautiful, or charming; besides, Leila is in Kuwait.' When my name was announced, she was very proud of me. She said it was natural for me, and it was the way I had chosen."

Mrs. Khaled, it appears, had by this time accepted her daughter's chosen role in life and was delighted with her. She, like the mothers in the Intifada, seemed to be able to set aside what one might consider the "normal" protective maternal feelings for the greater good of the cause.

On August 29, 1969, a TWA plane, Flight 840, en route to Tel Aviv from Los Angeles landed at Rome to refuel and pick up more passengers. It was scheduled to land again at Athens before continuing the last leg of its journey. The hijack was to take place between Rome and Athens.

In the departure lounge of Rome airport sat Leila and her accomplice, a young Arab man named Salim. They had met for the first time only a few hours earlier at the airport, recognizing each other from photographs and exchanging prearranged signals as identification. They had checked in together to ensure that they were sitting side by side in the aircraft; but in the departure lounge they studiously ignored each other.

She did not remember being nervous, although she had explosives and hand grenades in her handbag, and a gun tucked into the waistband of her trousers. She looked like a very wealthy young woman, part of her "cover," for she and Salim were traveling first class. She recalled every detail of what she wore: an expensive white pantsuit, matching handbag, and hat.

She had bought the clothes on a shopping spree in Rome to where she had flown from Beirut a few days earlier. Although she insisted that she had very little interest in clothes, and the outfit was a necessary item of equipment for the mission, she had particularly loved her white hat. "I made a ribbon for it so that if it was pushed off during the hijack I would not lose it," she recalled.

She had spent her time in Rome sight-seeing, and had enjoyed it. "Rome was such a beautiful city," she said simply.

It is hard to understand how someone could have strolled about a city, enjoying its sights just before hijacking an aircraft and terrifying people out of their wits. Miss Kim had passed the days before her mission in a similar fashion. Was it that these women were callous, or abnormal, or did the enormity of what they were about to do block out all emotion? Leila was not, though, utterly devoid of nerves: she recalled that she had been unable to eat for twenty-four hours before the hijack and did experience a few pangs of conscience as she waited to board the aircraft.

"I was sitting in the lounge, and there was a little girl playing happily with her sister. For the first time I realized that I would be endangering her life. If the plane blew up during our hijack, or if it was shot down by Israeli anti-aircraft fire, then those innocent children would die."

How could she have thought this and then calmly continued with her plans? Did she think that it was not really herself who was about to endanger these children? I wondered if it was significant that she had said, "If the plane blew up," rather than, "If I blew the plane up."

Her justification was again the extension of maternal feeling: "Then I remembered all the countless thousands of Palestinian children in the refugee camps. They were depending on me to tell the world about them. When I remembered their faces I was strengthened."

Her armor was to be dented once more as she sat on the bus taking the passengers out to the waiting airplane. Sitting next to her was a "very jolly Greek man" who struck up a conversation asking the young woman where she was from. She did not want to start talking to him because her mind was too busy with forthcoming events, so she just replied, "Guess!" He listed several South American countries, then Italy or Spain, but made no mention of any Arab nation. Leila was pleased: the less anyone suspected her nationality, the better.

Then the man intruded once more on her thoughts. He was telling her that he lived in America and was going home to Greece for the first time in fifteen years to see his mother. His words jerked her into realizing what she was about to do: "I was shocked. I was about to tell him to go away and catch another plane. I remembered my father going to Jerusalem in 1964 to meet his mother. He was given permission to meet her at the gate, and he waited three days but she didn't come. She came the day after he left in despair. She never even heard about his death. I knew very well what it meant to be away from home, from your mother and sisters, and I was thinking about that while this man talked to me. I wasn't listening to him anymore, but afterward he gave a newspaper interview saying that he had invited me to Athens to spend some time with him."

Leila did, then, experience guilt about the effect of her actions on the passengers, when she could directly identify with them. After the hijack, she had the chance to make amends to her Greek suitor.

She approached him as he sat crying and told him, "Now you are OK. We will send your mother a telegram, and she can meet you."

It was only afterward that she had time for emotions; as she prepared to go into action, she was icily calm. She was determined, she told me, echoing Miss Kim's words, "to achieve my mission perfectly." Her role in it was to be equal to, if not greater than, Salim's. She had the technical knowledge of the aircraft, and was to take over the control of the flight; Salim was the explosives expert who would blow up the aircraft once it had landed. The hijack was to have caused an even greater sensation than it did: General Ytzhak Rabin, then the Israeli ambassador to Washington, and former Israeli chief of staff, was supposed to be on board. The hijackers were to order the plane to fly to Syria, where Rabin was to have been put on trial at a revolutionary court. Unknown to Leila and Salim, he had switched flights at the last minute.

Their first-class seats were located near the cockpit of the plane. The hijack was due to begin half an hour after takeoff. "The air hostess kept coming over and asking us what we would like to eat or drink. We were not hungry, but in the end ordered coffees. I told the hostess I was cold and she brought me a blanket. I put it over my knees and then took my hand grenade from my bag to prepare it. The blanket covered what I was doing.

"Just as we stood up to run to the cockpit, the hostess came down the plane with a tray. She saw the grenade and threw the tray in the air and screamed. It was the only violence throughout the hijack. I asked her to calm down while Salim went into the cockpit and told the captain to listen to his new pilot."

She turned to follow him, but found her way blocked by Salim, who was tall and very broad. His bulk did not allow her to squeeze past. Undaunted, Leila crawled between his legs with her grenade clutched in her hand. She explained: "I had to get in there because I had the grenade and the pistol. At the time I was very thin so I could get through Salim's legs." One can only imagine the flight crew's reaction to the appearance of a giant closely followed by a small woman bearing grenades.

Leila herself did not notice any reactions; she was too busy fumbling inside her trousers. She giggled, rather inappropriately I felt, at the memory: "I stood up with the grenade and reached for my pistol but I felt it slipping down my leg. I had put it in my waistband, but I had not eaten for a day and the trousers were loose. I laughed and shook my leg until it came out. I picked it up and then

I turned to the pilot and told him, 'I am your new captain.' " His plane, she went on, had been taken over by a commando unit of the PFLP.

She then described in great detail, how she set about terrifying the pilot and crew. Such tactics might have been necessary in order to establish who was boss, but what she did was cruel, and furthermore she seemed to have been enjoying herself. Perhaps being in a position of such power is a heady experience, particularly if one is a woman.

"I took the pin out of the grenade and showed it to the pilot. I asked him, 'Do you know what this is?' He said no, so I showed him the grenade more closely; then he nodded his head."

He asked her what she wanted, and she told him to fly to Lydda in Palestine. The pilot looked confused. Lydda, after the creation of Israel, had become Lodd. He asked her if that was where she meant. She knew she was just playing a game, but one that she was determined to win. Lydda, she said again, adding that they would not be stopping at Athens anymore.

I asked her how she had felt at this moment, with her grenade in one hand and a gun in the other. Airily she replied, "It did not seem as if I was doing anything special; in fact, it felt very ordinary. This was the first time I had done this, and I felt very calm, but I always feel calm inside myself, especially when something violent needs to be done. It is so that I can use my mind fully and be cool." Absolute practicality, a characteristic that German intelligence officials told me was particularly noticeable with women revolutionaries.

She just wanted to achieve her mission in a perfect way. Then, forgetting the fact that someone could have jogged her arm and the plane would have exploded, she added, "Besides, we had very strict orders not to hurt anyone; only that we had to defend ourselves without exposing the plane to danger."

Salim turned off what she described as the gas valve in the ceiling of the cockpit, as they had been warned that the pilot could open the valve and the plane would depressurize. Without oxygen masks, she and Salim would faint. Leila herself sat down, took the earphones and microphone, and spoke to Athens control tower. At the same time, she wanted to impress on the crew that she was intimately acquainted with the aircraft, just in case they were thinking of trying any tricks. She asked the engineer how much fuel he had and he lied to her. She was, she remembered, utterly furious: "I told him, 'Lie to me again, and I will break your neck.' The engineer was very angry but the pilot told him to tell the truth. They understood then that I knew about the aircraft."

Having thus terrified the crew into submission, she turned her attention to the passengers. She seemed to be having such a good time that she wanted them to share it: "Relax and drink champagne if you want to," she told them.

The pilot was now putty in her hands. She replaced his flight plan with hers and ordered, "Fly on this line." She recalled him repeating parrot-fashion, "OK, on this line." They approached Lodd, where Leila had more fun with the control tower. She chuckled: "They were furious. I informed them, 'This is no longer TWA 840; this is Flight PFLP Free Arab Palestine.' Lydda refused to call us that. They told us: 'We are not talking to you.' The copilot asked to be allowed to speak to the tower to tell them to use the name I wanted, so I gave him the microphone. He almost screamed, 'This is Popular Front, Free Arab Palestine, and you have got to agree with this name. There is a hand grenade in here.' I was very angry with him. 'Why did you say that? Am I threatening you with the hand grenade?' "

Not much, the man could have replied. "He said, no, but Lodd have got to know how serious this is. Just then Lodd called us, using the right name." She, a Palestinian refugee, and a woman at that, had the enemy wrapped around her little finger.

She informed Lodd that she wished to land, and when, in response, three Israeli fighter jets appeared alongside the aircraft, she used her trump card. Switching on the intercom so that the passengers could hear every word, she warned Lodd: "We will blow up the plane. I told the control tower that the fate of the passengers and crew depended on their actions. The jets moved away."

Why did she subject the passengers to the added terror of this exchange? The answer was to remove any blame or sense of responsibility from themselves: "It was important for the passengers to know that we wanted to land peacefully, and that it was the Israelis who would not let us. I told the passengers, 'The Israelis are threatening you.' " It is possibly this sort of twisted logic that makes such people so hated and feared.

Then, just when I was finding her so hard to take, she became wistful and appealed to one's sympathy. "We were flying over Palestine, and until now I cannot describe my feelings. I was just looking at it for the first time and feeling what it means to be away. Then I saw my father's face. He was smiling, but he was dead. I could hardly speak. I wanted the pilot to land, but he said he could not because of the fighter planes. I got onto the tower and told them to take their jets away."

She paused, laughing at the memory: "They were shouting, 'You bitch,' screaming abuse. I was screaming and shouting back. I told the pilot to land—'no matter what happens, let it happen.' He begged me to wait for five minutes." Leila ordered the plane to descend to about 10,000 feet, and it flew over the runway. It was like a barracks, blocked with tanks and soldiers. It gave her a tremendous kick to see what she had done.

She had never intended to land, she told me, just to make a show of strength. Through the control tower she made a revolutionary speech to Palestinians, and then commanded the pilot to fly on to Damascus. It was quite noticeable that according to her account, she did everything. Salim does not feature in it.

Once more, she turned her attention to the passengers, urging them via the air hostesses to eat anything they wanted. She even joked, "It's at our expense." In the cockpit she had become irritated by the copilot: "The pilot was very calm, but the copilot was furious; it showed especially in his face. When he looked at me his eyes were full of fear and hatred. I told him, 'Turn your face away and your eyes away; I don't like them.' He was drinking, but his cup was empty. He kept on picking it up and putting it to his mouth." She had really found this very funny, telling me that she had asked the man if he wanted anything to drink, as he was only drinking oxygen.

It was an example of her inability to understand other people, as if they were there just as a foil to herself, and it was difficult not to dislike her. She wanted me to understand what she did, yet seemed incapable of doing the same for others.

The plane approached Damascus airport which was brand-new and about to be christened by the PFLP. The Syrians, seeing the Israeli jet escort, would have shot them all down if she had not assured Damascus that she had passengers on board. She could not resist a final twist of the knife at the very end. She warned the captain, "Land smoothly, because I might drop my hand grenade." When they landed, she cheerfully saluted him and thanked him for his help. He was amazed, she recalled.

"I went to speak to the passengers. I was still holding my hand grenade but I held it down by my side so they couldn't see it. I asked them to leave in five minutes and told the crew to prepare the passengers to climb out onto the emergency chutes. But the passengers did not listen. In one minute the plane was empty. I stood there saying, 'OK, don't rush,' but everyone was gone."

Salim now had his part to play. Leila gave him the explosives from her handbag, which he placed in the cockpit. The fuse was set, Leila jumped down the emergency chute, followed too quickly by the large Salim, who tore it and landed heavily on her. They waited for the explosion, but it did not come, so Salim ("He was very brave," Leila said generously) climbed back in to reset the fuse. This time it worked.

The Israeli fighter jets had also landed on the runway. The crews, four men and two women, ran for cover as the cockpit exploded. Leila, though, glorying in the moment of triumph, stood her ground, watching the fire. A Syrian soldier ran up to her, telling her to run and asking if she was not afraid. She was puzzled by his question; she said she had never been less afraid in her life.

The Syrians were not quite sure what had happened. They ordered the two hijackers to get on board the airport bus with the passengers. It must have been the ultimate nightmare for people who thought they had just escaped their tormentors. Several of them were crying; all were in a state of considerable shock. Leila noticed two women passengers clinging to each other and shaking with sobs. She had met them briefly in the Rome travel agency where she had bought her ticket, and now that the mission was over she was able to show compassion.

"I said, 'We are sorry.' One of them whispered, 'We have wet ourselves.' I told her it was OK, they could change their pants."

Leila could sense the hostility and fear in the bus and she did not like it. In some ways she had just finished the most glorious game of her life, and she wanted everyone about her to be happy. She was like a child, I thought. She apologized to the passengers again, explaining that it had been the "only way for us." Then she tried to win friends with that playground ploy of giving out sweets. In the handbag that had contained the explosives, she had cigarettes and sweets, and she started handing them out. She was hurt then, and still is unable to fully accept the reaction she got from some passengers. "Some looked at me as if they hated me and would not take anything from me. I did not understand their hatred."

Nor, it seemed, had the passengers understood why they had been hijacked. Leila had sat down in the bus beside a woman who suddenly turned to her and asked if she had not been afraid to hijack a plane. The question bewildered Leila, just as her answer shows what commitment to a single goal can do to the mind. Why, she responded, should she have been afraid? The woman sighed and shook her head. "I don't understand. Who are the Palestinians?" she asked.

The question stopped Leila in her tracks, even as she repeated it twenty years on. "It said everything—she did not know of our fight—no one did; she did not even know we existed. But after the hijack everyone knew. That is why we did it."

Both she and Salim knew that they had to report back to their military bases in Jordan as soon as possible. However, the Syrians detained them, at first accusing the pair of being terrorists working for Egyptian intelligence against "revolutionary" Syria. Then, when it became clear that they were PFLP commandos, they were castigated for embarrassing Syria by choosing to land there. It seemed that external pressure was being exercised either to put the hijackers on trial or extradite them to Israel, both demands being out of the question to the Syrian president.

Leila and Salim retaliated by going on hunger strike three times during the forty-five days of their detention. At one point, after refusing food for six days, Leila fainted and woke up in a hospital with IVs attached to her arms. Angrily she pulled them out and shouted at the doctors that she wanted to go home. In spite of everything, though, she was still in high spirits. Back at the prison an irate interrogator asked why they had chosen to land at Damascus, thus embroiling Syria in the Palestinian problem. She cheekily retorted: "I told him we didn't have airports in Palestine, and we knew Damascus had a new one. We wanted to test it out." The interrogator did not know how to respond; he was not accustomed to such jibes from prisoners, particularly female ones.

Mrs. Khaled, too, raised traditional eyebrows when she visited her daughter. One of the guards, distressed at the impropriety of Leila being held in a men's prison, urged her mother to get her transferred to a women's jail. Mrs. Khaled, the strictly conservative woman who had locked up her daughter rather than have her mix with men, now viewed Leila as a fighter well able to fend for herself. She responded tartly that it was only the guard's old-fashioned Eastern mentality that made him say such a thing. "I am proud of my daughter," she told him. "After what she had done, I am not afraid for her." She had, like Joan of Arc, "exceeded her sex."

Finally, the Syrian minister of defense ruled that the hijackers were free to go. Salim and Leila returned to their bases in Jordan, where the young woman suddenly found herself a celebrity. The PFLP leadership was delighted with the publicity and sent their star comrade on an extensive tour of the Middle East. They supplied her with her own retinue of bodyguards, well aware that she was at the top of the list for kidnap or assassination by the Israelis. To the Arab world, she was a heroic figure: students at the American University of Beirut mobbed her; parties and dinners were held in her honor. A British businessman who was introduced to her at an embassy party in Qatar commented, "She was feted like a visiting astronaut."

Leila remembered it as a wonderful few months that were, however, exhausting. "Yes, everyone was very pleased with me, but the Middle East tour was very hard work. I was giving lectures in all those countries, urging the masses to join the Palestinian struggle. I spoke about the need for the kind of mission I had just been on. It was important that there should be more such missions. For fifteen years we had been demonstrating, screaming, shouting for our land. The world answered us with resolutions that were never practiced. All they did was provide more tents, old clothes, sugar, and flour. Now we had a big question: Who are the Palestinians? Just as that passenger on the bus had asked. We knew there was no immediate answer, but the whole world awakened to the fact that there was something happening in the Middle East. It was the beginning."

A revolutionary woman could hardly have asked for anything more: she had not only led the way for other women, she had, to all intents and purposes single-handedly put the Palestinian problem on the world agenda. She was still not satisfied, however.

Back at her training camp in Jordan, she became increasingly worried at the publicity surrounding her. She had been promised that she would be going on an "even greater mission" in a few months, and she feared her face would be too well known to allow her to participate in it. She tried to dodge the journalists who swarmed over her camp with little success: "Once, an Italian film crew came to the house where I was staying. They knocked on the door and I opened it. They asked, 'Where is Leila Khaled?' I said that I didn't know; she wasn't there.

"My comrades were furious. I was ordered to report to the general secretary, Comrade George Habash. He was angry; he asked me what I was doing, refusing to speak to the journalists. He said, 'You went on this mission, and now you must explain why; this is an order that you speak to the film crew.'

"He told me it was my duty, that for the first time the world was listening, and it was me that they wanted to hear. I did not tell him the real reason; I started crying and said that I was afraid of making political mistakes."

The tears did not wash with Comrade Habash. Never had there been a comrade less likely to make such mistakes. He ordered her to go through to his outer office where the Italian film crew was waiting. Still crying, she obeyed. The crew did a double take. "You are the girl who opened the door!" they cried. It was not a successful interview. When she was asked, "How come a woman hijacked a plane?" Leila responded angrily and not very enlighteningly. "I am not afraid. I did it. I want to liberate our land." Then she said nothing else. "I just glared at them," she remembered. In the spring of 1970, she was ordered to report to a PFLP camp in Lebanon where, she was delighted to hear, she was to begin training for her second mission. In September she was to hijack an El Al plane, to make it clear to the world what the PFLP thought of Israel.

There was a hitch, though. Leila's fears of being too well known proved to be correct. Her superiors were worried about sending her; she could wreck the mission if someone recognized her. Calmly, she suggested that her face should be changed.

Although she did not admit it to me, it was quite clear that, seeing the chance slip from her grasp, Leila was prepared to do anything to get on that mission. She can hardly say that she was the only one who could have done it; there were dozens of other candidates who were as well trained, but much less well known than she. One concludes that she really loved the business, the power and thrill of being in command, and that she had become addicted to it.

Her commanders were still in some doubt as to whether facial surgery could really help, but confronted with her determination, they allowed her to go ahead. In Beirut she found a well-known plastic surgeon and visited his clinic. He knew who she was and was suspicious at once; he did not wish to be involved with the PFLP and their superstar. "I told him that my fiancé was studying in Europe and wanted me to go and join him so that we could be married. But because my face was well known to Interpol, I had a problem. They would probably arrest me on sight. I needed to change my appearance."

The surgeon, she knew, did not believe a word of it, but was probably frightened of refusing her. He took some photographs of her face to study and said he would see what he could do. When she went back to him he told her it was very nearly impossible to change her face because of her very strong jawline and cheekbones, and the unusual shape of her eyes. Doubtless, he hoped that would satisfy this potentially dangerous woman.

Leila was not so easily dissuaded. "No," she told the surgeon, "it is easy. Just put stitches by the corners of my eyes, here and here, and I will look like a Japanese."

The man was horrified. He told her not to be crazy; that if he did as she suggested her eyes would be either permanently open or permanently closed. Nothing was going to stand in her way. "OK," she said. "Let them be open all the time then." The surgeon refused, saying it would be inhuman to do such a thing.

They progressed, he reluctantly, she eagerly, to an evaluation of her nose. He thought perhaps that he could alter it a little. She remembered that he asked her what her fiancé would think of her new face, and whether he knew what she was doing. Coolly she replied, saying that of course her fiancé knew; they were determined to marry and this was the only way. She knew, she told me, that the man was hoping to catch her out. In the end, though, she wore him down; he agreed to the operation, making her sign documents taking all the responsibility. The agony she went through was tremendous: she insists that she was given no anesthetic at all.

"He operated first on my nose. It was very painful, because I did not have any anesthetic. The operations had to be done secretly, at the doctor's small clinic, and there were no facilities for giving an anesthetic. I could feel everything that was happening.

"The operation made no difference, so he did it a second time, but the change was still not enough. When I told him to try again, he said that he didn't believe I was going to get married." Leila was not about to be beaten by a plastic surgeon. She told him, "OK, whatever you believe, you have begun and you have to continue." The man looked at her and asked, "Are you threatening me?" Yes, she was, but she tried another tactic, appealing to him for help. "I begged him to do this for me." The surgeon gave in and carried out several more operations.

Eventually he seemed to take pity on his patient. Still maintaining the story they both knew to be false, he apologized for causing her such pain, "all because you want to get married."

"I looked at him. I knew he thought I was going on a second mission, and I asked him, even if he knew the truth, would he please carry on." To reinforce her point, she tried a little blackmail, telling him that she would keep his secret if he would keep hers.

The surgeon was up to his neck in it by now. Reluctantly he agreed to carry on but pleaded with her that after he had done what he could, he never wanted to see her face again.

After five months of operations, every part of Leila's face had been worked on, including her mouth. At last she and her leaders were convinced that only close friends and relatives would have recognized her. They were sure that an El Al security guard, relying on a photograph, could not have identified her.

It soon became clear to the hijack unit that such extreme precautions were only too necessary. In May 1970 Leila and her chief were working on plans for the mission at his home in Lebanon late at night. The house was hit by rockets, injuring the man's wife and only child but leaving the comrades unharmed. It was another Leila-inspired first: never before had Israel attacked inside Lebanon.

She and her chief spent the next few weeks at the hospital where the woman and child were treated. The attack, far from making them reassess the wisdom of their plans, had only served to infuriate them. A room at the hospital became their office and recruiting center, for it had been decided to expand the operation, and more hijackers were needed. The new plans included the seizure of Swissair and TWA flights as well as the El Al. It was to be a spectacular event.

Leila's face at that time, scarred, black and blue, must have been a horrible sight, and unfortunately an old friend of hers who was a nurse at the hospital recognized her. Not surprisingly she wanted to know what had happened to her friend, and Leila lied, explaining that she had been injured during training. She did it to protect her mother, she said.

"I did not want her crying over what I looked like or wondering why I had had my face changed."

It is curious that the chief did not reconsider sending Leila on the mission in the light of the nurse's recognition. It is particularly odd, considering that they believed the El Al flight would have an important Israeli on board, the chief of military security no less, who would surely have ensured that the flight was hijack-proof. Leila and her chief were also well aware that El Al's security measures had been tightened immeasurably since her last performance. On board would be the armed sky marshals, and passengers had to pass through stringent interrogation.

Due to these measures, only half of Leila's hijack team actually made it onto the flight. Two men were refused admittance, but they calmly bought tickets to a Pan Am flight, hijacked that instead, and blew it up in Cairo.

All this was unknown to Leila as she stood with her accomplice, Patrick Arguello, in front of the El Al counter in Amsterdam airport on the morning of September 6, 1970.

Patrick was a young Nicaraguan who had been recruited into the PFLP and had met up with Leila the day before in Stuttgart. He did not know her true identity, only that she was supposed to be playing the part of his girlfriend, and that her cover name was Maria Sanchez from Honduras. She was the senior ranking of the two.

Leila had once more slipped into her role of the cool guerrilla. The El Al flight, scheduled to depart at 11:20 A.M., was delayed for security checks, but she was not nervous. She was virtually a walking explosive: "I had hand grenades down my front and flight plans and instructions in my underwear."

As she stood waiting her turn (it was almost as if she were a beauty contestant waiting in the wings, I thought, as she recounted the story), she saw on the notice board something that reminded her of the last time. Pan Am Flight 840 had arrived in Amsterdam. "I remembered with happiness the TWA 840 mission of the previous year, not realizing that two of our comrades were about to hijack that Pan Am."

As the minutes went by, Leila became worried that they would miss the prearranged deadline for the hijack, 12:20 P.M. All the seizures were supposed to occur at the same time. Then, disaster nearly struck. Leila saw three Arabs approaching and recognized one of them. Frightened lest he should greet her by her real name in front of the El Al security guards, she flung her arms around Patrick and hugged him. "He was surprised, but he did not push me away," she recalled with a smile.

They passed through the security checks, Leila with her concealed armory, Patrick with a pistol. Their weapons, she said, were made of a special material that was not picked up by the scanners. She remembered that one security guard had asked her if she had any dangerous weapons. She laughed at him and replied, "Why would a girl like me have a dangerous weapon?" The oldest ploy in the woman guerrilla's handbook and it worked; the guard apologized.

Another guard suddenly asked her in English if she spoke Spanish. "*Si, Señor*," she replied, the only Spanish words she knew. Patrick was angry; he asked what she would have done if the man had started speaking in Spanish. Leila, though, was having the time of her life; she loved these little tests. "Relax," she told Patrick. "He knows no Spanish because he would have spoken to me in it if he did."

The couple went through into the departure lounge and once again Leila was confronted with the sight of the children who would be going on the flight. She steeled herself: "I promised to myself that I would make sure none of them was harmed. It was very difficult to watch those children; I felt as if I could not move." Just then the flight was called and the time for such promises was past; and she walked onto the aircraft.

She and Patrick were traveling in the tourist section. The plane sat on the runway for some time, and then an hour after the hijack deadline it finally took off. Patrick complained that he was hungry, but Leila, ever practical, warned him it was not a good idea to eat before action; he was just nervous, she told him. The young man got angry with his female companion. "Who do you think you are? Queen Elizabeth, or the queen of hijackers?" he hissed at her. Leila replied no, that she had had a little experience of hijacking and she had found that it was better not to eat before the mission. "So that your whole mind is alert," she told him. Patrick looked at her more closely and murmured, "Yes, I remember your face." Leila told him that in half an hour he would be able to eat and drink anything he wanted because the plane would be theirs.

She became suddenly and uncomfortably aware that a man sitting at the back of the aircraft was staring at her. She turned and returned the stare until he looked away. But she feared, rightly, that he was a sky marshal, who had found her face familiar. The time to act, she decided, was now.

She nodded to Patrick, and he got out his pistol. "I got out my two hand grenades. We stood up and ran through the first class to the crew cabin. The door was locked, and Patrick told a hostess to open it. I was holding the grenades and telling the passengers to be quiet." Lots of them were screaming, she said.

"Suddenly some people started shooting at us. They were sky marshals; one of them was the man who had been staring at me. Patrick had his pistol out and he defended me by shooting, but he was shot. I did not have time to help him; my chief thought was the mission and how it must succeed." Nothing, not even a wounded comrade, was going to stop her.

"I kicked at the door of the cockpit, holding my two grenades with the pins out. No one opened the door. The whole plane seemed to be full of shooting. I heard someone shout, 'Don't shoot her, she's got grenades.' Then two men, sky marshals I think, rushed at me and caught me, and they began to hit me."

She fell and one of the grenades fell from her hand and rolled onto the floor. By a fluke, it did not explode. "I thought it had, and that the plane had exploded, and that we were all just flying through the air. But when I opened my eyes people were beating me. I still had one grenade in my hand; I was holding it tight, and two passengers were holding it as well. Someone hit me on the head, and the two passengers were hitting me trying to get the grenade. There was a lot of shouting, and one man with blood on his face came toward me. He just wanted to kill me. He found a place free to hit me—it was my head. He took hold of my hair and pulled it. It came off; I was wearing a wig. He just stood there staring at it. I looked up at him and laughed and he jumped on me with his boots. I fainted, and when I came round they were still hitting me.

"In ten minutes the plane landed and at that moment the hostess asked the people to sing because they had conquered us. I could see Patrick. He was lying on the floor breathing heavily, his eyes were open, but he had been shot badly. A man came up with a gun. He kicked him and then put his pistol to Patrick's neck and shot four bullets into him—while he was lying there; he just shot him.

"When the plane landed there was a big fight at the door. The security men had tied me up with neckties—I was wrapped in them and couldn't move. A man, I think he was the pilot, came out and he picked me up and kicked me so hard I was thrown against the side of the plane.

"There was an argument going on. Some men speaking English came into the plane and tried to take me, but the security men were shouting, 'She is our prisoner; she is a terrorist and we are taking her to Israel.' The security men grabbed me, and the English grabbed me. I was fainting, and they were all pulling me in different ways, fighting. It was very painful. Everything in my body hurt, and I was covered with blood. One of the Englishmen on the stairs pulled me free and threw me out of the aircraft. He shouted to others to catch me and they caught me in their arms on the tarmac. Afterward the police told me that because the plane had landed in Britain, what happened to me was their responsibility. They could see that the passengers and the sky marshals might kill me; they had to get me out fast.

"I was put in an ambulance beside Patrick. He had a mask on his face, but I knew he was not alive. I thought, *he* was Nicaraguan; he was not a Palestinian: it should have been me to die, and I was crying for him. The men in the ambulance asked why I was crying, and who I was. I could not speak—all I could do was cry for Patrick. One of them said, 'Maybe it was her husband or boyfriend.' "

She was taken to the hospital and remembered that as she lay on an examining table, people kept coming in to question her. Even in such circumstances, her cheeky bravado was intact: "One of the men there asked me where I thought I was. I told him, England. He said, 'How come you know that?' so I explained, 'Because everyone is speaking English, so it is not France or Amsterdam.' "

The man asked her name, but Leila would only reply that she was a commando from the PFLP. Eventually a journalist who had interviewed her in Jordan arrived at the hospital, took one look at her and announced, "That is Leila Khaled." The plastic surgery could not have been that good.

"The doctor came to examine me. Here, in my front, I had put all the papers relating to the hijack. He tried to open my clothes, but I would not let him. He called to another man, 'There is something here,' and the police came and asked me what I was hiding. I just smiled at them. The doctor said that I needed an X ray—he was talking about my face, which was very swollen, because of the surgery still. But I told them I didn't need any X rays. I was afraid they would discover all the operations. The doctor said, 'Your nose is very peculiar because the bones go outwards.' He brought me a skull and showed me how it would look if the nose was broken: The bones would go in. 'Why is your nose like that?' he asked me. I replied that I didn't know, I was born like that.

"I remember one of the women cops in the hospital telling me that the doctor was a Jew. I said I did not mind. 'Are you serious?' she asked. I told her I was against Zionists, not Jews, and this doctor was British, not an Israeli. She did not understand the difference, and I was in too much pain to explain."

In the end, Leila had to surrender the documents that were hidden in her underclothes. Her cuts and bruises were treated, and she was taken to Ealing police station. She could not sleep, she told me, because every inch of her body had been beaten and she was so sad for Patrick. However, a truly wonderful piece of British bureaucracy brought a smile to her face as she remembered that night.

"At one point, the cell was opened and a man came in carrying forms. He told me that he was an immigration official, and he wanted to know why I had entered Britain without a visa. He had brought these forms, in Arabic and in English. He told me: 'You will have to go back to where you came from.' I laughed at him. He was accusing me of being an illegal immigrant. I asked where I was meant to go back to—Amsterdam? I hadn't planned to enter Britain, but if I had I would have got a visa. He said, all right, and left me alone with the forms."

Leila was to spend three weeks at the police station, during which time she earned the grudging admiration and respect of her captors. She was utterly fearless and totally unrepentant, and she played a cat-and-mouse game with her interrogators. The one she remembered most was Superintendent David Frew; she led him a merry dance. It was during this period that marriage proposals started arriving at the police station, and the British press took the imprisoned woman to their hearts. In headlines she was always referred to as "Leila"; there were reports on how she passed her time, what she said, and how she disliked compliments from men.

Leila began her first round with Superintendent Frew the day after she had arrived at Ealing. When he entered her cell, she told him, "I will not speak to you unless you recognize me as a commando from the PFLP." Frew withdrew gracefully, saying he would have to consult with his superiors. He did not reappear for five days, during which Leila went on a hunger strike. "I just used to drink water and smoke cigarettes. Whenever they brought me any food, I would cry. One woman cop asked my why I cried when I saw food. I explained because my comrade died when he was hungry. I could never forget that I had not allowed Patrick to eat before he was killed, so I felt I could not eat myself.

"There were two women cops in my cell and two men outside on guard. They were sympathetic toward me. They kept changing these guards, and other police kept coming and looking at me and saying, 'Is she the one?' I think they imagined that I would be a very huge person, and they were amazed to see a very tiny human being instead of a boxer. I spoke to the guards about why we did what we did. One of the women cops was very nice—I used to write to her regularly, but I lost the address in the end. But she told me, 'I don't think it's a good way, this hijacking of planes, because you make everyone afraid.' She used to tell me about what was going on outside."

On the fifth day, Superintendent Frew came back and informed her that there were certain things he wanted to discuss with her. She was taken into an interrogation room and left alone for a few minutes with a male police officer. Leila used those minutes well: "I read the laws on the interrogation of prisoners on the wall, and I realized that there should have been a woman cop in the room with me.

"When Mr. Frew came back, I said, 'I think you are breaking the law.' '*What?*' he shouted. I explained to him, 'According to your laws a female prisoner must have a woman police officer present during interrogation.' He had his mouth open. Then he said, 'Yes, we apologize.' He went outside to look for a policewoman but he couldn't find one of suitable rank, so they asked one of the cops who had been guarding me to come in. She was someone I didn't like. She made me wake early when I didn't want to because I used to sit up late at night thinking. Her name, I remember, was Hazel. I told Mr. Frew that I didn't want her in the room because I didn't like her, so he should bring another one. Hazel was upset. 'What did I do, Leila?' she asked. I just shook my head, and they brought another one."

She was surprised, she told me, that she had won this minor victory; but she was amazed when suddenly Mr. Frew and three other men in the room stood up. Mr. Frew addressed her thus: "In the name of Her Majesty and Her Majesty's government, we recognize you as a fighter from the Popular Front for the Liberation of Palestine and as a fighter for the Palestinian people."

"Thank you," she replied. "Now I have a question. In Great Britain, don't you have slippers? You have taken my clothes and shoes away and my feet are cold." Slowly but surely, Leila seemed to be gaining the upper hand. Frew looked at her feet and apologized.

For her part, Leila was determined to give nothing away. "I told them that as I was a prisoner of war they only had the right to ask my name and unit. Mr. Frew said, 'But we are not at war with you.' I disagreed and explained that since 1917, the declaration of the Balfour Treaty, the British had declared war against the Palestinians. Frew tried to argue that the Balfour Treaty was a long time ago and the British people had changed, but I insisted that they had not changed that much, and they still declared war against us by their policies.

"Frew was very cool; he was trying to get me to answer his questions. But I said, 'Because we are at war, I will only answer two questions. My name is Leila Khaled, and I am a member of the Popular Front for the Liberation of Palestine.' "

At this point, Frew seemed to tire; he ordered that someone should bring Miss Khaled her slippers. Then he tried another tactic.

"He looked at me very hard for several minutes then said, 'I don't believe you are Leila Khaled.' He had a lot of photographs in front of him and my passport photograph, which I had used at Amsterdam. He picked up a photograph and showed it to me. 'This photograph of Leila Khaled and the one in this passport of you are not the same person,' he said. I asked. 'Who am I then?' and he told me to tell him; he would like to know. I suggested that we should forget about names; he could just call me a PFLP commando. He told me, 'You know, you are an intelligent woman.' I replied, 'I am an Arab woman. We are a conservative people and I don't accept men's compliments.' He groaned. 'Look, my hair is gray.' He was trying to say he was old and I should help him, that he wasn't making compliments. I told him that the color of his hair was because of his wife, not because of me. I didn't want to talk to him.

"But he went on. 'You are a very important person, the same as George Habash, your leader.' I thought he was paying compliments again so I coldly told him that was his evaluation; I was only an ordinary member of the PFLP. He insisted, 'No you are not. Three days after your capture, the PFLP hijacked a British plane. They flew it to Dawson's Field, and they are now demanding your release for the passengers. Now do you understand you are very important?' "

Leila had been overwhelmed at the news; as she commented with a faraway look in her eyes, "A plane has been hijacked just for me."

"Frew then went on: 'Tell me, at least a hundred people must have been involved in planning your hijack. How come not a bit of information came out?' I replied, 'That's your problem. I don't think so many people were involved in planning.' He asked me to tell him about it. I explained: the chief calls me to him; he says take your passport, take the ticket, take the grenades, and go hijack a plane. Frew made a face, 'As I said, you are very intelligent.' I knew he was hinting he was experienced and didn't believe me."

Her interrogator had another policeman bring in a pistol and the hand grenade that Leila had let fall to the floor of the plane. They were in plastic bags. Frew asked her if she knew what was in the bags.

"I told him, 'Yes, that is a hand grenade.'

" 'Ah,' he said, 'it is your hand grenade that you threw.'

"I cried, 'I didn't throw any hand grenade. Are you accusing me of that? I want to go back to my cell.'

" 'No one is accusing you of anything; I apologize. We are not accusing you; but all the passengers said you threw it.' I told him that if I had thrown it, I wouldn't be here.

" 'Yes, possibly,' he agreed. 'But it did not go off. If I had been in yours shoes I would have thrown it to defend myself.' Then he asked, 'Were you afraid; are you a coward? Are you afraid to die? You were attacked; to protect yourself you have to throw one of the hand grenades, don't you?'

"I knew what he was trying to do—he wanted to provoke me to speak. But the reasons I had not thrown the grenade were that, one, I had strict orders not to blow the plane up because we are not killers, we are freedom fighters; and two, it would have been very easy to have blown the plane up while I was sitting in my seat. I told Frew, if he wanted to believe the passengers, he could, but they were our enemies and the British government was declaring war on the Palestinians."

Frew seemed to abandon hope of eliciting a full confession from his prisoner. He told her that he would put certain questions to her, and she should answer yes or no. "But do not lie," he warned. The effect of his warning was electrifying.

"I was very angry with him. I got up and shouted, 'Now you are accusing me of being a liar—but only thirty minutes ago you accepted my political position. I wish to go back to my cell.' I got up to go out of the room, but Frew begged me to sit down again.

"He asked me if I would like coffee or tea. I said I wasn't sure whether to accept a drink. He assured me that there would be no drugs in it. I told him, 'This is my first visit to your country, and you assume I think there will be something in the drink—is it your habit to put something in drinks?' He shouted, '*Visit?*' Then he went on quickly, 'No, it is not a habit. You are very intelligent.' Again I explained that I didn't accept men's compliments. The next day he brought a newspaper article about me, and at the end it read, 'Leila does not accept men's compliments.' 'All right?' he asked."

The only thing that Leila was prepared to talk about was her politics. When Frew asked her why she was on a hunger strike, she replied that she was used to hunger; she was hungry to go back to her homeland, she told him; she had been hungry all her life. He tried to break down some of her defenses by telling her that Israel wanted her extradited. To which she answered: "That's all right; I want to go to Palestine. I will be going sooner now rather than later." Frew thought she had misunderstood the danger to herself should she be sent to Israel. He explained that she would be tortured and imprisoned. Leila replied, "So you know that they torture us? That's why we tried to hijack the plane." Frew, she remembered, sighed deeply, saying, "Again you are speaking politically, and we don't want political speeches."

Leila shot back: "Yes, I'm involved politically. Do you expect me to speak about fashion?"

What made her goad this policeman so, I asked her. "I was able to speak like this to him because the other hijackings had given me confidence, and because of the exchange he had told me about. I knew it was only a matter of time."

After about a week, Frew seemed to resign himself to the fact that he would get no information from her. He arranged for her to have exercise, playing table tennis with the policewomen; to have a daily shower; and to be brought newspapers. To her fury, she was at first supplied with women's magazines, and she complained loudly that she wanted "newspapers, not knitting patterns."

She remembered reading on September 17 about the fighting in Jordan between the Palestinian guerrillas and the army. She commented: "It was terrible to be in my cell and not be able to fight.

When we were thrown out of Jordan, I thought, Where am I supposed to go back to? No country will take me back if I am released." She was determined, though, not to show Frew her fears; when he told her that the Palestinian resistance was finished, she perkily responded, "OK, I will get out of here, get married, and have lots of children so I can make a new resistance." Frew did not know whether to believe her or not, she said.

As the days went by, letters began arriving at the police station for the prisoner. Some of it was hate mail, but in other letters men asked to marry her. Frew read them all, asking whether Leila knew these people, and why they were writing to her. He had not appreciated her notoriety.

After three weeks she was told she was to be released, and Frew asked her where she wanted to go. Palestine, she answered. Just before she left, she could not resist teasing him a little further: "I told him, 'I like this hotel. It is awarded ten stars; the service is very good, and I will ask my comrades to come here. I hope you have had a good impression of me.'

" 'Perhaps,' he replied, 'but I beg you not to come back.' I promised to write to him and the other cops and send them Christmas presents."

True to her word, she sent greeting cards to Superintendent Frew and his colleagues at Ealing police station. The cards were written on mock airline tickets and she enclosed photographs of the aircraft blown up at Dawson's Field.

On the morning of her release, Frew explained that he would open a door of the police station that led onto the street. She was to walk straight to the Land Rover that was waiting, get in and lie down on the floor. These precautions were for her own good, he told her, as there were concerns that she might be kidnapped. "Who by, the Zionists?" she queried. "Then it's your responsibility to make sure they do not." With what relief must Frew have finally bade her farewell.

"When I got to the door I saw a lot of photographers waiting, but I walked through them and into the Land Rover. I was wearing the same clothes as a woman cop—a black skirt and jacket, and nobody realized who I was. There were two armed men and four police officers with me. I was taken to a military airfield, then by helicopter to an airport, where I got on a Royal Air Force plane."

The policewoman guarding her warned jokingly that Leila

should not do anything on this plane. "No hijacking," she said. Leila laughed at that. She wanted to have a little fun with the pilot; she told him she hoped they were going to Haifa. The pilot was not amused, and Leila was disappointed. "He was very serious and would not talk to me."

The flight landed first at Munich, then went on to Zurich to collect other Palestinians who had been freed from jail in order to save the lives of the hijacked hostages. The plane flew to Cairo, with each Palestinian under heavy guard and sitting several rows apart, just in case. They were handed over to the Egyptian authorities, who kept them at a safe house for eleven days. The other hijackers who had successfully brought aircraft to Dawson's Field joined them, and it was a time for rejoicing. Leila, who had secretly feared that she would be in disgrace over her failed mission, found she was still a hero for the cause. The world's press again clamored to interview her.

She and the other guerrillas returned to their units, now based in Lebanon. Every Palestinian was needed to fight Israel which, after the hijackings, had vowed to eradicate terrorists once and for all. Leila joined a combat unit and in between fighting would tour the refugee camps urging women to join her. She was an inspiration: "Because of what I had done, the women listened to me and believed they should do as I told them."

Her mother came to visit her shortly after her return to Lebanon. "She came at midnight, but only for fifteen minutes because of security reasons. She looked at my face which she had not seen since before the operations and cried. 'What have they done to you?' she asked. I explained it was because of the fighting and that it would be all right. She said, 'You know I am so proud of you, but I didn't sleep for many times.' She had heard rumors that my eyes had been taken out and my ribs were broken."

In November 1970 Leila suddenly married a fellow fighter, about whom all she would say was that they spent a week together before returning to their separate combat units and that the marriage did not work.

Leila was, she admitted, more interested in fighting than setting up housekeeping. She had been told, and had accepted the fact, that there would be no more hijackings; the PFLP had decided they had served their purpose. She wanted to be on the frontline in other missions (what these were she would not say), but she found that her face, even the surgically altered version, was preventing her from doing so.

Resolutely, and to the man's horror, she returned to the Beirut plastic surgeon. "He was not very pleased to see me," she recalled with a smile. "He told me not to come to his clinic during the daytime in case someone saw me. He was afraid that he would be implicated. I promised that our secret was still safe and told him not to be frightened. He carried out several operations on me again, mainly on my nose and cheeks, and although my face did not look as it had done before, it was more how I once looked."

Israel had made a public declaration that she would be caught and brought back to Jerusalem to stand trial. Less publicly, it appears that Mossad simply wanted to kill her: "Once I was coming back to the apartment at midnight, and I don't know why, I looked under the bed, maybe I was looking for slippers. I found a box stuck to the bed. I left at once and went to the office; it was a secret office and my comrades were angry that I had come so late—I might have been followed, they shouted. I had broken the rule. I explained, 'There's something in my apartment.' Someone went immediately and when he came back he said, 'It's explosives. If someone sits on the bed, it will explode.' "

The assassination attempt had frightened her masters, so Leila was ordered to disappear. For a year, she stayed at different secret addresses, moving constantly so as to avoid detection. She was only allowed out to fight when the guerrilla camps were attacked.

Leila claimed not to remember whether she killed anyone in these desperate battles. She sighed, "It is a difficult thing to know what you have done when you are fighting like that. Either you kill or are killed. When there is shooting you hide and shoot. It was very different fighting in the street from fighting as a guerrilla in the mountains, as I had before. In the middle of gunfire, when you have shot someone, you do not have time to look to see if he is dead. You have to move on to the next one."

For the next few years, Leila's lifestyle was one of guerrilla fighter, recruiting officer, and trainer. On Christmas Day, 1976, her younger sister and the sister's fiancé were killed in Leila's house. "I went home because we had arranged to go to Tyre for their wedding. I found their bodies; they had been shot; it was a big shock to me. I had been preparing myself for my sister's marriage. Our mother was waiting for us in Tyre. I do not know if the Israelis thought they had killed me because it was my home."

Two years later, she accepted an invitation from the Soviet Union to continue her university education in Moscow. The invitation coincided with both her wishes and those of her commanding officers. She still very much wanted to get a degree, and they wanted her to be safe. She spent two "very happy" years in Russia, but again failed to complete her studies. This time her education was interrupted by a call from the PFLP to all students to return to defend their bases in Lebanon. She went back to the battlefield.

She was married again in 1982 to a physician, Dr. Um Baader, who was also a PFLP comrade. It was the time of the Israeli invasion of Lebanon, and the couple were living and fighting in Beirut. Leila remembered her frustration at being forced to hide and not kill an Israeli who was standing just a few feet from her—in case she was captured and recognized.

By now she was pregnant and the city was under bombardment by the Israelis. After three months, Leila and her husband, along with thousands of other Palestinians, fled the city and sailed to Damascus. Here she gave birth to her first son at a friend's house.

When the baby was a few months old, she went back to work for the PFLP. In 1986, the Palestinian Popular Women's Committees were established, and she was elected the first secretary. Much of her time is now taken up with improving conditions for women and children in the camp, albeit that the final goal is to free mothers from traditional tasks so that they can support the Intifada. PFLP nurseries, catering to children aged two months to six years, have opened in the camp, each one named after a martyr for the cause. The children are taught Palestinian freedom songs and chant, "We will grow strong so we can be fighters too."

Did she miss those days when she was feted as the girl hijacker? Her eyes slid away. "No," she said slowly. "That was the time for doing it, and I was glad I was involved. I do wish I had some photographs of me in those days to show Baader, but they were all destroyed in Beirut. My mother kept every one, but her flat was attacked."

Being a freedom fighter, she continued, meant everything to her. Now, in retrospect, she could understand that the passengers she hijacked must have been terrified: "If it happened to me, I would be like them; I would say my prayers, but I am not afraid to travel.

"My work as a freedom fighter has given me happiness; you identify yourself with the struggle. It is the difference between a freedom fighter and an ordinary person. As a Palestinian I wouldn't be happy with myself unless I was a freedom fighter. I am glad I have done so much."

In the end, I came to the conclusion that Leila Khaled was not a cruel or heartless woman, however much her actions and her behavior during them might suggest otherwise. She did seem to have an inability to put herself in anyone else's shoes, and her delight in recounting the way in which she had terrified people was disturbing. However, she had been utterly without guile in talking to me so frankly, and I think the most lasting impression I had of her was of a woman who was almost childlike in her single-mindedness. It is surely this that made her so dangerous.

Chapter 5

✾ THE WOMEN OF THE IRISH

REPUBLICAN MOVEMENT

"Fighting the oppression of women must go together with the Republican fight."

Albert Cooper looked at his watch when the white Vauxhall Astra pulled into his garage; it was 9:45 A.M., and the young woman who had telephoned half an hour earlier was, as he called to one of his employees, right on time.

She got out of the car, a small figure dressed in a black bomber jacket, black ski pants, and with her dark hair swept back into a ponytail. She smiled and stood chatting to Mr. Cooper for a couple of minutes, then, arranging to collect the car later, she walked away.

Seconds later, the car exploded. Mr. Cooper, who had been backing it into his workshop, was killed instantly. He was forty-two and left a wife and three young children. A few hours later on that day, November 2, 1990, the IRA claimed responsibility: Albert Cooper of Cookstown, County Tyrone, Northern Ireland, had been a part-time soldier of the Ulster Defence Regiment. It is thought that he was killed in retaliation for the death of a member of Sinn Fein, the political and legal wing of the IRA, who was shot by Loyalist paramilitary forces a week earlier.

The woman bomber, who had fled the scene, got more space in British newspapers than is normally reserved for such sectarian attacks. IRA WOMAN IN BLACK MURDERS UDR SOLDIER, said the *Times* headline. The dead man's MP, the Reverend William McCrae, was quoted: "It is hard to believe that a woman who, under God, can give birth to a new life can be so twisted and warped by hate that she can bring forth death to an innocent victim."

The conflict in Northern Ireland has been going on for nearly four hundred years, and women have always played a part in it. The women interviewed in this chapter have been involved in the most recent and arguably the most bloody stage; they have taken up arms in the fight against the British Army, first sent to Northern Ireland to protect the Catholics from Protestant mobs.

It was the women who made soldiers cups of tea when the first of the British troops arrived in Derry and Belfast in 1969. Photographs of the time show the Catholic women smiling and relaxed with their protectors, but this honeymoon period did not last long.

The soldiers, in Northern Ireland to "aid the civil power," were soon sent into the Catholic housing estates to find caches of guns and ammunition, which had been stockpiled to defend the community against Protestants. Some of the arms searches were brutally carried out, and by the summer of 1970 many Catholics were beginning to regard the British Army with hostility. Catholic girls who dated British soldiers were tarred and feathered by other women in their community.

The IRA, shamed in 1969 for failing to protect the Catholics and taunted with the graffiti IRA—I RAN AWAY, began to reestablish itself. The army, in a series of incidents, including house-to-house searches, killed and injured a number of Catholic civilians. By 1971 the British forces had come to be seen by some as an army of occupation, there to preserve the status quo and enforce the Protestant domination of Northern Ireland. Friend had become foe. In that year, a woman called Maire Drumm, a member of the executive of Sinn Fein, who was later shot dead by Loyalists, addressed a rally thus: "It is a waste of time shouting 'Up the IRA.' The important thing is to join." Afterward, apparently, recruits lined up to enlist in the ranks of "volunteers"—the men and women soldiers of the Irish Republican Army. The "Troubles" had begun again.

Over the last twenty years, IRA women have played an increasing role in "frontline" actions against British troops and Protestant paramilitary units—and against the British public too. Initially women were used as bait to lure British soldiers, on the promise of a good time, to a rendezvous where they were shot by gunmen. Other women carried "baby bombs" in prams into shopping centers. Any initial reluctance by the IRA's leadership, the Army Council, to expose women to the danger of direct action was soon overruled by the women themselves. They wanted to fight, and they wanted to be treated as equals.

Mairead Farrell, who was shot dead by the SAS (army special operations group) in Gibraltar in 1988, said in an interview a year before she died that she was attracted to the IRA because she was treated the same as "the lads." Her death has made her a martyr, with children of Republicans being called "Mairead Farrell O'J" in her memory.

Before her death, Farrell had been known for her strong feminist views: while in prison serving a fourteen-year sentence for bombing a hotel, she had campaigned for equality for women within the IRA structure. During that sentence, Farrell was put forward by Sinn Fein to stand as a candidate in the Cork elections. The campaigners used a picture of her as she then was—filthy and disheveled as a consequence of taking part in a "no-wash" protest in Armagh women's prison, which is now closed. Farrell's father was upset at the photograph and had tried to have it substituted by another that showed his daughter as the attractive young woman she was. Farrell complained: "My father was running around saying, 'Don't be showing that . . . that's horrible; don't be showing that photograph of her. Here's a lovely wee photograph of her, here, you know.' All prim and proper taken. He didn't want to accept the reality, you know, because it's so hard to accept. I suppose from an emotional aspect as well. Show the pretty picture because this is the daughter he wanted portrayed, not the actual reality. I think that society in general also found it difficult to accept."

Society did indeed find it difficult to accept the first IRA women. When the Price sisters were arrested for their part in the 1973 bombing campaign in London, in which 180 people were injured, they were called "the Sisters of Death." The detective who arrested nineteen-year-old Marion Price recalled how she had looked at her watch and smiled when the Old Bailey bomb went off. The two young women were reviled by the media as inhuman and unwomanly, descriptions still applied to today's generation of IRA women.

When asked, the Northern Ireland Office claimed that the IRA has virtually stopped using women volunteers—a claim that I found difficult to accept after interviewing numerous women, including one currently on "active service." Looking back over the last twenty years, women have consistently played an important, sometimes central role in IRA operations.

Dr. Rose Dugdale hit the headlines in the early seventies as the daughter of a wealthy English family who had rebelled and joined the IRA. She stole paintings from her father, hijacked a helicopter, and tried to drop milk churns filled with explosives onto RUC (Royal Ulster Constabulary) barracks. When she was arrested, she was pregnant by Eddie Gallagher, one of the IRA's most notorious "hard men."

Gallagher, however, proved rather less hard than another IRA woman, Marion Coyle. In 1975 the two of them kidnapped a Dutch industrialist and demanded Dugdale's release from prison as part of the ransom. During his thirty-one-day ordeal, the victim said that he established some sort of rapport with Gallagher, but that Coyle remained cold and aloof throughout. When the pressure mounted it was she who took charge of the gun and the negotiations; and when the police finally stormed the house, Gallagher lay terrified on the floor while Coyle retained her aggression and control right up to the very end.

In 1983 Anna Moore was sentenced to life imprisonment for her involvement in the bombing of the Droppin' Well pub in Ballykelly, near Derry, in the northwest of Northern Ireland, close to the border. It was a popular haunt for British soldiers, who went there to meet local girls. Twelve soldiers and five civilians were killed.

Ella O'Dwyer and Martina Anderson were also given life sentences in 1986 for their part in the plot to bomb London and sixteen seaside resorts. O'Dwyer's fingerprints were found on a "bomb calendar" hidden among explosives when police raided the unit's safe house in Glasgow. Anderson, who was twenty-three when she was arrested, had been a former local beauty queen.

The case of Evelyn Glenholmes has become a cause célèbre to the IRA and a bête noire to Scotland Yard. Glenholmes is wanted in Britain for questioning over a series of bombings, including: a nail bomb at the Chelsea Barracks in London, which killed two civilians; a car bomb attack on Stewart Pringle, the former Royal Marines commandant general; another bomb attempt at the home of Sir Michael Havers, then attorney general of Britain; and an explosion at a Wimpy bar in Oxford Street that killed a bomb disposal expert.

In 1986, Scotland Yard issued nine warrants seeking her extradition from Dublin; she was to be the first alleged IRA terrorist to be extradited by Dublin for trial in Britain. Owing to legal technicalities the court ruled the warrants were unlawful and freed Glenholmes. Furious Special Branch officers chased her through the city center, and she tried to hide in the women's department of a branch of British Home Stores. She was rearrested and put before another judge. He freed her again, ruling that her arrest had been unlawful. Since then she has been on the run.

The bare facts of the crimes and atrocities that these women have been involved in are chilling. Yet the women I met were not monsters. Some were friendly, some less so, but they were all ordinary. Most of them had become involved in IRA activities as teenagers or in their early twenties; most had been unmarried when they were active, although not all. None of the women had been persuaded to join by a boyfriend, although some of them had clearly been brought up in strongly Republican homes and had doubtless been influenced by friends and brothers and sisters. There was an almost universal response to the question "Why did you join?" It amounted to: "How could we not?" Again and again I was told of the treatment of the Catholic community by the British soldiers; of raw, powerful memories of events such as Bloody Sunday, when British paratroopers killed thirteen civilians during a civil rights march; of the terrors of children facing Protestant bullies; of feeling despised and wanting to fight back. All of the women shared a hatred for the British Army and an unshakeable belief that they were justified in using violence. Interestingly, many of them cited the foul language and manners of the British troops as a reason for that hatred. Such behavior engendered in these women the same disgust as that expressed by the Palestinian women toward Israeli soldiers in the West Bank.

These interviews were probably the most difficult in this book because I was more afraid of the IRA than any other organization I had approached. Fear can make one less objective, so it had to be overcome. I had interviewed many other women who had killed or taken part in actions designed to kill, but none who saw me as their enemy. However many times I was told by the Republican women that when they said they wanted to kill as many "Brits" as possible, they did not mean me but British soldiers, I still felt that I was an enemy by birth.

All these interviews were granted on the understanding that a copy of this chapter would be shown to Sinn Fein before publication.

Outside Sinn Fein's press center on Falls Road there are boulders on the pavement to prevent car bombers. Concealed cameras relay your picture onto a small TV screen in the reception room, and once given clearance you are admitted to the building through two wire-mesh doors. The interior is dark—there are few windows—and the lights are on all the time. The reception room is also a drop-in center for members of the Catholic community who need advice on claiming social security or compensation for damage to their homes during a search by the Brits, and a meeting place for the unemployed. Upstairs are the press offices and rooms set aside for interviews.

At about 11 A.M. on a Saturday morning I arrived, as instructed, at the offices. The young woman Sinn Fein worker who had arranged other interviews for me in the previous few months was waiting. Together we set off on a journey that ended in a quiet housing estate where an Alsatian dog slept in the wan sunshine of the front garden. Inside the house, in a pleasant, well-furnished room, sat a twenty-eight-year-old operational woman volunteer.

The owner, who had opened the front door, asked no questions and left us alone. At some point during the interview a youth in his teens came in, served us with tea, cheese sandwiches, scones, and Penguin biscuits, and quietly retired.

The volunteer was an attractive woman with dark hair and large dark eyes, wearing jeans and a sweatshirt. She seemed composed and relaxed, and appeared calmer than I felt. I kept thinking how surreal it was to be eating Penguin biscuits with a woman who had proved her ability as a member of an IRA active-service unit. The woman seemed remarkably honest. She described her underground life as restricted, disturbing, and a bit boring. Particularly irritating, it seemed, was her inability to go into town to a good, boozy party for fear of being arrested or killed. She came across as a dedicated person who was well prepared for the interview and had thought things through for herself. She was rather likable, in fact . . . and then she chuckled over the freezing conditions on the night she laid a land mine for some British troops, and I wondered how many people she had killed and would go on to kill.

She had a list of questions that I had submitted to the IRA

Army Council a month before. Some of them had a cross beside them—for example, "How many women in the Republican movement are operational?" These would not be answered.

In a businesslike manner she read out the first question: "Why did you become involved?"

"I felt that I could help remove the British from Ireland and that it was right to use any means at our disposal to do so—explosives, bombs, and so on.

"Throughout my life I have seen the way that the British people abuse us, educationally and culturally they are endeavoring to wipe us out. I have seen them harassing and murdering some of my friends and family, and I have seen the way they use the Loyalists to help them.

"Certain things happened in my childhood. At one stage my family was living in a mainly Protestant area, but our street was Catholic. The UDA [Ulster Defence Association] or the UVF [Ulster Volunteer Forces] put our street under siege. They marched up and down, and all of us had to stay indoors. There was a fierce gun battle between us and the Loyalists, who were trying to burn our houses. At about three o'clock in the morning the British Army arrived, and they and the residents of the street decided it was too dangerous to stay. There were a number of children in the street, and we were to be moved to an army barracks on foot. We had to run down the alleyways, hiding and waiting for the shooting to stop so that we could cross a short distance. I was a child of nine or ten years old, and I realized we were in danger, but not the full extent of it."

Under fire from the Loyalists, did she not see the British troops as saviors, rescuing the victims from their attackers? "No," she replied firmly. "They were the orchestrators, the dividers of our community. Before they came, we were allowed to play with Protestant children; we went to their Twelfth of July bonfire. After the soldiers came that was not the case anymore. The communities were divided.

"I do not have any bitterness towards the Protestant people, although I know there are some very dangerous Loyalists. Their understanding of the situation is absurd. They view everything in a totally different light to us, and they are trying to take away our identity.

"As I was growing up, in the second house, we were put out again. Once again, I saw the British Army and government, who had initiated the move, as intimidators. They saw themselves as our masters, who had the right to intimidate my family. I thought if I could do something to help remove them, I would do it.

"I approached someone I knew was a member and asked if I could join, too. I opted for the operational end of the movement because I believed we had the legitimate right to use arms in our struggle." She paused for a sip of tea, then resumed.

"I was fully trained in the use of explosives. I was taken to a camp—I don't know where it was. A camp is just somewhere we meet, and the locations are changed constantly. Sometimes it is held in a disused building, or one is constructed for the use of the camp. There is a training officer and usually an equal number of men and women. There are several different categories of training—just basic, or if you want, more detailed. Because I was fully trained, I was not frightened when I was handling the explosives. I learned how to prime a bomb and detonate it, and at a number of camps I learned about the booby-trap bomb, micro switches, relay switches, and remote controls.

"At the camps we would also be given political training, and there would be discussions on how you view certain things. The camps would last for several days. If it was a weapons camp, there would be a training period and then the camp would end with a shoot-out."

She referred to it so matter-of-factly, this "shoot-out," that she could have been talking about a cocktail party. Just as calmly she explained that she had been trained in handling weapons as well as explosives, so that she would be fully able to protect herself on an operation. "If, for instance, you are doing a car bomb, you need to be armed, too, so it is necessary to have training in both fields. I wouldn't say I was an expert in either field. You are always learning, and you gain experience with the number of operations you partake in.

"At first you do lack confidence. You have been shown the basic equipment, and you know the components of a bomb, but you need to take part in operations before you are fully confident or competent."

Once trained and operational, the volunteer awaits orders. In the majority of cases he or she will still be living in the parental home. "My family didn't know at first," she recalled. "When I went off to the camps I can't remember what I told them. It was certainly not, 'I'm off to get trained.' In the end I told them—I think life would have been too hard otherwise, always trying to think up excuses. While my mother and father were worried about my safety, they understood what I was doing and the reasons behind it.

"Because everyone who is actively involved expects either to be killed or to go to prison, there is a great comradeship between the volunteers. For a variety of reasons I prefer not to stay at home. I would not sleep there for more than two nights in a row, but I try to visit my mother's house regularly. If I know they are safe from the Crown Forces security, it makes me feel better."

She did not, however, leave home at first, even after participating in an operation. It seems that there is a sort of honeymoon period during which a new volunteer remains undetected by police and army intelligence. Eventually, however, depending on how, as she put it, "active you are," it becomes crucial to leave one's family. "In a lot of cases, something happens to give you an indication that the British intelligence is onto you. You might be stopped in the company of a known IRA volunteer, or someone might tip you off. You have to get out then. All volunteers are targets for Loyalists and the Brits, and if they can pinpoint you to an address, you are setting yourself up for assassination. And if the British Army simply wants to arrest you, it is very convenient for them to know just where you are."

The woman explained that she had lived with her mother until she was arrested. After a number of years in prison she was released and rejoined the movement, but as a well-known figure she had to go underground. From that point on, home became a number of different houses of friends and comrades willing to take her in.

It was hard, she admitted, getting used to this eternal guest existence: "It is a big disturbance in your life, but at least I know there will always be somewhere to sleep. I have got clothes all over the place, and there are houses I can go to in lots of areas, so I can live where I happen to be working. This moving about is quite normal for us."

Although she was careful not to criticize her enforced lifestyle, an element of longing for a normal life now crept in. "Not being able to move about freely restricts you in your social life. It means you are confined to the movement's areas when you want to socialize. You can't go into the center [of Belfast] to nightclubs or parties because you would come across Special Branch people or the RUC standing at the bars. You would also come across Loyalists, and coming home from the center of town can be dangerous. If there was an RUC roadblock they would harass you, and if they got you in an isolated spot, they would harm you.

"So we have to stay here. It's very local, and it's a bit boring. We have different clubs and bars, but you are always meeting one type of people, you are not broadened . . . There are parties that take place in this area, but because of the British licensing laws they don't go on for that long."

Perhaps realizing that she sounded a little resentful, she hastened to praise her lifestyle, too, in terms that reminded me of the young Palestinian fighter, Bana, fourteen years this woman's junior and engaged in a different war hundreds of miles away: "It is nice and safe to socialize with your comrades and fellow volunteers. I don't miss going into the center and traveling to parties elsewhere. I did all that before I became a volunteer, and when I was relatively unknown. I'm lucky, at least I was able to have that time; other volunteers haven't had it. I don't feel I am missing anything that I want to do." I did not think I believed her.

She went on to recount one of her operations, as I had asked in the list of questions. "It was a land mine against a British Army foot patrol. A number of people, including myself, met at a safe house and discussed the operation from beginning to end. We thoroughly discussed the risk to civilians in the area, and we decided there was no risk, so we would proceed with the operation. Someone would be on sentry duty, and if a woman or a child appeared, we would halt. We obtained all the materials we needed and got the detonator and timing devices that made up the bomb. We all wore dark clothes because it was nighttime.

"The operation involved the laying of a command wire, which had to be buried in the ground because the particular area where we were laying the wire was overseen by a British Army observation post. It was in a grassy area, and there was a stream, so we had to lie down on our stomachs and crawl through the stream, dragging the command wire and burying it as we went along.

"We had people in the area with walkie-talkies and a safe house nearby. If a British Army or an RUC patrol came, we could be radioed and would have to leave everything and run into the safe house. That happened twice. We got so cold and wet crawling through that stream. But eventually everything was in place; it had taken two hours to lay the line and attach the command wire and firing set to the bomb. Then all the equipment was tested and everything was passed in working order and the bomb was put in place. We called the scouts in, and all the people involved in the wire-laying operation returned to the safe house. One person stayed with the device, and some others kept a watch. If any civilians came along, they would radio an instruction not to detonate the bomb. We waited in the house to hear what happened to our target."

She stopped. And what did happen, I asked? She shook her head: "I can't say any more because no one has ever been charged for that operation." I wanted to know the answer to this question, though, and after some persuading the volunteer said she would contact me later. She did. It had been agreed that I could be told simply that the operation had been successful. No other details were given.

I wondered whether that operation had been chosen for the interview because it had not involved civilian deaths or injuries, and because it seemed careful precautions had been taken to ensure that. What was her attitude toward operations when civilians were killed? "IRA operations have never been directed against civilians— only British soldiers or the UDR, the UVF." How about Enniskillen, or Harrods?* "I cannot answer that question, Eileen," she said softly, as if ordered not to do so.

She was, however, perfectly prepared to answer the next one: "Would you kill?" "Yes," she said simply. "There is no point in being operational if you are not prepared to kill—as long as they are legitimate targets." Had she ever killed? She looked me straight in the eye and said in a tone that brooked no argument: "I am not prepared to answer that question, Eileen."

But she did have something to say over the matter of innocents being injured and killed in IRA attacks. It was an answer I had heard before from other groups and would hear again: "The reason is that the Brits don't act on our warnings. If a bomb is directed against a commercial target in the center of town, a warning is always given in plenty of time—ample time for the area to be cleared. The person who is given the job of telephoning the warning always makes a mental note of the time at which he or she made that call. It is always forty-five to sixty minutes before the bomb.

"It is in the interest of the Brits to have people injured, and on numerous occasions they have not acted on IRA warnings. It is so

---

* At Enniskillen, an IRA bomb killed eleven and injured sixty-three at a Remembrance Day service on November 8, 1987. An IRA car bomb killed eight and injured eighty on December 17, 1983, outside Harrods department store.

they can blame us." She believed it, or she was giving a very good impression of believing it. Apparently it is unheard of for the IRA to phone a bomb warning direct to the British Army—the normal procedure is that either a newspaper, a radio station, or, on occasion, the Samaritans are alerted. The problem is in distinguishing genuine warnings from the hoax calls with which the authorities are plagued every day.

We moved on to violence. Define violence, she demanded. "In this context, violence against soldiers," I said. "I suppose you mean the Brits?" she queried coldly. "Obviously I don't like to see anyone killed or injured as a result of war, but until the British government recognizes they are the root cause of violence and decide sincerely to remove that root and reunify our country, removing the British presence—only then will there be an end to violence.

"I long to see the day when the British presence is removed from my country, and I think it will be in my lifetime. For that reason, I'm prepared to remain a volunteer for this stage of the war. At some stage my personal life might change, and I may not always be an active volunteer, but there are different jobs in the movement, and I hope I would be able to find a suitable one. I believe we all have to work together within the movement to remove the British presence from Ireland."

"All" very much included women, she insisted. The pattern seemed to be that women joined young, and if they were not either killed or jailed—although some, like this woman, went back to being operational on their release from prison—they stayed active until they married and/or had children. A few women even carried on with their operations when they were mothers. This volunteer, who only a few minutes before had been a fearsome soldier, took on a maternal air herself as she talked of the difficulties of being a "mummy" and an IRA woman.

"If a woman volunteer with children is captured and put in prison, her family generally look after them. But if there is no relative to do it, fellow Republicans take the children in. There is one girl in prison at the moment, and her friend is looking after her two children. There is always someone to advise on financial matters, and a guardian is appointed to get the guardian's allowance from the British government—it is the same as if a child has been orphaned. The children of captured volunteers are always spoiled by everyone else; we are a big family.

"It causes problems when the mummy comes out of prison, because the children have been used to one sort of discipline and they see her as an intruder. Lots of mothers in this situation try to buy them with sweets and money and wee presents, but it doesn't work. They have to slowly work their way back into the family. The worst thing for a woman in prison is if anything happens to her family."

Apparently there are no objections raised by the IRA leadership to a woman being both a volunteer and a mother, if that is what she wants. "Everyone is treated the same. During training men and women are equally taught the use of explosives and weapons. I have personally never come across any sexism in the movement, but that is not to say that it is exempt from it. Some men may be sexist, but it is only the way they have been brought up. It is an educative process, and they learn about women through their roles in the movement." Her words echoed those of the ETA women, whose male comrades were apparently educated in the same way.

"The Brits treat women volunteers just the same as they do men. There was a woman who appeared in court with bruises and a black eye. I saw her being dragged up the steps and battered. When I was in Castlereagh [the interrogation center of the RUC near Belfast] on the evidence of a supergrass [informer], I was deprived of sleep, kicked off a chair, and beaten up. The Brits know that the women are just as dangerous as the men."

Did she see herself as dangerous? She laughed wholeheartedly at the very suggestion. "What me, dangerous? I know I am not dangerous, but the Brits would think I am. There are files on me. In Castlereagh, notes are made of anything you say. When I was being interrogated, all I would say was my name and address. That's all I said for seven days.

"They have another file, a security one, which details your movements and associates—things like where you go each day, where you socialize. There are photographs of you in the company of other people.

"I am very suspicious of everyone; of course I am suspicious of you. I was detained in Castlereagh after a very good friend of mine betrayed me. I don't trust anyone, and that is sad.

"When I went on my first operation I was frightened and extremely nervous and lacked confidence. But at the back of your head you always think about why you are doing what you do, and that gives you confidence. After the first one, you are still nervous about operations, but not enough to stop you continuing what you are doing. As long as you get back and don't get caught . . ."

Rita O'Hare was a married woman with three children when she was involved, "with a person unknown," in the attempted murder of two British soldiers. The details of the incident are hazy because she jumped bail and fled to Dublin before she could be tried. She refused to talk about it, except to maintain that she was not carrying a gun when the shooting took place. She herself was shot by the soldiers in the head and nearly died. It was partly the thought of her children that kept her alive.

Three years after her flight to the South, she was imprisoned for being in possession of explosives. It was rumored that she had smuggled gelignite into Portlaoise prison, hidden in what newspapers described coyly as "her body," but she was never charged with that offense and angrily denies it.

Today, still a wanted woman in the North, Rita O'Hare is the editor of *An Phoblacht*, the newspaper of the Republican movement produced in Dublin. It is not a job she relishes, but she sees it as a political obligation. She would prefer to be writing herself.

She is a small woman with red hair and a fiery temperament who is said to have close associations with the IRA Army Council. At forty-seven she is divorced and a grandmother several times over. She has been described as "a grown-up"—a lifelong member of the Republican movement who can take criticism of the IRA without getting a dose of the "political sulks." Certainly, when she talked about young soldiers' deaths she seemed genuinely anguished, and she remembered the terror of the soldiers, fearful for their lives, as she lay nearly dead at their feet. Her plea that the army should get out of Ireland does not have the didactic quality that the rhetoric of many of her compatriots displays. Rather, she seems truly to believe that this is the only way to end the violence.

She agreed readily enough to an interview in her newspaper's office in Parnell Square, but she warned me that I had better not be writing a book about criminals or crazed killers.

Her involvement with the Republican movement came about through her association with the civil rights marches. She was twenty-six, and not only married with three children but also studying languages at a university as a mature student. In the civil rights movement she met, for the first time in her life, staunch

Republicans. She was born to middle-class parents in Andersonstown in southeast Belfast and recalled that her childhood was very happy and normal—with one exception: her father, a first generation Scottish Protestant, had in his youth been a communist, and their house was filled with books on revolutions across the world. Politics were freely discussed, but not Republican politics. "I knew about every revolution except my own," she commented.

Through her contact with Republicans, she became aware that the civil rights movement was not going to get results: "We might achieve a few meaningless reforms, but it was obvious that the northern state was not going to change. To me it became clear that a military fight was the only way in which things would change."

It still took her some time to decide to join the IRA. She had to weigh her decision that direct action was the only way against her responsibilities as a mother. She was one of the very few women in this book who was a mother when she opted for direct action. Most of the other women were single and considered that having children might detract from, or impinge on, their ability to be fighters. It seems, though, that Mrs. O'Hare felt she could juggle the two roles successfully: the battle was raging outside her front door. It was the late sixties, and there was real warfare, she recalled, going on in the streets; everything was extremely intense. "People were being batoned in the streets, everything was happening very fast—nowadays the nature of the war has changed.

"There was a great need for people to join the movement in those days—it was 'sixty-nine, and the IRA was virtually nonexistent, and Sinn Fein was very small. I talked to some people who were of the same opinion as myself, and then I joined. I was given some training, but I cannot say anything about that.

"Nowadays membership checks are much more stringent; then there was a terrific openness. People did not care who knew they had joined. The people in the community knew who you were; in those days you could have gone to just about any door as a member of the IRA; there were only a few houses where it was not safe. In a way the openness was extremely bad—it gave the Brits the opportunity to plant spies and so on. People had a very rosy view of things then. It was thought that the whole thing would be over very quickly. Something big was happening every day."

She remembered a terrific sense of being part of something. She supposed that some of the younger volunteers thought it was a game, although no one had a flippant attitude to the fighting. "It was not all gloom and doom; we laughed a lot . . . But certainly there was a very strong feeling that you were in the middle of history being made."

Women took control for the first time in those days because so many men were imprisoned or interned. Historically and traditionally, with the men absent, the women were allowed to take their place, even in repressive societies. The same was true also of the Palestinian women in the Intifada, and like them, the Republican women enjoyed the power that had been given them. They had to look after themselves, sort out finances, and so on. It also meant that women came out onto the streets and got directly involved in the struggle: "No matter what action they took, even if it was just standing on the streets, watching, or taking part in the marches, curfew-breaking, women were really aware that they were doing something themselves on their own initiative. I am not saying that it was all good, but it was happening."

The emergence of these women as active participants caused the IRA to change its structure regarding women members. Until then, there had been separate women's sections within the movement, but in the late sixties all the different departments were merged into one IRA—everyone was needed for the guerrilla war.

Mrs. O'Hare said that her husband knew that she had joined the IRA, but nothing else. He was not privy to his wife's actions, particularly since at the time he was himself interned. She would soon join him in prison—she was sentenced to six months for wearing a paramilitary uniform.

"It was actually just an ordinary combat jacket with fur around the hood, but that was enough to get you six months. If you were seen carrying a hurley stick (hurley is a Gaelic game), that was deemed to be an offensive weapon. That offense was rescinded later because there was a national outcry, but in those days there were a lot of women in prison for carrying them or wearing combat jackets. It was very sectarian—those laws didn't apply to the UVF or the UDA, who could wear masks.

"When I was in Armagh I realized a lot of things—that this was a struggle for an oppressed people, not just about the British occupation. The great majority of the women prisoners were no possible security threat to the state, and when you saw the viciousness and callousness with which they were treated the whole struggle became redefined. Those six months were a tremendous turning point for me. I had gone into the movement from the standpoint of civil rights; I had been an intellectual socialist before. I mean, I had done a bit before going to prison; I had helped out, but it was prison that really decided me."

When she was released, she became far more active than before, and in October 1971 she was shot. "It was in Andersonstown and it was nighttime—I cannot tell you any more than that. No, actually I was not carrying a gun. A soldier was shot, too, but not very badly. I was shot in the head, stomach, and leg, and almost died. One of the reasons I didn't was I was very strong and fit in those days. I didn't smoke or drink; I was very conscious of keeping fit. Another reason was that I didn't conceive of dying. I didn't realize how badly hurt I was. It was quite a few minutes before I felt any pain—at first I didn't know I had been hit; I thought a soldier had hit me on the head with his rifle butt.

"I was captured and taken to Musgrave Park Hospital, the military hospital. They would not take me; they only took the soldier who had been shot. They said they didn't have the facilities to treat me, which was not true. Maybe they hoped I would die, I don't know.

"Jesus, I was in terrible pain by then. I was given a shot of morphine by a medic but I puked it up. I was in the back of an armored personnel carrier, PIGs, we called them. I did notice how terrified the soldiers were; they were trembling. I suppose they had been shot at a lot that night. They were absolutely terrified. I remember their scramble into the PIG after they had put me inside. They were so anxious to get into it that they were trampling on me. They couldn't avoid it; they had to get inside to safety.

"I remember so clearly that a very young soldier straddled me. I was on the floor, and he crouched with his arms and legs over me so that the others wouldn't walk on me. I will always remember that. He put his hand under my head—it was a metal floor and my head was banging up and down on it as the PIG drove off. He took his hand away and said, 'She's been shot in the head.' It was only then that I knew what had happened to me.

"A medic came and opened my coat. I had been hit by SLR bullets—they are small but they spin and explode on impact. I had been saved partly because I was wearing a big, heavy duffel coat, and it had acted like a big bandage on the arteries. It is the shock that kills most people who have been shot. Most people think, 'Christ, I'm dying' and then they die, but I wasn't thinking that way. I was dying and my mind was saying, 'Oh God, the kids; I'll have to get home.' " It appears that, far from being a hindrance to a female fighter at moments of crisis, children can be a positive advantage.

"Everyone thought I was going to die. In fact word went to my husband in the Kesh [near Belfast] that night that I had died. Then in the morning they told him it was a mistake. At the Royal Hospital, where I was finally taken, they thought I was going to die. I was operated on, with soldiers in attendance in the theater.

"I was in the Royal for a month. My parents came to see me, and they were absolutely shattered. They had no idea I was even in the movement. They looked after my kids while I was in the hospital. I was actually charged in the hospital with the attempted murder of a British soldier and about twenty other charges—I can't remember what they all were. They wanted to move me, and they couldn't do that without charging me so they set up a sort of court in my room to do it.

"I felt very detached during that month. I kept cool and calm about it all because I knew if I didn't it would hamper my physical recovery, and I had to keep my wits about me."

She was sent to Armagh prison, and on Christmas Eve got bail. She considered that bail was granted because she was such a nuisance in prison: she had to be assisted up and down stairs, and the doctors who had to come into prison to treat her posed a security risk. She attended court twice, and then at the end of January, just as she was leaving the court, she overheard something she was clearly meant to hear. "It was still inside the court precincts, and there were judges and lawyers and the RUC standing about. One of the soldiers said as I was going past, 'We should have finished off that bitch when we got the chance; but we'll get her in the end.' Then he said something about my kids, too, and I thought, Even if I beat this court case I will be waiting for a bullet in the head. And I was terrified for my kids."

She insisted that until that moment she had not entertained the idea of jumping bail; it was the threat to her children that galvanized her into action. The desire to protect them overrode any other consideration. She discussed her plan to flee south with them—the oldest was eight years old—and they wanted her to do it. The IRA advised her against flight: they thought that she had a chance of winning the case. But her children overruled that advice: "They wanted me to come south because they thought I would get better, and they were frightened of me being in prison.

"I was obviously still quite ill at the time, and that must have played a part in my decision too. I came south. Somebody drove me over the border. It wasn't like it is today, with surveillance of everything on the border. I was sitting in the car, not hidden in the boot [trunk]—it was amazingly easy. I think that because I had appeared twice in court since getting bail they didn't think I would run. I came to Dublin first, and then the children were sent down."

She laughed when I asked her if at that point she considered she had done enough. "I did think of going to live in a thatched cottage and taking up weaving, but it wouldn't have worked. I wanted to be in Dublin because at least I could keep in contact with what was happening in the North, although it is difficult. Things are happening every day up there."

She admitted to missing Belfast very much, especially her parents, who were now old and found it difficult to travel to Dublin for visits. Then there were her friends and "just being there, being in your own place." She was horrified when her children started speaking with a Dublin accent, but when she chided them for it they asked her how else she expected them to speak. As soon as her eldest daughter was old enough, she went back to Belfast. "I have been back myself, very occasionally, but I stand the risk of being arrested and facing trial." She smiled. "When I do go back it is not for social occasions, shall we say?

"I thought at the beginning that things might be all over in a couple of years, and I would only have to be on the run for a short time. But that was 1972, and I'm still here. I don't travel abroad much in case I am recognized. I am not saying that I am paranoid, and that every policeman in the world is waiting for Rita O'Hare to step over the border, but I have to think about extradition treaties and that sort of thing, and then there is Interpol.

"I know I am under surveillance here; they make it pretty obvious sometimes. If they knew I was going to France, for instance, they could notify the police there. Perhaps France might not want to bother extraditing me, but there is the international agreement on terrorism that they have signed and they might be constrained to."

When she first arrived in Dublin she spent some time in a hospital and then got various jobs before starting to work for Sinn Fein. She bitterly recalled those early months of scraping by on what is "the excuse here for social welfare."

Her husband at that time was serving a sentence in Portlaoise

Prison in Dublin. When he was released, Mrs. O'Hare continued to visit Republican prisoners whose families could not make the journey. After one such visit, she was arrested and charged with being in possession of explosives—the newspapers claimed that she had tried to smuggle gelignite in and leave it with a prisoner.

She heatedly denied the allegation: "There was no evidence. I knew it was because they knew who I was and had tried to extradite me twice before and failed. Explosives were found in the prison after I had been there, and the story was that I had left them with this fella—I hadn't even been visiting him . . .

"At my trial a warder said he had seen one of the women visitor's hands touch a prisoner, and he thought it was my hand. I was found guilty of possessing explosives at a time and place unknown, although even the judge said there was nothing to support the allegation that I had smuggled explosives into the prison."

She served two years in Limerick Prison, and found conditions and her time there far worse than the six months she had lived through in Armagh. Limerick was small and isolated, and she was only permitted visits from immediate family. She worried about her children constantly. She was allowed to write two letters a week and asked if she could write a page each to each child, and if those three pages could be treated as one letter. She was told that would be all right. It was only much later that she discovered one page was always confiscated so one child would think he or she had been left out.

There was no doubt that her children did suffer. Dublin was not Belfast, where having a mother in prison for possessing explosives was a perfectly acceptable circumstance. Her children were shouted at in the street, and there were no Republican women to look after and comfort them, as would have happened in Belfast. They asked her why she had to be in prison, and she tried to explain that it was the price of being a Republican. "I didn't try to justify it to them because they were already feeling it too deeply, but I said, 'At least I will be coming home to you,' not like some mothers they knew who had been killed. It was a very hard time."

When she came out of prison in 1977, she took in the son of one of the women prisoners she had met and raised him as her own. It took her a year to sort herself out, she said, during which she and her husband divorced "for a variety of reasons." She would not explain what those reasons were.

She was working then in the administration and accounts departments of *An Phoblacht,* and when the editor died in 1979 she took over the job. She would like to see more articles relating to women in the paper, and would write them herself if she had the time.

On the whole, she thought that women were probably "more human" than men, because they were carers. It was different for a woman to join an army, she reckoned, because armies were seen as such an exclusively male preserve. But liberation armies were different because they had a different goal: "Liberation armies have to make a conscious effort to be different. That is not to say that there are no men in the Republican movement with bad attitudes to women; of course there are. But I think that has changed in the last few years in the same way that it has changed in society as a whole."

She pointed out, for example, that traditional rebel songs about "the lads" and about a mother losing her sons for Ireland are no longer written—and "that is no accident." It is no longer assumed that warriors are men.

On the subject of violence, Mrs. O'Hare freely admitted to having opposing viewpoints. First, there was violence in the home: "I hate it. I abhor the use of personal violence of any kind. I would never hit my kids. I am vehemently opposed to corporal punishment either in the family or institutional, and of course to violence against women. I hate the acceptance, particularly in Western society, of beating and smacking kids."

Then political violence. "I hate the war and the killing that is forced upon us. But I see violence against an armed enemy very differently. In Ireland's and other countries' freedom struggles, it is a people's only weapon. It is the only context in which I see violence being justifiable."

She paused and without prompting broached an unasked question: "Face to face is difficult. That time I was shot, I was in a wee room off a ward and there were a lot of young soldiers in with gunshot wounds. Half of them told me they had shot themselves because they were so frightened of being killed on the streets. It is very difficult when you are talking to a twenty-year-old working-class fella who is prepared to be open with you, very difficult.

"They in themselves are not the enemy. I could feel sorry for them because they did not know that the line about them being peacemakers was guff. Do you think that we rejoice when a busload of young Yorkshire soldiers gets blown up?" She looked agitated and distressed when she asked this question.

"It is the people that use them that are the enemy. They are being used to keep the state a sectarian state. Because they are here as an army, they are the enemy. But one to one, you know, you can't see them as that. As an army, it is an army of shoot-to-kill and plastic bullets, and I hate that.

"People make the mistake of thinking that we take pleasure out of death and killings, but no one hates this war more than us. It is our country, and we hate the bloody war. I wish the soldiers would go. But if they do not go, we have come too far and gone on too long to give up. It is not just the membership of the IRA that feels that, it is the whole people.

"If the Brits were serious about wanting peace they would stop creating laws to try to abolish Sinn Fein's political thrust. Ireland is the last outpost of the empire, and we will be free; it will happen here in the end. There is so much pain and misery, that they are going to have to go. This time, this uprising has gone on for twenty years, and this time we are not going to give up or be crushed."

In 1976 the special status of "political prisoner" was removed from those sentenced for terrorist crimes. Henceforth terrorists would be treated as ordinary criminals. Privileges such as the right to wear civilian clothing and not to work were abolished, and the IRA's prison structure of having an OC (officer in command) as the sole representative for the Republican prisoners was also supposed to be dismantled.

Inside the jails, the IRA fought back. In the H-Blocks the men went "on the blanket": they refused to wear prison uniforms, wrapped themselves in blankets, and stopped washing. They emptied their chamber pots onto the wing and smeared excrement on the walls. Then, in 1980, the hunger strikes began. A year later ten men were dead.

In Armagh Women's Prison, similar battles were engaged. Led by Mairead Farrell, the OC, the women instituted a "no-work" protest, which they later amended to a sabotage campaign. Then they went on a "no-wash" strike; and finally they began their own hunger strike.

The women in Armagh had another fight to win—that of convincing the men in the Republican movement that they should be allowed to participate in the protests. At first, the response had been horror that the "girls" should even contemplate such a thing. It was never, as several ex-prisoners pointed out, "the women" in

Armagh, always "the girls." Sinead Moore, who served seven years for possessing revolvers, explained: "The movement said, 'Poor girls, it is bad enough for them to be in prison; they shouldn't have to take part in the no-wash.' It is inbred—no matter what they might say—the men wanted to protect us." It is a problem that men in traditional armies have faced too. The Israeli Army stopped the practice of having women in the frontline because the male soldiers would rather risk their own lives than have a woman injured or killed. According to a British policewoman, it is considered unwise to have a female officer present at a scene of danger because her male colleagues will try to protect her rather than concentrate on the job in hand.

After much debate between the women inside and the men outside, it became clear that it was menstruation that was the problem. The men were embarrassed to say so but worried that infections would occur if women did not wash when they were bleeding. The women, however, stood firm, and the men capitulated in the end, though not without much wringing of hands. Soon the Republican women's section in Armagh resembled a cesspool: warders came in to work every day clad in protective suits and masks to hose down the urine and excrement from the walls. Only one prisoner became ill during the thirteen months of the no-wash, and she apparently had been unwell before the protest started.

The first hunger strike in the H-Blocks had been going for about a month, when the women decided they too would refuse food. The movement again reared up in shock and begged the women to reconsider, but to no avail. There were only twenty-seven Republican women prisoners, so they decided among themselves that just three would start. Mary Doyle was one of those.

She was twenty-three years old and was serving her second sentence in Armagh. The first one, for causing an explosion, had been passed in the "holiday camp" atmosphere when political status was still enjoyed. Her subsequent detention, for planting incendiaries, occurred a year after the special privileges had been removed. At once she joined in the no-work and no-wash protests, and when the decision was taken to start the hunger strike she put her name forward. She was selected together with Mairead Farrell and Margaret Nugent.

"We started on December 1, 1980. We had all volunteered, but it seemed sensible to start with three of us, so that when one of us died another could take her place." She spoke simply and unemotionally, but went on to reveal just how much she had agonized over such a step.

"It was not something that any of us took lightly. We had been speaking about it for months, once we knew that it had to come to that, that the hunger strike would be the only way to get our demands met. We were all told to talk about it and to take the idea of going on hunger strike very seriously—to think about the consequences. The likelihood of dying was very strong. The Brits were not going to give in to our demands after one week of a hunger strike.

"You did not just think about yourself; in many ways you were the least important person. You had to think about the effect it would have on your family and friends. I had to think about my father; what my death would mean to him.

"I remember thinking about wanting to have a baby. Supposing I survived; would I have become sterile through loss of weight?" Her conflict was of course a peculiarly female one: that her role as a fighter might endanger her future as a mother. After the battle was over, or at least her part in it was concluded, Mary wanted to be able to be just like any other woman. "We tried to get hold of as much information about starvation as possible so that we would know how to cope with the different stages.

"On the morning of the first of December 1980, Mairead, Margaret, and I all refused food. The screw said, 'It's your choice,' and left us. The announcement that we were going on hunger strike had been made on the radio news, so I suppose they knew. They put the three of us in one cell.

"We were drinking water and taking salt tablets. Every day they took blood samples. They said it was to assess the state of our health, but we thought it was also to check that we had not been eating.

"The authorities decided that we must have food in our cells at all times, to tempt us to eat. We would laugh about it. When we were on no-wash, prison food was cold and the portions were very small, but as soon as we went on the hunger strike they would come in with great plates piled high with hot, steaming chips, and the smell would be all over the room. They would only remove the food when the next meal was brought in.

"By the eighth or ninth day, I suppose, we were beginning to feel weak. At the beginning I was about nine stone [126 pounds];

Mairead was the lightest, just over eight stone. But for weeks beforehand our comrades had given us as much of their food as they could so as to build us up. Mairead's natural weight was really only seven and a half stone; she was very slim. Gradually we became dizzy and got weaker."

They talked about their families, about politics and religion, and about who would be the first to die. In the second week they were moved to the hospital wing. They all got depressed. One of the men on hunger strike was very ill, and they were waiting for the news that he had died. Mary Doyle told me: "We thought that we were definitely going to die. On the eighteenth day we heard on a radio that had been smuggled in to us that the men had called off their strike because guarantees had been given that our demands would be met. We decided to wait until the next day for definite word. We learned later that a priest had come to see us to tell us that the calling-off was genuine, but he had not been allowed in. On the morning of the nineteenth day, the prison governor came in and said, 'You might as well eat your breakfasts because the hunger strike is off.' By lunchtime we heard from our people that it was true. We were delighted; we had been preparing ourselves to die."

The women had all lost about a stone in weight, but suffered no long-term effects from the fast. The delight in their victory, however, was short-lived. On Christmas Eve Farrell discovered that the Northern Ireland Office was denying it had agreed to any demands. A second hunger strike of the women was discussed, but it was decided that all attention should be centered on the men's second hunger strike. Mary Doyle remembered that the movement was greatly relieved—she even had a letter from Bobby Sands saying he was delighted that no women were going to take part in another strike. To ensure that all publicity went to the H-Block hunger strikers, the women also called off their no-wash protest.

Few of the women were sorry to see it end, Mary included. She was sitting talking to me in her spotlessly clean home, cradling her seven-month-old son, Seamus, in her arms. Her daughter, aged four, sat beside her.

"It's hard to put into words what it was like; I often sit and think about it. I used to worry about infection when we were not washing, especially when I was having a period—you could not help but worry.

"We used to empty the chamber pots out onto the wing. I wonder how we did it. If I had been told a few weeks before what I would be doing I would have said I did not have the stomach for it. I would much preferred not to have done it."

She was thirty-three at the time of the interview and due to get married in a fortnight's time to her fiancé. The wedding would take place in Crumlin Road jail, where he was being held in connection with the killings of two British soldiers who had been shot dead by the IRA after being dragged from their car. She faced a married life of prison visits, but seemed quite cheerful at the prospect.

Although Mary was released from prison in 1983 and has not been arrested since, she has remained "very Republican" in her outlook, although having two small children means that she is now more restricted in her activities. Nowadays, she gives any free time to working for Sinn Fein.

However, the mementos of her life as a former volunteer are all about her. Her house is a veritable Fort Knox, with bullet- and bombproof glass in the windows, and steel plates reinforcing the front door. "In case of Loyalist attacks," she explained to me as she heaved the door open, cursing me jokingly. "Most people use the back door, but you would never have found the entrance."

In the sitting room, tucked in beside the mirror over the fire-place, was a memorial card for Mairead Farrell. What was she like? I asked. "Good-natured, good-humored, a very caring person. If you had any problems you went to her with them. She was a committed Republican; her whole self was dedicated to the move-ment, one hundred percent."

Mary herself had joined the IRA at sixteen for the "usual reasons: as a teenager, seeing what happens to your friends and their fam-ilies; internment; Bloody Sunday; friends being harassed. I grew up in Greencastle, about two miles outside Belfast. I came from a Republican family, but it was my own decision to join; we were not brought up with politics. It's the way it happens.

"Sometimes a couple of friends talk about it and join together; others do it on their own. You begin training as soon as you join; some things take longer to learn and of course some people pick things up more quickly than others. Basically, you are under train-ing until whoever is over you feels you are safe. You are not usually asked to do something you don't want to do or feel capable of. That is the whole meaning of being a volunteer.

"If it does happen that you do not feel happy with what you are doing it is much better to say so because otherwise you are endangering not only your own life but your comrades'. It is far better if you feel inadequate in any way to say so. It's just common sense."

Although men and women received equal training, there were certain operations for which women were better suited, she said, echoing the words of the ETA women, and of a German male revolutionary, that undoubtedly the assumption of women being innocent was useful. "For instance, if someone is to carry a bomb in a pram, it is better that a woman is pushing the pram, because a man doing that might attract attention. Also, if bombs are going to be placed in boutiques, it is better that women do it."

When she was arrested at eighteen on the explosives charges, her parents were not particularly surprised: Mary, who worked as a telex operator, must often have been unaccountably absent from home. "They had their own suspicions that I had joined, although I had not told them. When you join you have to be very secretive; there is hardly anyone that you do tell. You just try to live a normal life; you go about your own business, but your life revolves around the movement.

"Being a member of the IRA is not a nine-to-five job. It is up to you in many ways—how much time you can give the Republican movement. You can't plan ahead. You are on call all the time because you want to be, not because you are forced."

Her first arrest, in 1974, was for laying a booby-trap bomb for the RUC. No one, Mary said, was "seriously hurt." She was caught shortly afterward. She was quite philosophical about it: "I was part of the team responsible; I lived at the top of the street near to where the bomb had gone off. I was questioned, and it was my own fault; I made a statement."

As a political prisoner she passed a relatively bearable two and a half years in prison, reporting to the OC and attending weekly meetings. She recalled that "the screws were quite content to leave us alone."

She was released in 1976 and a year later was caught putting incendiary devices in shops. She received an eight-year sentence. "I was not a bit pleased when I got to Armagh to find I was no longer a political prisoner. The governor said to me on the day I arrived, 'You are no longer running this jail. You are criminals now as far as we are concerned.'

"One of the first things I noticed was that the screws would try to get us to talk to them, not like before when we only communicated through the OC. Now, if the OC went on your behalf about something, they said, 'She must come herself.' In the end, though, they had to accept our way, otherwise they couldn't have run the prison."

The no-work protest resulted in loss of remission and the confiscation of parcels. The women were locked up during working hours and only allowed out for meals and "association" in the evening. Sometimes the prisoners got depressed. "Nobody wants to be locked up—unless they need to see a psychiatrist. You just had to get on with it and serve your sentence; there was no use crying over spilled milk. Of course there were days when I would be a wee bit down, or somebody else would be, but then everyone else rallied round. There was great comradeship."

There were also clashes with the Loyalist prisoners, particularly when the governor of the jail decided to try integration. It was bad enough, she said, to hear Loyalists singing their songs without being forced to mix with them. In Mary's opinion, the warders were behind the Loyalists and against the Republicans.

"Our view was that the only way we were going to get the Brits out was by sending them home in coffins." Sitting just a couple of feet from her, I must have gulped. She laughed. "Oh, I don't mean you, I mean the British soldiers!" She continued, but it was still difficult to disassociate oneself from that term, the target, "Brits."

"You see, if when we were in prison we heard that a Brit had been shot or killed, we did not celebrate the death as such. But the Loyalists would try to aggravate us when they heard a Catholic had been killed. That was the difference between us; we did not take it personally; we viewed the killings as a hazard of the situation."

Her own mother had been killed by Loyalists in 1975, when Mary was serving her first jail sentence. She recounted the death without bitterness, rather as though such things were commonplace: "She was in a bar, and they burst into a room spraying the place with gunfire. I was given twenty-four-hours parole to attend the funeral. I didn't want it; I didn't want to go because I thought if I didn't it wouldn't be true." She sighed. No, her mother's death had not made her hate Loyalists more. "I had been brought up in an area where I had seen what they were capable of doing. They were real bigots."

She hoped, she said as she smiled down at the baby, that things would be different when he grew up, but if they were still the same, she would not discourage her children from taking the path she had chosen. "If my kids wanted to join when they were old enough and things are still the same as they are now, I would not stop them. It would be up to them." They were free to choose—to an extent. Her face clouded. "But if Seamus ever told me he wanted to be a British soldier, I'd kill him; I'd strangle him."

She followed my gaze to the infant in her arms and shook herself, laughing. "Jesus, what a thing to say about your baby!" She leaned forward, the better to emphasize her point. "We don't like to see any killings, but they are necessary; there is a war on. The Brits are here. If they were not here, it wouldn't happen."

Geraldine Crawford was heartily thankful that she missed the no-wash protest in Armagh. "Oh God," she said with a laugh, "I don't think I could have stood that."

She had been in prison twice. The first time she was eighteen, and she was arrested after being shot in the legs by a British soldier.

Twelve soldiers were flown from West Germany to Belfast for her trial (a common practice) and the one who shot her gave evidence. He had fired twice at a group of girls after he saw Geraldine aiming a rifle at a military post in West Belfast.

Geraldine was a cheerful woman, and she launched into her own account of her wounding matter-of-factly and without rancor. "I was shot by the Brits in both knees; I lost the kneecap in my right leg altogether. It was a Saturday night, September twenty-second, 1973, at ten-thirty P.M. I had a rifle, and I was standing in Suffolk Road, near Andersonstown. There was another girl with me and three fellows, but I was the only one with a gun. It was the first thing I had done.

"My group had gone round first to see if it was all clear; then I was going to take a snipe at the army barracks. They said it was clear, so I went up with my rifle and the other girl came with me. Before we even fired a shot, some Brits in a hedge on the other side of the road shouted a warning: to halt, or they would open fire.

"I was standing at the corner of the road, and I turned round. They shot at us; they weren't intending to kill us, although they could have done. They aimed to stop us. I was shot in the back of my left knee, and through my right knee. It felt as if this huge blast had hit me, a big smash that knocked me to the ground. I was wearing these dusty pink trousers, and they were covered in blood, I remember that.

"A bullet went through the other girl's trousers, but it did not hit her. One of the three boys was also hit, but they all got away.

"I dropped my rifle and fell on the ground with the other girl. The Brits called to us to walk towards them, but I said I couldn't walk. They told us to crawl towards them then. I had to shuffle on my bum using my hands to push myself forwards. The Brits came over to me and one of them put a rifle to my chest. He said that if I had any other weapons to throw them out, but I had nothing other than the rifle. I asked him to give me a field bandage—I knew they always had them in their kit—because of the blood. He didn't seem concerned that all this blood was pumping out of my leg. He threw a bandage over to me and I had to put it on myself. He was not violent or abusive in any way, very professional.

"I was screaming with pain. I've heard other people say that when they were shot, they didn't realize it. I suppose it depends where you are shot, though. I remember being very aware of what was going on. I was shaking and very cold, lying on the ground. The Brits had surrounded me and the other girl. Then this woman came out of a pub and managed to get to me through the soldiers. She was very drunk, but I told her to go down the road to where my sister Maureen lived and tell her I'd been hit. Maureen came, but she just stood there, staring at me while a neighbor bent down and talked to me. I couldn't understand why my sister was just standing there like a stranger, but I know now that she was in shock."

An army Saracen Red Cross ambulance arrived, and Geraldine was placed on a stretcher and lifted inside. She had to wait there until a civilian ambulance arrived. She was then taken under military escort to the Royal Victoria Hospital and operated on immediately.

The next morning she awoke to find Special Branch at her bedside, but she refused to answer any questions. She was in a main ward, and at the bottom of her bed there was "a great big Brit. He was in full gear, fully armed. The other patients were glaring at me, and I was glaring at him, and everybody was glaring at everybody, so they put me in a single room. On about the third day I was charged with being in possession of an Armalite rifle and ammunition with intent to endanger life."

She was in the hospital for ten days and remembered her embarrassment that a trainee nurse, a girl her own age, had to wash her. "I told her I could sit up a bit and do it myself, so she left me and closed the door for a bit of privacy. The next minute, the Brits kicked the door in. I went on hunger strike in protest. I was eighteen years old, and I think I was only the second woman to have been shot."

Geraldine was moved to the security wing of Musgrave Hospital, and after three months there, to Armagh on remand. She had to walk with a stick, and she dismissed the prison doctors as "quacks," but she was among friends in the Republican wing. Those were the days of political status, and everything including security was, according to Geraldine, very lax. "Each morning at ten A.M. the OC came in, and we had cell inspection and had to stand to attention. Then we did drill in the yard for fifteen to twenty minutes, and the screws left us alone and never bothered us. If we wanted anything like writing paper we would go to the OC and ask her to put in our request to the screws. It was like a holiday camp."

She had been sentenced to eight years, but with remission she was released in 1977. Four years later, while attending the funeral of a hunger striker, she was arrested again.

"I was caught in a house where the men who fired the shots over the coffin were staying. After firing the shots, they came to the house with the guns. The army surrounded the building and then burst in, firing everywhere. They nearly shot me again.

"I was upstairs in a bedroom and the Brits burst in, firing, and the plaster was falling on me. I thought, Oh no, not again. I've been hit.

"I was feeling for blood, but I couldn't find any. I was scared that time; I thought they were going to shoot me. I was in a confined space and there were no witnesses. Some of the men were injured; one lost the sight of his eye. The soldiers could do anything.

"They beat the shit out of me. I made a complaint but never heard anything about it. I was charged with being in possession of a weapon because the guns were downstairs." It made no difference, she assured me, that she had not actually been holding a gun. "If the Brits came in here now and there was a gun downstairs, we would all be charged."

She received another eight-year sentence. She arrived back at Armagh to find she was now regarded as a criminal, and that the warders, who had seemed content to leave the Republicans well alone before, were openly hostile.

The no-work protest had stopped, but in its place was a sabotage campaign. Geraldine explained: "Our aim was to upset the system as much as we could. We had to make trousers; the screws had a quota of, say, fifty trousers a week. We used to wreck the sewing machines and rip buttons off the trousers. It meant that we only made about five pairs a week. We used to bring our knitting out in the work room and make our own clothes.

"Before, we had been allowed up to seven people in a cell at nights and we had booze so we could have parties. This time, we were locked up at nights in our own cells and the screws used to order us to go to work in the mornings. But we used to wait until our OC, Mairead Farrell, would enter and tell us to go. It was an easy life for the screws if they left us alone."

If they did not, the Republican women were quite capable of inflicting a degree of terror: "We used to have the kettle on all the time in the work room to make tea. One screw once told us that we were not allowed to make tea. We just sat and stared at her. Ten Republican women who didn't give a shit sitting staring at her. She got scared and let us make the tea."

Geraldine's voice was low and quiet; often she had to repeat something so that I could hear what she said. She spoke softly, she told me, as a result of her imprisonment. "There is another girl who was in with me and we can have a conversation now just with our eyes."

She has never been charged with membership in the IRA, but was willing to explain why she had taken up arms. Again, it was the hostile attitude and the abuse handed out by the British soldiers that had angered her as a teenager. Her resolve to use force against the British presence was strengthened when in 1975 her twenty-five-year-old sister, who was a volunteer, was killed in a premature bomb explosion.

Since her release from prison in 1986, she claimed to have been stopped on an almost daily basis by the security forces. "I work for a company selling taxi parts, and yesterday I was driving my boss to get some bread and milk when an army jeep pulled me over. They have taken my car apart in the past. Often they say, 'Hullo Geraldine. Have you got your ID?' It's just harassment. The intelligence officer is always the first one to ask questions, but all you have to say is your name, address, and that you are over twenty-one. One of them asked me once, 'How is your leg, Geraldine?' Then he said, 'You have got some fucking history.' I always refuse to get into a bantering match with them, or to take notice of their verbal abuse: whore, slut, etc.

"The Brits take it all so personally. They were in the work yard one day, and we had Gerry Adams's* armor-plated taxi in. This Brit asked the mechanic if he was scrapping it, and the mechanic said, no, it was a good car. The Brit said, 'We will have to scrap the fucking bastard who owns it.' "

She did not hate the soldiers, she insisted, but she did feel sorry for them. However, she reasoned they did have the option not to be in Belfast, and therefore she considered that any British soldier serving there must be naïve. Although she was getting married next month, she did not expect to be any less committed when she was a wife. Children, perhaps, would make a difference, particularly as she wanted to have ten. "I do think that you are here to look after your children, and it would be difficult to have them and to be in prison. But I think that is something I will only be able to know for sure when I have them.

"There is someone I know who wants to give it up and lead a normal life. The trouble is that here, what is a normal life? I can think of only one or two people who are not affected by things here."

By the time I got on board, the blue minibus was already half full of relatives and parcels for the visit to Maghaberry Prison on the outskirts of Belfast. The other passengers were mainly women, one red eyed, another morosely silent, but on the whole a cheerful, friendly crew, swapping bits of local news. Between the seats, a little girl showed off to two small, solemn boys, who sat sedately with their father.

More parcels of home-cooked meals and biscuits were being stowed under our feet. Outside, two youths were touching up a mural of armed and hooded men which adorned the wall of the Sinn Fein press center in Falls Road. One boy, perched high on his ladder, was applying a fresh lick of paint to a necklace of golden bullets.

I was on my way to meet Jennifer McCann, who was serving a twenty-year sentence for the attempted murder of a policeman in a shoot-out. She was also OC of the four sentenced IRA women prisoners at Maghaberry.

Maghaberry Prison is a series of long, low buildings, shrouded in wire, with cement blocks placed strategically along the perimeter

* President of Sinn Fein, the IRA's political wing.

fencing to prevent attacks by vehicles. It is surrounded by green hills and at first sight looks as if it might be a poultry farm. The bus bounced us over speed bumps in the road leading to the high metal gates and deposited us there swiftly before driving off—no waiting was allowed.

Entry was through a number of gates that opened automatically with a warning screech and clanged behind you. Inside the prison grounds, a row of warders looked over, through, and beyond the visitors as if any eye contact was simply not worth the trouble. The little girl piped, "I hate them"; her mother giggled proudly and shushed her.

First of all, the parcels that we carried had to be searched; it meant a long line at two counters—one for men, another for women—for a meticulous search by two prison guards. Everything had to be checked, weighed, and marked down on printed forms. One of the women guards, a motherly-looking woman, attempted to be friendly. "Hullo, dear," she exclaimed to my Sinn Fein escort, Marie. "You have lost weight!" Marie grunted something noncommittal and then explained to me that she had served a sentence here; it was her first trip back in two years.

After the parcels, it was our turn. One by one we were called, identified only by the name of the prisoner we were to visit. Two women warders made a rather perfunctory search, finding a house key and a five-pound note, which they confiscated. "We'll pop it into Marie's handbag for you, dear," said one. Nothing was allowed inside that might be used to bribe the guards, Marie told me. After the search came the wait in a room where a television sat on a high shelf relaying the Saturday afternoon horse racing. No one watched it, though. Instead, all eyes were glued to the door where periodically a guard appeared shouting prisoners' names. When Jennifer's and two others' names were called, a little group of us went forward and were shepherded onto another bus for the two-minute journey to the women's prison. The children, getting excited, tried to peel the laminated plastic from the windows; they failed; we could see nothing outside.

We were disgorged outside a large, new, brick building, then ushered through automatic doors, past more women warders—a more grim-faced crew than the ones at the gate—and into another waiting room. This time the television was on BBC2, showing a documentary with subtitles about an Indian poet. Everyone sat glumly watching it. Marie could not remember the exact layout of the prison; she thought the visiting room was around the corner to the right. She pointed out the design of the bars on the windows— straight verticals interlaced with circles. "When we came here from Armagh, we couldn't believe it. They had really tried to make it better; even pretty bars."

Finally the door opened, and we were collected up for the visiting room. As we entered, four prisoners rose to meet us from separate tables. Jennifer McCann walked toward me, smiling warmly. She was thirty but looked older, her black hair sprinkled with white, and the whites of her eyes a pinkish color. She knew my name, knew what I was doing, and she utterly ignored the glass cubicle in the room packed with watching guards. She motioned me to her table, on which was set out a flask of hot water, tea bags, coffee, milk, and biscuits. "Now, what would you like?" she asked, for all the world as if she were a waitress fussing over the silver service.

It was difficult to see this woman as part of "a bomb team intent on causing death and destruction on the widest scale"—the words of the judge as he sentenced her in 1981. She had been found guilty of possessing five firebombs, and a gun and ammunition, found after a high-speed chase through Belfast. The van, which had been hijacked, crashed near Divis Flats on Falls Road after smashing through an RUC checkpoint. Shots had been fired from the passenger seat of the van during the chase and wounded a police reservist. Jennifer McCann was the only passenger in the van; the weapon had been found on the floor where she had been sitting.

Jennifer would not talk about "the incident" very much. "I was caught while on the way to an operation in Belfast. We had bombs in the back of the van—they were for commercial targets and there would have been a long warning given so no civilians would have been injured. We were stopped at a roadblock, and there was a shooting incident. A policeman got hit, and I was grazed by a bullet on the ankle and the fella with me was hit too. I could have been killed, either shot, or the bombs could have gone off in the back. You do close your eyes before each operation and think, This could be it; I may not get back alive. You put up a sort of mental block. If you were thinking too much about what might happen, you might panic, and then you would be no use to anyone. You have to be calm."

Like Geraldine Crawford, she has never been charged with membership in the IRA. She described how her own initiation into the

Republican movement took place: aware from a young age of injustice; seeing the soldiers on the streets around her home; sickened by abuse—all these things made her want to fight back. "My family was thrown out of our home by Loyalists, and we moved to West Belfast when I was a child. I went to a convent school and had to pass through a Loyalist area. My sisters and I were punched and abused on the bus, and in the end the teachers had to drive us to and from school.

"There were four girls and one boy in my family, but only I became involved—I don't know why, we were all very different personalities."

The last nine years of her life had been spent in jail, so it was natural for her to concentrate more on that, and her new passion—women's rights. Her eyes sparkled as she spoke of what she had learned inside and explained that she now regarded women criminal prisoners as victims of society and injustice by men. She had become a kind of sociologist, having ample case studies around her; she was also taking an Open University degree in social welfare and was considering becoming a rape center counselor on her release.

"Before I came to prison, I suppose I thought of myself as a feminist in a vague sort of way because I was independent. Now I have become aware of the world struggle for women's rights and see that the Republican movement must fight for women's equality at the same time as we are fighting for freedom." She was in contact with a network of women prisoners from Chile ("On International Women's Day the Chile women sent us these beautiful earrings.") and the Baader-Meinhof, or Red Army Faction, group. The contact with the German prisoners had been set up by IRA women who had been in the same jails.

She was delighted to hear about the women of the Intifada and their charter for equality in their yet-to-be-born Palestinian state. She questioned me about how they participated in fighting and organizing the uprising, and applauded the way in which they flouted traditional Muslim values to gain their independence. Like the Palestinian women, she considered that the struggle for independence had to run parallel with the fight for women's rights.

"I agree with all these women on feminist issues. When I was outside, I thought that we could wait until we had won the battle and got our own state before we sorted out women's rights. Now I see there is no way that we can wait for that. Fighting the oppression of women must go together with the Republican fight. If we leave it till afterwards we could lose it."

She would not criticize the movement for male chauvinism, only saying that it "is getting better in its attitudes towards women. Now men in the H-Blocks are taking classes in women's issues and in child care. You wouldn't have caught them doing that a few years ago; they would have been horrified!"

In an article in *The Captive Voice*, a magazine written by IRA prisoners, she and the other women at Maghaberry had written about the need to merge both fights, for women on one hand and for a free Ireland on the other. The article had ended on a positive note, which promised that such a joint assault on injustice would not dilute the armed struggle, but rather would strengthen it: "The military campaign need not suffer as a result. In fact, it should benefit as women shun the subordinate roles which constrain them and engage more fully in the Republican movement in all aspects." The theory, then, seemed to be that liberated women made better fighters, a fact born out by Jennifer's view of the ordinary criminals who surrounded her.

"They are in here because of the same oppression that made us fight. I see so many examples of the way in which women are oppressed here. The juvenile prisoners—girls of sixteen and seventeen that no one cares about, the drug addicts. They come here very young; they end up in this place and nobody cares; the welfare officers don't care. A lot of them have been raped or sexually abused, often by their fathers or uncles. Then you have the old ones: there is one wee women aged about fifty-four, a wino. She was sentenced to a week in jail for failing to pay a fine of twenty-five pounds for shouting at a peeler. It was terrible. She did not know where she was or what had happened to her.

"We listen to them, but we are not trained counselors. We do tend to keep to ourselves, although some of the other prisoners like to come and talk to us. We realize that we are not above them; we are not superior, it is important to remember that.

"Maybe when I get out I will do some counseling work in a rape center. I don't believe it is enough to say, 'I am a woman,' and then do nothing for oppressed women." I wondered how the prison authorities would view the little enclave of IRA women counseling the other prisoners, and also whether the movement itself would appreciate this work.

Jennifer did not find her job as OC very onerous: there were only three other sentenced Republican women currently under her command, although there were three others on remand in the same wing. "When I first came to prison, there was a sort of military style of doing things among the Republican prisoners—drills, cell inspections, that sort of thing. That changed after 'eighty-three, when things were relaxed. Now we share everything; we have a kitty for food and clothes; it is like a community. I am OC, but that really just means I am the spokesperson for the group. We make decisions collectively, and then I speak to the prison authorities. We no longer have orders coming from the Republican movement outside.

"We are a very small group, and at first it was difficult for us sentenced prisoners to talk to the three on remand—they are on the floor above us. Now we have educational classes and we meet at those.

"We cook for the whole wing, and we are allowed to wear our own clothes. We also insist on our community life and the OC structure. It is done to protect ourselves; if someone is down the others support her. If everyone spoke to the screws and one of us got depressed, the screws would try to isolate that person and try to break her. Their aims are, one, to contain us, and two, to break us. They hate to see our community working, but they leave us alone most of the time. Sometimes they try to break us by putting one or two of us in isolation from the others, so it is important to retain our structure.

"Once they tried to break us up by putting three of us into a Loyalist wing. We lost so much remission then because we were always fighting with the Loyalist prisoners. The screws can also be very petty; one girl lost a week's remission for dancing.

"Officially, we are not recognized as political prisoners, but everything is agreed de facto—it gives them an easy life."

She did not regret the last ten years. "I can really only see good things have come out of my time in prison. I suppose other people may think that I have changed for the worst, but I certainly don't. My eyes are now open to social deprivation. I never thought, Oh no, twenty years; what will become of me? I didn't feel frightened."

And of her future after her release (she was due for release at the end of 1990)? "I certainly can't see myself getting married when I get out of here. Apart from anything else, I would have to find a man first!" She laughed, and really it was impossible not to like her—even though she was not telling the truth. Her release came a few months early, and in the autumn of 1990 she was married to her fiancé of long-standing, a Republican man serving a prison sentence.

As the interview came to a close and the visitors rose to go, Jennifer said that she was not the longest-serving Republican woman prisoner in Maghaberry. There was wee Mary over there; she was serving life. "What for?" I asked. "Murder," came the reply. I later learned that Mary McArdle, at the age of twenty-five, had been involved in the murder of a magistrate's daughter. The victim, a twenty-one-year-old schoolteacher, had been leaving church with her father after mass, when two gunmen opened fire. The girl, Mary Travers, was shot dead, and her father was seriously injured. Her father remembered the gunmen telling him, "It's you we want," and his daughter warning him, "This man has a gun," before she fell to the ground.

The gunmen ran off but stopped beside a girl out walking a dog. They gave her their weapons and escaped. Mary McArdle was arrested minutes later, and the guns were found under her skirt, strapped to her legs with surgical bandages.

As I looked over at Mary, I thought she looked too small and too tired to have carried a gun.

Chapter 6

✿ *SUSANNA RONCONI*

"As a lonely woman I had a particular relationship with weapons."

"All my recollections, even the most beautiful ones, are marked one way or another with death."

Susanna Ronconi had been a happy and dreamy child whose love for her family, particularly her mother, increased as she grew older. She agonized over leaving home, and when she finally did, it nearly broke her heart. Yet she went on to become one of Italy's most notorious and skillful political revolutionaries, a woman whose dedication to her cause led her to kill and maim time and time again.

Of all the women interviewed, she spoke the most freely of the psychological impact of her activities on herself, from the schizophrenic state that resulted after witnessing her first murder to the security that the gun came to represent to her. She did not believe that the ability to commit violence had anything to do with gender; it was far more connected to one's own makeup, background, and experience.

She had been sentenced to life imprisonment several times over for her part in the "years of lead" that scarred Italian life in the seventies. At the peak of the violence, there were an average of seven terrorist attacks a day, and in one year alone, 125 deaths. Prominent businessmen dared not venture outside without their retinues of bodyguards and traveled in armored private cars.

Susanna had been a member of the most infamous of all the revolutionary groups, the Red Brigades, which kidnapped and killed the ex-premier of Italy, Aldo Moro, and had also cofounded and led the second most feared band, Prima Linea (Front Line).

She had been found guilty of the murders of three men, one of them a comrade suspected of being an informer. She had also been involved at the highest level in the planning and execution of six other men, among them two judges and a criminologist, who was considered to be showing an unhealthy interest in the revolutionaries. She had shot several other people, who survived, and had kneecapped ten members of a business school as a warning to others of the dangers inherent in choosing such a profession. She broke into government offices to obtain false documents and carried out numerous armed bank robberies to fund the group. In 1983 she was given an additional thirty years for breaking out of prison, in the course of which a man who was walking past the prison had been killed. It was the only time that Prima Linea apologized for one of its actions.

She was speaking of this incident when she lamented that all her recollections were touched by death. Her escape, which had been masterminded and executed by her lover, had been "the most wonderful moment of my life"—sullied by the death of the passerby. Her other cherished memories were of her mother, with whom she had a very close relationship, but who died while Susanna was on the run. Then there was an earlier lover, a youth whom she had met in the Red Brigades, and by whom she became pregnant, but who was to die in prison of leukemia.

As she talked of her eight years as a revolutionary, it became clear that she had loved the camaraderie of her group so much that she had refused to abandon that way of life when she had an opportunity to do so. "I could not leave my comrades," she explained simply, although the alternative resulted in more shootings and five years on the run. Just before her first arrest, when her then lover, now husband, quit Prima Linea because he felt it was finished, she remained because she was too emotionally attached to the group she had formed. Her memories of those years, riddled with bullets and death, were also happy memories for her because she had felt so at home with others who were as committed as she was to the armed struggle.

She was a small, neatly built woman of thirty-nine, with dark shoulder-length hair, a very pale skin and gray eyes. Most of the time she looked sad and drawn, but when she smiled she was suddenly radiant and pretty. By the time of this interview she had served ten years in prison; two of these before her escape in 1982 and the remainder after her recapture. Originally, she had received several thirty-year concurrent life sentences, but the term had been reduced to twenty-two years and six months after she had declared that she had become "dissociated" with her past. Under the Italian Dissociation Law any convicted terrorist who renounces violence and whose change of heart is attested as genuine by prison authorities and magistrates is entitled to a reduced sentence. Susanna could have gone a step further and taken advantage of the Penitence Law, which requires that a terrorist make "an active contribution to the prevention of further acts of terrorism," i.e. name names. The reward for this is a drastic reduction in sentence, but Susanna refused to entertain the idea. Not only does she have a fierce loyalty to her former comrades, but she believes that, in the context of the times, violence was justifiable.

Her claim of dissociation has been completely convincing, even to the extent of allowing her, in January 1990, to get a job outside prison. Six days a week, early in the morning, she leaves her cell at Le Nuove prison in Turin, where warders allow her to keep a gang of stray cats, and catches the bus into the city. There, in a pleasant office in a prosperous quarter, she works from 9 A.M. until 7 P.M. It is a job that she loves, writing press releases for a center for dropouts, drug addicts, and ex-prisoners, and for which she is paid a regular wage. She also receives forty-five days vacation a year. When I made the initial request to interview her, she said that she could see me any Saturday, but warned, "Come before August eighth, because I am off on a three-week holiday."

Her vacation was to be spent with her husband, another convicted terrorist, whose life sentence has been reduced to thirty years because he too has become "dissociated." Every day the couple are allowed an hour alone together at Susanna's office.

It was a large, sunny room on the fourth floor of an old building. There was no elevator, just flight upon flight of stairs, a journey cheered by brightly colored posters proclaiming "Ciao!" on the walls. All the offices were built around a central courtyard, and there appeared to be no other exit, not even a fire escape. Susanna was sitting behind her desk and seemed nervous at first, but as the day wore on, and the temperature rose to 90 degrees, she became quite relaxed.

She was not as free to come and go as I had thought; she was under constant guard. I had not noticed, but she pointed out of the window to where two men were standing below on the pavement.

They were leaning against a concrete block, dressed in jeans and T-shirts, and looked as if they were waiting for a friend, or a lift—but they waited all day. During the week they must have had an excruciatingly boring time as Susanna was not allowed out of the building all day, but on Saturdays at least they could follow her to the café a hundred yards away, where she was permitted a two-hour lunch break.

As we walked there, with the two men at a discreet distance, I asked Susanna whether anyone had ever recognized her. Turin, after all, was in her time and largely due to her activities, a war zone, with running street battles between the revolutionaries and the police; the road signs were pockmarked with bullets. No, she swiftly shook her head, no one had yet stopped her in the street. She seemed quite horrified at the prospect, and possibly it was for this reason that she absolutely refused to let her photograph be taken.

It became apparent in the café that these two hours were normally spent catching up with news from her friends; several people approached her and after an hour she left our table to join them. In the afternoon, the guards sat down in the parking lot opposite her office; I asked her what sort of security there would be on her vacation. First of all, she informed me, she and her husband were not allowed outside Italy; then the police would check up on where they were staying and drop in during the evening to make sure they were in the hotel. She seemed to have a good relationship with her watchers; occasionally they would come into the office for a spot-check, and they appeared to have a grudging respect for her. She smiled, "Once, one of them said to me, 'At least when you lot were running around, we had something to do.' "

In her time, Susanna had given the police plenty to do. She had been an activist from the age of seventeen while still at school, going on demonstrations, joining picket lines outside factories, and participating in various school "sleep-ins." It was an exciting time to be a student—another Red Brigade woman member said it would have been difficult not to have been involved "with so much going on." In 1968 there were student protests, followed the next year by factory workers' demonstrations and strikes—all of which led to violent clashes with the police. The students, inspired by Marxist-Leninist teachings, and condemning all political parties as a sham, agitated for revolution; the workers, demanding better pay and improved working conditions, seemed to provide the necessary popular support required for the students' dreams.

Frightened by such a prospect, which suddenly in 1969 seemed a distinct possibility, the state returned to its old fascist ways, abandoned only some twenty years before. Fascist squads sprang up, with, some believed, the covert backing of certain members of the establishment, including the judiciary, police, and security forces. Their aim was not only to restore order but also to fight the left, often in street battles and hand-to-hand fighting. These neo-fascists wanted to create a state of chaos, their so-called strategy of tension, which would force the army to take over and impose mar-tial law as a precursor to overthrowing democracy. In December 1969 fascists performed their first "strage" (slaughter) by planting a bomb at the Piazza Fontana in Milan, which killed seventeen people and wounded eighty-eight.

The terrorism allegedly practiced and funded by some sections of the establishment fueled the unrest. A sizable proportion of the community believed that it was their right to fight force with force, as their fathers had done with Mussolini. Around 250 revolutionary groups were formed encompassing every political persuasion from Trotskyism to anarchism; some were political parties with a mili-tary wing, others were autonomists, holding power in a factory, port, or university department; some lasted only a few weeks, oth-ers several years.

Padua University, where Susanna had enrolled as a student of political science in 1969, was at the forefront of the protests. She joined Potere Operaio (Workers' Power), a revolutionary move-ment which argued for mass agitation and violence. She also en-gaged wholeheartedly in a new area of protest—militant feminism.

In Italy at that time, women were certainly one of the most oppressed groups in society. Until 1975 an Italian man could legally beat his wife; a woman's adultery was punishable with up to three months in prison, while a man's infidelities were only considered a crime if they caused a public scandal, and abortion was illegal until 1976. Italian feminism at last emerged during the late sixties, and the groups that Susanna joined were angry and violent. Some fem-inists formed female vigilante squads, attacking doctors who spoke out against abortion, cinemas showing sex films, and shops that displayed live models of women in their windows.

Susanna poured all her energies into the protest movements and became known as a thoroughly devoted militant. When the Red

Brigades were formed in 1970, she was still living nominally with her parents, but a considerable part of her time was spent in feminist households. She was greatly attracted to the Red Brigades and knew several people in her circle who had joined, but she was also aware that if she did the same she would have to abandon her militancy in the feminist arena. Eventually in 1974 she made her decision; the Red Brigades were well organized, shared her political beliefs—including the one that violence was necessary to overthrow the state—and moreover were fighting for such groups as the feminists, who were being brutally repressed by the police. Furthermore, the Red Brigades were, out of all the groups that had emerged, the ones most likely to win.

She joined and in June that year was present at the Brigades' first murder. It devastated her, this initial contact with killing, and in a state of shock she left home and went underground with the movement. She quickly realized that she had made a mistake: she came from a different background, both socially and politically, from most of the other members, and she was deeply lonely. Throughout her adult life Susanna craved companionship and a warm living environment with lots of people from many different walks of life around her; in the Red Brigades there was a strict policy of no contact with outsiders. Nevertheless, her determination to succeed as a militant forced her to remain for a year, during which time she fell in love with a young comrade and became pregnant by him. Then she and her boyfriend left.

They spent several months living together, and Susanna had an abortion—by law illegal—which was botched and nearly killed her. After she recovered, she made fresh revolutionary contacts and in 1976 helped form Prima Linea.

The new group believed firmly in violence but differed from the Red Brigades in its structure. It was loosely knit, a kind of melting pot for militants and included some feminist fighters. There was much emphasis put on the necessity of maintaining contact with what was deemed to be the group's supporters—the working-class population, who had begun to question the brutality and necessity for some of the terrorist outrages. Susanna was much more relaxed with such a group; she was able to have the social interaction she needed so much.

Initially, Prima Linea restricted itself to skirmishes with the fascists, but it soon moved on to armed robberies, shootings, arson, kidnapping, and murder. In its four years, the group killed sixteen people and wounded twenty-three more. One of the most brutal actions occurred when a Prima Linea gang, led by Susanna, raided the Turin School of Industrial Management, took 190 students and lecturers hostage, and kneecapped 10, 5 from each group. It was a warning to all trainee managers, the "oppressors of the people," of what they could expect, but it revolted the Italian public. The same disgust was displayed when Judge Emilio Alessandrini was executed by Prima Linea. Alessandrini was respected by many on the far left for his investigation into the Piazza Fontana bomb attack and his insistence that it had been perpetrated by the neo-fascists. It is believed he was killed because he had started to investigate Prima Linea, and also because he was bringing a measure of honesty and accountability to the judicial profession—regarded by the revolutionary groups as beyond the pale. Susanna was convicted of this murder, a charge she vehemently denied, pointing out that under Italian law one can be condemned for a crime by simply being a member of the group that committed it.

She was, nevertheless, one of the four leaders of Prima Linea and admitted that, apart from the judge's murder, she had been involved at the most senior level when decisions were taken to shoot and kill particular targets. I asked her if she had ever made the decision not to kill someone because he had aged parents or small children. She flinched visibly, "Oh, yes," she whispered, and her eyes pleaded with me that she was not such a monster.

She had been born in Venice in 1951 to middle-class parents; she was the middle child of the family with an older brother and younger sister. She described her childhood as one of idyllic happiness, although of great loneliness; she remembered that she spent many hours alone in the garden listening to music, with her dog lying beside her. It seemed that at this stage she enjoyed solitude, for it enabled her to indulge in her great passion—making up stories. "I had a very vivid imagination, and I would try to write down what I thought. I kept tons of diaries."

Her enjoyment of her own company continued throughout her childhood; as a young teenager she recalled how much she had loved visiting Venice on her own. It gave her a sense of freedom to be alone, and she was particularly fond of Venice because it had been her mother's city. "When I needed to be alone and feel good,

I went to Venice," she said. "It has always been a special place for me." Seventeen years later when she escaped from prison it was to Venice she fled for refuge.

When she was a young child she experienced the "classic thing" of falling in love with her father, but the most important parent in her life was to be her mother. Mrs. Ronconi was something of an oddity in provincial Padua, to where the family had moved when Susanna was small. She was an atheist—and proud of it—in that most Roman Catholic and traditional area. "She was not ostracized, but she was known to be a bit different. None of the Catholic traditions were ever observed in our house.

"My mother had a deep passion for many things, but she only talked about them at home; she had a rather restricted social life. She was vaguely socialist and had a very optimistic outlook on life. No doubt her socialism is something she passed on to me."

When Susanna was fourteen years old she rebelled: she chose to go to the "wrong" school. It was hardly the traditional teenager rebellion against parents, more one against herself. A psychologist suggested that perhaps the reason for this was that she, as the daughter of an atheist, had no religious background to rebel against. One might also speculate that her lack of a "belief system" resulted in her far greater rebellion later in life—but it is only speculation, and it is probably reading far too much into the decision of a young teenager.

Susanna herself described her choice of academic career as one based on pure contrariness and a desire to be noticed. In opting to go to the scientific high school, rather than the classical one, she was flying in the face of tradition. Girls "of good family" in Padua went to the classical school; those whose backgrounds were not quite so middle class went to the scientific. "For me the classical school was the obvious choice, taking into account the amount of writing I did, all those diaries and stories. I chose the scientific school as a way to distinguish myself. My choice was wrong, and it could not have been more so, as I hated scientific subjects."

Nevertheless, she attended the school and in the end came to enjoy the subjects, describing her acquisition of new knowledge as "more and more entertaining." Just as important, the high school introduced her to other people whom she instinctively liked and got on well with. Suddenly her childhood love of loneliness evaporated, and in its place came "something like a hunger," to be involved with other people. This hunger was something that was to be the dominant theme in her adult life; never again would she crave solitude; in fact she would flee from it, as if afraid to be alone.

She began to spend less and less time at home, preferring instead to immerse herself in school life and eagerly accepting invitations to parties and concerts. In 1968, when Susanna was in her penultimate year of high school, the student riots started, and with her new friends she was swept along on the tide of militancy. It was not a violent movement, but the potential for violence was there; the students' heroes were Che Guevara and other revolutionary leaders who had won freedom struggles in third world countries. To Susanna it was all tremendously exciting and enjoyable: "I remember sleeping inside various schools, and there was this sense that you were occupying your own space, the space of your peer group. We were all together, and we all felt the same, that changes were going on, and we were part of it. I met people from different social classes, different cultures, and felt as if I had left behind my own social class.

"Whatever I did in that year, I remember doing it with joy and feeling good because I was with the others. I think this was the richest time of my life."

She took part in the open warfare between the students and the neo-fascist youth groups; sometimes the opposing sides resembled street gangs, fighting over disputed territory. But there was a far more serious side: the way in which elements inside the police and the security forces seemed to provide backing and cover for the fascists. There was a genuine fear that the far right would orchestrate a military coup and impose a fascist dictatorship. A number of police officers and security men were attacking those suspected of left-wing activities, and some of the Italian populace responded by acquiring guns to defend themselves.

That period of terror culminated in 1969 with the massacre at the Piazza Fontana, which was originally blamed on the left. When it became apparent that it was the work of the far right, including a member of the security services, the war on the streets took on a new dimension. Susanna summed it up: "One could sense an atmosphere of tragedy, and what I remember very clearly is feeling that one had a great sense of responsibility. I said to myself, 'Now, either we are united or goodness knows where we will all end up.' "

This feeling of having a responsibility to be involved was one that she referred to often, and it seems as if other political women revolutionaries shared it. The German law-enforcement agencies pointed out that women, more than men, are led into violence through a conviction that they must change society for the better. Astrid Proll, a former member of the Baader-Meinhof gang, once described herself and her comrades as being "very well-armed social workers."

Susanna had just enrolled at Padua University and joined Workers' Power. Although she was still living at home, she devoted most of her time to the group, immersing herself as she had done in her school days in the community of militant students. She noticed that in spite of there being many other women students in Workers' Power, it was the men who did most of the talking while the women worked feverishly and got things done (another common theme, running through such groups, from the extremists of the animal liberation movement to the fighters of the Intifada).

"I was one of those; silent yet I worked a lot. This capacity of mine to work so hard and be so militant came to be noticed, and I was soon identified as 'the comrade who can be trusted.' I lived totally for the group; I did nothing else, and I slept very little.

"I remember that a crowd of us would be together from four o'clock in the morning, when we started distributing leaflets, to late in the evening. We would end up singing songs in the tavern until midnight. There was no time during which we were alone, from giving out the leaflets to eating; it was an incredible experience."

She spent two and a half years with Workers' Power, then came a period in which she admitted, "I don't have all the right answers in the right places."

"Some of the choices I made are still very difficult to explain. There were three things going on at the same time. One was dissatisfaction with Workers' Power—it stopped being militant and eventually dissolved in 1973. Secondly, there was still the problem of the fascists and the urgent need to do something about them, and I started having contact with the Red Brigades. The third thing was my involvement with feminism. The feminist debate had started within Workers' Power, and a group called Lotta Femminista (Women's Struggle) had been created. I did not know what to do— whether to join the Red Brigades and the armed struggle or remain with the feminists, so for two years, between 1972 and 1974, I floated between the two groups."

The decision was made more difficult for Susanna because she had more or less moved into a feminist household and felt very relaxed there. Also, the feminist movement in Italy had a lot of battles to win, and Susanna enjoyed fighting. "I remember that when we were demonstrating against the anti-abortion law, the police would take their belts off and hit us with them. They wouldn't use their batons, as they would have done with a student demonstration, because we were all women.

"There was a court case of a woman charged with having an abortion. We occupied the courtroom—it was the first time I had been in court, and I can still recall the policeman's uniform and the barrister. We had two big sit-ins in the square outside the court and did round dances and sang songs. For me, it was the first time that I realized the crucial difference in being born a woman; it was very important."

Perhaps the most agonizing part of her decision was the knowledge that if she chose life with the Red Brigades she would lose contact with her mother. Susanna was twenty-three at the time, but since the age of fifteen the relationship with her mother had grown particularly close, and the bond had been further strengthened when Susanna became involved in feminism. Her mother, perhaps out of a genuine sympathy but possibly also to maintain contact with her daughter who was so seldom at home, became interested in the movement too. "I used to take her to the meetings and demonstrations and at one point when she was sick I proposed that she should come and live with me.

"She was not militant, but her interest in feminism helped consolidate our relationship, and it helped me to clarify my own thoughts on the subject. We were like two friends, two adult women.

"I was never at home during the day, and I remember the times at night when I used to come back home, sometimes very late, one or two o'clock in the morning. My mother would be there, awake, waiting for me with a little glass of grappa. We would have half an hour together when we would very quickly tell each other all our news. Then we would go to bed. When I was trying to decide between feminism and the armed struggle, it was also a choice between living with or leaving my mother."

One does not expect such revelations from a hardened political killer: that she was tied to her mother's apron strings. It is often said that the European revolutionaries were little more than spoiled, middle-class kids, kicking out at the values instilled in them by their parents as much as at society. Obviously, nothing could be further from the truth in Susanna's case. She was deeply attached to her mother, and the prospect of leaving her was a traumatic one. It is interesting that throughout her life she became as deeply attached to her political movements, as if she had transferred that filial devotion to her beliefs and to her comrades, and the prospect of abandoning them, as with the militant feminists, seemed to wrench her apart. It might be that she was always searching for the idyllic happiness of her lost childhood.

I asked whether another problem for her in choosing the Red Brigades had been their dedication to violence. No, she responded, "It was not clear-cut like that. There was a wide spectrum of feminist groups, some of which were prepared to use violence, and others not, but there was a constant debate on the use of violence. So it wasn't that the Red Brigades meant violence and the feminists didn't; it wasn't as if one day I had to make the choice between violence and nonviolence—it was always there.

"I did not, and do not, see myself as a violent person, but I believed that under certain conditions, when one class held power and the other didn't, the use of violence was legitimate. Our most important role model was the struggle against fascism during the last war, which was of course still vivid for our parents. So we had heard stories of how violence had been justly used in the fight. When we talked of it, violence was always put on an ideological footing, so it was sort of filtered and you felt justified in using it."

Finally in 1974 Susanna, worn out trying to split herself between the organized revolutionary movement and feminism, opted for the Red Brigades. She joined with a group of friends—two women and three men—and she spent a few days in the mountains, learning how to shoot. The training for actual "military operations" she said casually, one learned on the job. Her first action was armed robbery soon after she had joined; then, in June 1974, she was part of the gang that performed the Red Brigades' first murders.

Three weeks before a bomb had exploded during an anti-fascist rally in Brescia, near the Italian lakes. Eight people were killed and ninety-four wounded. It was the work of the Social Movement Party (Movimento Sociale Italiano, or MSI), the Italian neo-fascists. The Red Brigades decided to strike back. Their Padua column, which included Susanna, the new recruit, raided the offices of the MSI party in Padua intending only to steal documents. However, the gang was disturbed by party officials, and they shot the officials dead. In claiming responsibility for the murders, the Red Brigades for the first time declared war; the statement urged all revolutionary movements to take up arms in the fight against "fascist barbarism."

Susanna was deeply traumatized by the deaths: "I had not taken part in the killings directly because I had not been in the same room, but I was only ten meters away. Afterward, I wandered around in a state of shock, wearing the wig I had used for the operation; then I took it off and went home. There was a meal waiting for me; the radio was on and giving details of the operation . . . I felt I was in a state of schizophrenia; it was really heavy.

"The older comrades were very good, very understanding and sympathetic, and they talked about the incident and our right to use force, based on the anti-fascist tradition. I started to recover a little, and realized that I had joined this new war."

Until this point, Susanna had still maintained contact with her parents, but now she felt that she had to make a complete break and go underground with the Brigades. "I did not want to live a half-life anymore: the parents, home, and the 'good girl' on the one hand, and 'the rest' on the other.

"I remember so well the moment that I left. I took my suitcase and a comrade took me to another town, gave me false documents—I tore up my real ones—and there I started a new life. I didn't go back to Padua for thirteen years. I told my parents that I had to leave home for political reasons, but gave them no details. I went away saying to my mother, 'I'm only going for a month.' I left one night at six o'clock, and the last thing I did was to go to a women's demonstration, a torch-lit procession. I was crying because I felt so torn apart, but I was also very resolved. Nobody could understand why I was crying. I left with a suitcase containing a few clothes and the covering from my bed, a red quilt filled with goose feathers.

"After I had left, my mother just collapsed; our relationship soured."

The snapping of this most important emotional bond, by her own hand, had a lasting effect on Susanna. She was like a child who had left home with her red quilt and it seemed to be significant that she described her old life in the terms of being a "good girl." Having severed her connections and opting for the role of "the other" (the "bad girl," one wonders?), she expected a great deal from the group she had sacrificed everything for; she wanted a new family, love, and support. In this respect, she was like Ulrike Meinhof of the Baader-Meinhof gang: Ulrike's mother had died when she was a teenager and Ulrike sacrificed her own family, including her young twin daughters, to join the revolution. She seemed to want love and attention in the gang; like Susanna, she did not get it.

Susanna's new life was well organized and secretive; she was given a car with false license plates and false documents. "I felt a bit like a traveling salesman, everything was false," she commented. She glossed over what actions she actually did in her year with the Brigades, saying, "I grew up fast in military aspects," and concentrated on describing her swift realization that she did not fit in with her new comrades.

She had no complaints with the way in which the group treated her as a woman; both sexes were equal as far as the leadership was concerned, although she admitted there might have been subtle undercurrents that led the men to be dominant. Another former Red Brigades woman declared that if women in the group showed any hesitancy or expressed doubts, their wavering was taken far more seriously than that of their male colleagues. It seemed as if women had to be doubly tough.

Susanna's problems with the Brigades, however, had far more to do with her feelings of loneliness. She was outnumbered; there were many more men than women in the movement (only 10 percent), and as everyone was underground they were very isolated from the rest of society. No one else in the Padua column shared Susanna's background, and there was none of the camaraderie that had so marked her political activities both at school and in the university.

During the course of Susanna's time with the Red Brigades the group became rigid, rules had to be obeyed and were strictly enforced. If the leadership decided that a new column had to be set up in another part of the country, and that meant splitting up a couple who were having a relationship, then so be it. Susanna commented: "I started realizing that I had made the choice to join more on a wave of haste than out of a real political identification with the Red Brigades. My problem wasn't criticism of the armed struggle; more with their rigidity.

"My first few months were marked with great solitude. However, I threw myself into the militancy in a very determined manner—I was deeply convinced of the need to work for this organization, and I had a great need to be utterly involved." Her deep commitment to the group overrode any personal feelings of unhappiness.

"Then something happened that broke up the loneliness; I started having a relationship with a young man in the group whom I had met after joining. He was very young, younger than me, and had gone underground before his eighteenth birthday. He was quite different from me; he was a very lonely man. It was a very important relationship from the romantic point of view, but full of conflict in all other respects. My relationship with him helped me get through my first year in the Red Brigades."

She became pregnant by her lover, Fabrizio Pelli, and at about the same time they both decided that it was time for them to leave the Brigades. The leadership had decreed that henceforth they needed to become even more formal, virtually a political party and more Leninist in outlook; they would be the armed vanguard of the masses with whom they had so little contact. Susanna said: "I was not strictly Leninist, and my education, formation, and political culture was not one of rigidity. I wanted to be much more involved with people, fluid and elastic, in terms of the other movements that were around at the time."

Susanna, her boyfriend, and another friend announced that they wished to leave; there were no hard feelings, but a request that the three should isolate themselves for a few months to allow the organization to reshape and to make sure they did not know "certain things." Susanna admitted that she could have gone back home because there had been no warrant issued for her arrest, but "I was scared, and I did not want to leave the other two." She was too emotionally involved, but one also wonders whether she had become addicted to the life of the outlaw.

She was also ill; she had had an abortion that she realized had been badly performed, and she needed to do something to rectify matters.

Many of the women interviewed, in choosing the path of violence and revolution, had either opted to delay or not to have children, or as in the case of Ulrike Meinhof mentioned above, had abandoned their children. Susanna, by having an abortion, had gone one step further, in deciding, sensibly one might think, that the life of the revolutionary was not one for the child. Yet, she had given much thought to maternity; it was a theme she was to return to later.

Her ensuing ill health made things very difficult: not only was she living underground, but in having the abortion she had broken the law, and it was risking arrest to approach a doctor for help. Eventually she forced herself to act. "It was awful. Neither I or the other two knew what to do, so I ended up traveling from clinic to clinic, all by myself, half dead, with a temperature touching one-hundred six degrees. Eventually somebody said, 'OK, here is a bed, come on . . .' "

She paused, then added, "It was the only memory I have in which I was scared of death in spite of seeing it so many times later in my life." It was also the only time that she was in a position where she was confronting death because, and only because, she was a woman.

When she had recovered, Susanna wanted to see her parents. She discussed it with her two companions, and they pointed out the dangers that such a visit would entail, possible capture and questioning by the police. Eventually, they all agreed it would be safe enough, so she contacted her parents and told them she would meet them for Christmas at the family house in the mountains. There was a joyful if guarded reunion; obviously Susanna could not answer many of the questions she was asked. Then on Christmas Day disaster struck: "While I was sitting round the table with my parents, just a little family enjoying their Christmas dinner, I saw the photograph of my boyfriend on television. He had been captured, and the house where we lived had been raided. I had to decide immediately what to do next because I had left my documents in the house and knew that the police would be able to trace me very easily.

"I turned to my father, who on that occasion was splendid. I called him into my room and told him briefly what had happened. I said, 'You must take me to the railway station.' He did not argue, he didn't say a word, he just did it. His last words to me were, 'Let me know something.' I got to Turin the next morning, dialed a number, and met up with some comrades."

It was the start of Prima Linea. Susanna and a group of similarly minded activists were committed to the necessity of violence, but saw themselves as coming into existence only to serve (with weapons) the needs of the working classes. Their motto was "Prima Linea is founded to prepare its own destruction"—after the revolution the group would dissolve and would not seek power as the Red Brigades intended to do. Its structure was informal, and it welcomed other guerrillas from different groups. Susanna was able to meet a lot of people, and she was happy. The new group formed "proletarian bands," which patrolled the working-class districts and attacked police stations and bars where drugs were sold. They saw themselves as the protectors of those unable to defend themselves and extended their actions to those whom they considered were polluting the environment.

It was 1977, sometimes referred to in Italy as "the year of the P38"—the name of the most commonly carried handgun of that time. The numerous revolutionary groups, including Prima Linea and the Red Brigades, who carried out the frequent violent actions, became known collectively as "the '77 Movement." Dozens of groups suddenly decided that violence got things done, and streets seemed to be filled with young people looking for confrontation. The police, taken by surprise and unsure who was responsible for the increase in armed activity, arrested hundreds of people, only in many cases to be forced to release them for lack of evidence. By the end of the year, there had been nearly two thousand terrorist actions and thirteen deaths. Susanna commented: "We all agreed that 1977 had been a point of no return. It had laid a foundation of a new way to express oneself, to fight."

During the year a number of Prima Linea members had been arrested, and Susanna and another comrade decided that Turin was becoming too dangerous a place to live. They moved to Naples, where she was one of the top three of four leaders within the movement, and as such responsible for all the decisions that were taken. I asked her how a target was chosen.

"The first thing was to decide which institution should be chosen, and within that who was to be selected. Then a military assessment of the target had to be carried out. Sometimes it was impossible to carry out an attack on the person we had chosen because his habits were too regular or he had too much protection.

"I was always nervous before any action. I lived with fear; it was something I lived with for ten years. Every time, before an action, it was a challenge for me. It is not something that you get used to, handling violence. You feel normal human emotions; violence is not something to be undertaken lightly. Preparing for an action involves all sorts of mixed feelings, but in the end you have to carry out the decisions that have been made."

One such decision was to kneecap a woman prison guard who was responsible for security in the maximum security wing of a Turin prison, where many women terrorists were being held and allegedly badly treated. It was the only action Susanna said in which it was decided that the "firing group" should be composed of just women. "I did not agree with that, that no men should be involved, but it was a decision that had been made.

"There were four of us in the group, and we waited for her outside her house. I did not shoot her; I was covering for the others that day. When she came out, she saw us and about two seconds before she was shot, she realized who we were and started calling us 'tarts.' "

Susanna and the others had been outraged at being called such a name. One had the impression that if the victim had screamed "murderers" they would have preferred it: "It was the worst insult she could have used; it was a direct insult against our womanhood."

The fury at being reviled in such terms was also shared by other, less militantly feminist women from traditionally repressive societies: the IRA and the Palestinians. Why should it matter so much that the enemy calls you names? Particularly when you are about to drill bullets into them. Is it that such name-calling drives home to the women society's view of deviant females, when they see themselves as sexless fighters for the cause?

The punishment shooting apparently had the desired effect. The women inside the prison reported to Prima Linea that conditions improved dramatically.

It was 1978 and Susanna was by now one of the most wanted faces on the terrorist posters. She lived under the constant threat of arrest and the tension that that inspired, but at the same time, she said, there were also the mundane aspects of everyday life to contend with—shopping and cooking, friendships and lovers. With Fabrizio in jail (he was to die there the following year) Susanna had a succession of relationships. She explained that as she moved around, so she changed lovers.

I suppose one could say that this demonstrates the popular view of such women: that they are not only violence crazed but, like their male counterparts, sex crazed. However, it seems far more likely in her case that these casual affairs were the result of her craving for affection. She went on to say, in the most conservative of ways, that the only relationship she had ever seriously worked at was with the man who was to become her husband.

Life on the run was not only stressful, it was lonely, and Susanna had grown fearful of that state. However many casual relationships she might have had, she found that her greatest source of protection was her gun. "Those years were very hard, but also beneficial in helping me to grow up. I was in a situation where I had to fend for myself, both in the political meetings and in the military actions.

"As a lonely woman I had a particular relationship with weapons; for me to carry a gun was a defensive action and a protective one as well. I spent seven years going around armed, yet for me the chief importance of my gun was that it defended me. It was an exception when I used it offensively."

When she spoke like this, she might have been an ordinary, fearful woman describing how she decided to carry a gun to protect herself from rapists, instead of a woman who should be feared in her own right. Even in admitting this she insisted that the primary use of the gun was to protect her:

"I had many experiences of direct operations but often the gun was only used as a deterrent. I did, of course, experience wounding people and killing. It was an atrocious experience, each one very different. It is very difficult to describe, partly because one thought about it so much beforehand and then afterwards.

"In a sense committing violence is a violence against yourself because it is not something you would naturally wish to do. Because you have to put something of yourself to one side when you do it, you are forcing out the desire to preserve life. It is one of the reasons that it is impossible to go on doing it for a long time. You know that there is a price to pay, and at a certain moment that price becomes too great, and you have a personal crisis. You become aware that the costs outweigh the benefit. You always knew that there was a choice in what you did, that no one forced you to do it.

"Those operations only lasted a few minutes, yet my reaction to them was always one of total suspension of all emotions. The most dominant feeling was fear, but not only because it could have gone wrong; it was something deeper, you were crossing a threshold. There was the moment before, then afterwards was the suspension of everything. I seemed to have stopped breathing; everything around me was soundless, noiseless, colorless; there was emptiness.

"I have read in many books descriptions of courage—personally I don't know what it is. The only thing that I know is that moment when everything is suspended, the use of the gun and the picture of the gun's flash when it has been fired. The rest of the thoughts, sensations, come later."

Clinical psychologists say that the feelings she described of pushing aside the life force and crossing the threshold are exactly in keeping with many soldiers' reactions after killing. The difference is that if you are a political killer on the run you cannot seek psychological help, and as Susanna rightly said, the ultimate consequence of this can be personal crisis.

"You keep these things firmly locked inside you and ignore certain aspects of what you are doing, but you can't eliminate them. Then they start to come back, very slowly and painfully."

At the time, she added, no one discussed their feelings about violence; it was as if the subject was taboo. Did she think that she and the other women found it more difficult to be violent?

No, she shook her head; she had her own theory about the female relationship to arms: "The whole idea of violence is linked to maternity. It is the woman who gives life; it is the woman who also takes life.

"There are many examples of mothers killing their children before committing suicide themselves, so the traditional view of the mother as incapable of using violence does not correspond to the facts.

"I do not believe that the experience I have described of blocking the life force, putting aside emotions when you are being violent, is exclusively male or female, or that it is something that women find more difficult than men. I have known quite a number of men who have told me that they could not have shot people."

Her last view was one that I was beginning to share myself: that the propensity to commit violence was not governed by sex. However, I was not so sure about her denial that blocking the life force, or the instinct for life preservation, was as easy for women as for men. Surely women have a deeper, almost instinctive desire to preserve life? Perhaps I am simply expressing a stereotypical viewpoint, but what about the number of occasions we hear of when women have confronted danger to protect their children? A lioness and her cubs—is this all wrong?

Susanna clearly thought so, as her theory that mothers give and take life shows. It is true, as she said, that there are examples of mothers killing their children, but it is undoubtedly only a very few mothers who do that. However, I talked to a criminologist who agreed with Susanna on the point that mothers have the ultimate power of life or death at the crucial moment of birth. The criminologist pointed out that in societies like Italy, where it is traditional for the woman to give birth at home, the midwife and mother may often conspire to kill an infant if it is deformed or simply unwanted. One also thinks of societies where the mother will kill her newly born daughter because she is not a son. There did seem to be an element of truth in Susanna's linkage of motherhood to violence.

She and her women comrades, in fact, used to laugh at a lot of the men, especially the younger ones, who loved to strut about wearing leather jackets and brandishing a gun. She felt that some of them had joined the group because it was the macho thing to do, not out of any deep sense of commitment—and here they differed from the women who had only joined after a lot of soul searching.

One was reminded of the words of the ETA woman who claimed that women were far more committed to the cause than men because in choosing to join they had so much more to lose. The relatively shallow male allegiance to the movement that Susanna and the other female revolutionaries observed, was reflected, she said, in the way in which men reacted when captured. "Some of the younger men had a mania for guns and treated them a bit like a fetish, in a sort of slightly infantile, typically masculine way. It was never the same for the women; they put much more of themselves into the experience.

"As a result, there is a relatively small percentage of women who have become *pentiti* [repentant], because for them to collaborate would be denial of their whole being."

She did not mean to imply, she went on, that the women comrades were a dull, serious bunch who did not share any of the thrill associated with the revolutionary lifestyle. She asked about the other women I had interviewed, how had they viewed what they did? I mentioned the longing that Leila Khaled had shown for her days of glory, and she nodded sympathetically:

"I am not saying that there were not times when what we did had its own sort of excitement. It was not continual excitement, but there was a heroic dimension to it. The main thing was that you felt you were able to influence the world about you, instead of experiencing it passively. It was this ability to make an impact on the reality of everyday life that was important, and obviously still is important."

I wondered how much more significant to women in an oppressive society was this feeling of being actively involved in changing the world. After all, at the time of Susanna's activities, Italian women were expected to be totally passive; the law allowing their husbands to beat them had only just been abolished.

Looking back, she considered that 1977 had been the best year for Prima Linea and the other revolutionary movements; 1978 was the beginning of the end. In March, ex-premier Aldo Moro was kidnapped and fifty-four days later murdered by the Red Brigades. There was intense public outrage, and those who had previously nurtured a sympathy for the revolutionaries began to see them as cold-blooded murderers. Many who had eagerly joined in the street demonstrations of 1977 abandoned revolutionary ideals, leaving the underground fighters more isolated than ever, and inside the groups themselves the comrades argued fiercely over whether Moro should have been killed.

As the year progressed, the war between the state and the revolutionaries intensified, with both Prima Linea and the Red Brigades deciding that they needed better weaponry than their small handguns to continue the fight. Prima Linea bought around fifteen AK-47s and two Soviet missile launchers, a consignment that came from Lebanon and that cost the group about 100 million lire. In order to finance their purchases dozens of bank robberies were carried out; but when the shipment arrived the guns had been ruined by salt water. Hardly any of the costly weapons were ever used and most were buried in the ground or hidden in cellars where they were discovered years later. The quantity of bank robberies had resulted in many arrests, and many of those captured militants had begun to talk.

Susanna recalled the terror of those days; the disintegration of the group she had come to see as her family, the sense of alienation from the masses: "There was a hemorrhage of militants and a great disenchantment; we began to ask ourselves, 'Where are we going, what are we doing?' But the waves of arrests did not give us time to think. For some time before, I had been living only in the present; the past justified what I was doing, and the future was a time I could not live. Now, suddenly even the present seemed impossible, a time in which we could no longer exist."

I asked her whether she had felt trapped and resentful toward the movement that had made her life so difficult. She had not. Such feelings would have been impossible for her; the movement to her was like her baby: "I think it is possible that other people felt that way, but I was one of the founders, a leader, and I was in a position of responsibility. I do not think I could have felt resentful because I had made the choice that had led to the position I was in."

Her chief solace became Sergio Segio ("he became the core of my life"), a man who was a joint founder of Prima Linea, although the two only met for the first time during 1978. Susanna recognized that her feelings for Segio were much deeper than for any of her previous lovers. She commented: "This was the first time in which I tried to build a relationship that might last, that might endure difficulties." They lived together and ran the organization together.

In 1979 Susanna was involved in the murders of three men in Turin—a prison guard, a bar owner suspected of being an informant, and the director of the Fiat motor car company. She was also held responsible for two killings the next year: a former militant accused of betrayal, and the director of a chemical firm that was guilty of releasing poisonous gases over the town of Seveso in northern Italy. It is not known whether she and Segio committed their crimes together, but they were both considered to have planned the killing of two judges in 1979. When four years later they stood in the dock to receive their life sentences, they had just become man and wife, the marriage ceremony having been conducted in prison.

The relationship survived in spite of a fundamental change of heart by Segio, just before Susanna was arrested. He felt it was pointless to continue with Prima Linea and decided to leave. He wanted his girlfriend to quit, too, but she refused, feeling that she owed greater loyalty to the group than to her lover. Her feelings toward Prima Linea were similar to those of the traditional mother to its child: she had to protect it, particularly when it was in danger.

Her decision resulted in a heated discussion at the end of which he left, and she chose to stay. "For me this choice was partly political, and in part due to emotion: for me it had been a group experience, one in which I had personally been involved from the very beginning and had helped build up, so I did not feel like abandoning it. Sergio still reproaches me a lot about this decision; he said it showed a lack of clearheadedness. But it was a choice related to the experience of my life."

Three months later, in December 1980, Susanna was arrested in Florence. She was asleep when the police broke into her hideout in the middle of the night and dragged her from her bed. She was given a few slaps ("nothing too heavy-handed") and then taken to a police station where, because of a lack of high-security cells, an office was cleared out especially for her. She spent five days handcuffed to a chair during the day and a cot at night; she recalled feeling very exposed because her hands were always locked behind her, and she had nothing to protect herself with. "I was lucky; they could not really beat me because I was due in court so soon," she explained.

She was remanded in custody to a series of women's prisons and pointed out that she had learned a lot about how violent women could be from the warders. "Here is another aspect to women and violence," she said. "The female prison warders had no difficulty using violence. In fact, the violence shown to us by the women guards was much worse than that of the male warders." The ETA women had said something along the same lines; that they had found the women torturers worse than the men. Susanna also expressed disgust, as the Basque women had done, at the way these women could be violent to other women.

"The women used violence neutrally, as a type of control, and the amount they used, just doing a normal job, showed what truly violent people they were.

"We were searched. I had to stand naked and one wardress would search me physically, and the others would stand around and make comments. It was much worse than if it had been done by men. If men had done such a thing and acted in such a way, you would accept it, it would be logical. But it was difficult to accept women behaving in such a way toward women.

"I suppose there was more violence shown toward us than towards ordinary prisoners because we behaved in a different way to the other inmates. We were haughty and stood apart; we did not fit into what these women expected from prisoners. We had a completely different way of looking at things and came from a different background and culture to the wardresses, most of whom only had a primary school education.

"In the male prisons there was a military way of doing things. The prisoners were kicked, but that was expected; there were definite rules. But the female prisons were more subtle: you got kicked one day but the next the wardresses would try to be nice to you."

Susanna was put on trial in Turin, accused of several murders. Through the barred cage in which terrorists are tried in Italy, she managed to communicate via intermediaries with Segio. He told her that he was going to get her out; he had a plan, the details of which he passed onto her. She could hardly believe it: "The hope of escape, by Sergio, made my life worth living. Most of my waking hours were spent checking the changing of the guards and observing the weak points, to see how it was going to be possible. I used to cling to the prison windows, trying to figure out how he was going to rescue me. At first, I kept the secret to myself; then I told two other comrades.

"Outside, Sergio was planning every detail. I was very moved because he had left Prima Linea, but he came back for me." Her eyes were shining; I asked whether she saw him in the role of the knight rescuing his lady in distress. She laughed. "Obviously there was some political point behind it, but it was much more an act of love.

"He sent me a package of books with a message inside. On the day of the escape, he was going to send me a bunch of roses. I never actually got them, but I was told that they had arrived, so I and the two other women knew it was the day. While we were out in the courtyard during exercise, we went to the exterior wall and waited. We heard the explosion and started to run through the hole that had been blown in the wall.

"It was one of the best moments of my life, to escape the prison in that way." She did not know until she listened to the news that someone had been killed, and it was then that she insisted an apology should be made to the dead man's relatives.

She and Segio, now truly a Bonnie and Clyde couple, fled to Venice, the city she knew and loved best. Almost immediately, the two other women who had escaped with her were recaptured, but Susanna was to spend ten months as a fugitive until someone tipped off the authorities as to her whereabouts.

She referred to those months as a time of desperation. No one seemed to believe in the armed struggle anymore, so many comrades had been arrested and many more had fled abroad. Susanna, though, rejected such a solution for herself: her emotional bond to the group went far too deep. "I was not that lucid," she admitted. "I felt too torn by duty and sentiment to leave everything. I was always saying, 'No, we can't do that.' " She and four or five others managed to keep the group together. She remembered herself and another female comrade laughing over the fact that now most of the men had been imprisoned; it was time for the women to take over; traditionally this was their opportunity, when in war women were allowed to fight. But they had been fighting for a long time and few had the spirit to continue. There were virtually no actions.

Susanna wanted to rescue the comrades she had left behind in prison; indeed, she felt "a great emotional burden" to do so, but no one dared to carry out such a venture with the police net tightening around them. There was the added fear of what would happen if they were captured again, because stories were coming out of the prisons of systematic torture being practiced on their comrades. The diminished band spent hours debating how they would cope personally with such brutality. Then one comrade committed suicide, and the group's morale sunk even lower.

Susanna was in a far worse emotional condition than most of her friends. Just before her escape she had learned that her mother was seriously ill with cancer. She could not risk visiting her as she knew she would be recaptured, but her failure to do so still haunts her today. "It is something I find very difficult to talk about because I loved my mother so much and wanted to see her, but dared not. I felt I was dealing her such a cruel blow."

In October 1982, as she sat having a drink in a bar in Milan, she was rearrested. She braced herself to resist the torture, but found that she was treated kindly by her captors. Gently they told her that her mother had died two months earlier. "I was in a terrible state when I heard that news, and I was also in despair over Sergio. For the second time I was inside, and he was out there without me. I was very scared for him and wondered constantly what he would do." Three months later Segio was arrested, too, after he had apparently exposed himself to needless risk, as if he no longer cared for his own safety. Perhaps with Susanna gone, he did not; the couple by this time certainly seemed to need each other in order to carry on. She commented, "It was as if he had grown fundamentally tired."

Later that year they were married in prison while standing trial for murder. The ceremony lasted two and a half minutes exactly, she recalled, and was conducted by the councilor of traffic, or senior traffic official, in Florence. She laughed. "I think I was the only bride who has had her honeymoon in reverse, because from the women's prison to the men's prison the road was too narrow for the armored vehicles to do a U-turn. This meant that the driver had to drive in reverse, while I just sat there clutching my little bunch of flowers."

I suggested that it seemed out of character for her to commit such a bourgeois act as marriage. She looked a little embarrassed and hastened to explain: "There were two things. One was that at that time in 1983 it was very difficult to have any kind of meetings in prison with someone unless they were your husband. Secondly, the marriage was a kind of reaffirmation of our relationship, which we probably wouldn't have felt we needed if we had not been in prison. It was a source of comfort to us in the isolation of prison to know that we were married."

She spent the first year or so of her second imprisonment dreaming of escape and being infuriated by her comrades in the adjoining cells. These women over whose freedom she had agonized in her ten months on the run seemed concerned with just one thing—how to have babies in prison. "I had been worrying about these people, how to get them out, and that is all they could talk about. I don't have anything against babies, but I didn't want one, and I felt like a stranger for some time."

For three years Susanna was moved around Italy to stand trial in Naples, Padua, Turin, Milan, and Florence. She joked that the only occasion she was not in a courtroom was at Christmas and bank holidays. Slowly she began to question her commitment to the armed struggle, and over the course of twelve months she became "dissociated." For her, who had given up so much for the cause, it was a time of personal crisis.

"It was a very painful process for me; life and militancy were so much intertwined. It was not just a case of making a simple decision. I suffered a great deal trying to separate myself from what I had done and believed in. Sometimes I felt so bad that I did not think I could hold myself together any longer; I thought I would crack.

"Now I have, to an extent, worked it out, but I am not one of those people, and there are some who say, 'We were mad. I have woken up from that nightmare and realize how crazy we all were.' I don't believe that. I believe that we were part of a culture that thought we should reconstruct another political identity and in the context of the times, violence had its part to play. It had a logic then. I am not saying that what we did was wonderful, but I do not think it is right to deny everything that happened and pretend that past doesn't exist. I see what I have gone through as a process of growing out of the way of thinking that I had then, that particular political identity. It was not a case of black one day and white the next.

"There are things that I would much rather not have done, particularly actions involving people, and of course my other big regret is not visiting my mother. But I do not regret that I worked and struggled for a principle." To do that would be denying her whole self, and yet she did feel guilt: "Where people were hurt . . . having hurt them it is something obviously I cannot undo. I caused great suffering to people—I regret that."

Had she, I asked, received any psychiatric counseling? She giggled. "In Italian prisons you are obliged to meet a psychologist every now and then. But the woman I have talked to occasionally treats me very much on an equal footing. She does not attempt to psychoanalyze me, and she has found me quite normal!"

Susanna also denied that her past violence had created any barrier between herself and other women. No, there was no awkwardness, no difficulty, she insisted. In fact, her closest friends were the ones she met here, in the center. "I don't think I am any different to anyone else," she said softly.

That was really the tragedy of her: that she appeared to be so like everybody else and yet could never be. I felt pity for her, while at the same time reminding myself that she had killed and injured so many people. She was such an intelligent woman, yet she had wrecked her own life and the lives of countless others. If she had chosen differently she could have done so much good; it seemed a waste. However, she clearly did not want pity.

Segio would be arriving soon for their hour together, and she was becoming slightly restless. Did she envisage a time when they would both be out of prison, living the quiet life of an elderly couple? She found the idea amusing: "It's almost impossible in prison to think more than one month ahead, let alone so far into the future. I mean, it is difficult to imagine that when we get out we will not be involved in something, but I do not know what that will be. It is hard enough just living at the moment."

Chapter 7

GERMAN WOMEN AND VIOLENCE

"They have to become better than men."

I happened to be interviewing the director of Hamburg's intelligence gathering network on terrorist activities, when a statement arrived from the Red Army Faction (RAF), Germany's most notorious and feared revolutionary group. The communiqué claimed responsibility for the murder in a bomb explosion a week earlier of Alfred Herrhausen, chief executive of Deutsche Bank and one of the country's most powerful businessmen. Herr Christian Lochte, director of Hamburg's Office for the Protection of the Constitution (the equivalent of the British M15 or FBI) read it and sighed. "The same old thing, anti-capitalist," he said. Did he think that any women might have been involved in the killing, I asked.

He looked up in surprise. "But of course," he replied.

Of the eight people on Germany's current "Wanted Terrorists" poster, five are women. Friederike Krabbe, now aged forty-two, and a member of the Red Army Faction for many years, has been hunted since 1977. She is thought to have been involved in at least three murders, including that of Hanns-Martin Schleyer, an industrialist kidnapped and held captive for forty-three days before being killed. Ms. Krabbe wears a sort of Mona Lisa smile in her "wanted" photograph. Today, she is believed to be living either in Iraq or Lebanon.

Next to her is Barbara Meyer, one of the RAF hard core, and

married to another member, Horst Meyer, whose photograph is beside hers. Mrs. Meyer's first RAF action was in 1974, when she was involved in the murder of Berlin's senior judge. She was just nineteen years old and was described as having "the face of an angel." Eleven years later she and a male accomplice shot dead a German industrialist. Mrs. Meyer had lured their victim to his front door by pretending to deliver a letter that needed his signature.

On the top row is Andrea Klump. She was suspected of leading a young American soldier to his death in 1985 in order to obtain his identity card. It is believed that the card was then used by an RAF commando to gain access to a U.S. military base, where a bomb exploded, killing two and injuring sixteen. In 1988, Ms. Klump took part in a shoot-out with Spanish police after she and two men had left a bomb (containing eleven pounds of iron nails) at a disco frequented by American soldiers. It seems that she was the most coolheaded of the RAF unit when it came under fire; she hijacked a camper van belonging to an English couple and took them hostage, thus ensuring her own escape and that of her comrades.

All these people, warns the poster, are likely to be armed, and there is reward on each of their heads for 50,000 DM (about $32,000).

There are so many women who have chosen the path of revolutionary violence in Germany that one is really spoiled for choice in selecting a few to concentrate on. Women form about 50 percent of the current RAF membership and around 80 percent of the group's supporters. Traditionally, new commandos are drawn from the pool of supporters, so it is possible that women may in future years dominate the RAF even more.

It is not just in the ranks of the RAF that women abound; they also feature in the revolutionary cells and until recently there was a group called Red Zora, which was more or less exclusively female and bombed sexist targets. Women have also been members of neo-fascist groups: in 1980 a young woman was sentenced to life imprisonment for the murder of two Vietnamese boat people.

Why should German women, in particular, be so drawn to causes that espouse violence? Is it part of the national psyche? Or have they got more to be angry about?

The head of the country's anti-terrorist squad, a white-haired gentleman with a goatee beard, attributed it to the advanced state of emancipation among his countrywomen: "German women are more liberated and more self-aware than Italian and French women; the Italians still have the image of the woman as the mama. One could say that the emancipation of women is not so advanced in France, Italy, and Britain as it is in Germany, and that is why there are fewer women terrorists in those countries."

German women have thrown off the shackles of the traditional woman in society and have realized that there is no reason why they should not be violent. They were several steps ahead of, for example, the ETA women, who admitted they had only just "stepped into the street."

Another man, a former leader of yet another revolutionary German group, seriously believed that women in his country had been influenced by SCUM, the Society for Cutting Up Men. SCUM was the idea of an American woman who shot Andy Warhol. In the German guerrilla circles of the late 1960s the idea was very popular, particularly among the women. The theory was that, as men had created the problems of the world, they should be killed off. Michael "Bommi" Baumann recalled the reaction of his female comrades to SCUM: "They said the left was as bad as the right in exploiting women. A lot of them thought SCUM was a good idea and said, 'Sure, let's do it. Yes, that's very reasonable; off we go. Cut off their pricks.' "

There are, however, no references to emasculated men littering the towns of Germany. The castration was metaphorical: the women intended to snatch the controlling reins of the revolutionary movement from the men's grasp. This they succeeded in doing.

Astrid Proll, an early member of the Baader-Meinhof gang (the original name for the Red Army Faction) and now a journalist, suggested another reason for the dominance in women in the German groups. She had been visiting a photographic exhibition of the Gestapo, where she saw plenty of examples of men in uniform, but no women. She commented: "That is one of the reasons why so many women joined the RAF." German revolutionary women were convinced that if they had had a voice during Hitler's time, many of the atrocities would not have happened. Their mothers had been excluded from the army, but they were determined that at last they would have a military role to play in overthrowing the German state.

Astrid Proll's suggestion did seem to suggest that German women had more to be angry about, and that their anger might be part of a national guilt complex. She appeared to be closer to the truth than blaming the phenomenon on an increase in feminism.

Whatever the reasons might be, one of the consequences of the numbers of female revolutionaries is that no one in Germany seems to raise an eyebrow when a woman, or several of them, participates in a terrorist action. This is reflected in the country's newspapers, which do not, as a whole, revel in descriptions of "gun girls," or ask, "How could a woman do this?" It is too normal an occurrence for journalists to pay much heed.

The head of the anti-terrorist squad commented: "I think the way in which the British press treats similar attacks says more about your society's attitude to women than anything else." He might well be right, but it also should be pointed out that German journalists have grown weary of exclaiming over women revolutionaries. There is little more that the German media could say on the subject.

Back in the early seventies, in the Baader-Meinhof heyday, there were certainly shrieking headlines asking how could a woman do this. Most shocking was just who Meinhof was: a society journalist and a household name who had abandoned her twin daughters for the life of an outlaw. To the police and to the media, she was credited with being joint-leader of the group; in fact she had a dog's life.

Like the Italian revolutionary Susanna Ronconi, Ulrike Meinhof craved love, comradeship, and emotional support from her comrades. Such qualities were sadly lacking in the group. Andreas Baader, a rather nasty chauvinist who called all women "cunts," particularly seemed to hate Ulrike. He screamed and swore at her, belittling her for her technical clumsiness and condemning her for "over-intellectualizing." Far from being a leader, Ulrike was the whipping boy.

Her decision to join the revolutionaries was not out of love or respect for Baader, nor the result of strongly held feminist views. A couple of years previously, she had interviewed Baader's girlfriend, Gudrun Ensslin, who was serving a prison sentence for arson on some department stores. She had been deeply impressed by the young woman, who seemed to share her own political views on the corruption of society, but unlike herself had done something about it.

Her childhood and adolescence had been disturbed. Her father had died when she was six years old, and she and her older sister had been brought up by their mother, who also died when Ulrike was fifteen. A woman friend who had lived with the family for several years became her substitute mother and, later, a close friend.

Ulrike studied education and psychology in the university, and it was here that she became involved in politics. Her views on social injustices and the nuclear issue were at first very much linked to her deep Christian faith: she was remembered at the university for saying grace before meals in the dining hall. She was elected spokeswomen of the student's branch of the Social Democratic Party, and it was felt by many who knew her at the time that she had a great career ahead of her in politics.

Her first job, though, was with a left-wing literary magazine called *Konkret*, and it was here that she met her husband, one of its editors. She became a columnist for the magazine and quite a celebrity in the media world; it was fashionable to have Ulrike Meinhof as a guest at your party. After interviewing Gudrun Ensslin, she became sympathetic to the young woman's cause and through her met Andreas Baader. Although part of her longed to join them, she had her twin daughters, then aged seven, to consider. She finally took the plunge after helping to free Baader from jail, an escape planned and led by Gudrun.

Gudrun was once described as the soul of the Baader-Meinhof group, with Ulrike as its head and Baader as its engine. She was a young woman of passionately held beliefs, who inspired others. Bommi Baumann, who knew and liked her, said, "You just didn't say no to Gudrun."

She was the daughter of a pastor, who throughout her childhood and adolescence was, like Ulrike, a dedicated Christian. She continued reading the Protestant Girl's Club paper, *Be Armed for the Day*, until she was twenty-two years old.

In the university, where she read educational theory, German and English, she met and became engaged to a fellow student. She was extremely active in left-wing student politics, and when she had a baby by her fiancé, she took her little son with her on demonstrations. In the mid-sixties, she went to Berlin to study for a second degree, and there she met Andreas Baader. Until this point, although she had become known as one of the students' most politically aware radicals, she had not been involved in any violent action. Shortly afterward, she also abandoned her son, then aged eleven months, and moved in with Baader.

The couple became inseparable, she delighting in his dedication and longing for violent action, he admiring her grasp of political knowledge.

Baader seems to have been, by most accounts, a rather unpleasant character, ill-versed and little interested in revolutionary ideals, and far more concerned with action than debate. His father had died when he was a toddler, and the young Andreas had been reared by his mother, aunt, and grandmother, who had spoiled him. He had rebelled from an early age, been expelled from several schools, where he was considered intelligent but lazy, and had already served prison sentences by the time he met Gudrun in Berlin. He seemed to delight in telling stories and being the center of attention—at times he regaled his audience with his illustrious past: how he was descended from a famous Baader who was a philosopher, and how he himself had challenged international philosophers when he was a boy of sixteen. On other occasions, he bragged that he was an expert burglar and car thief. He wore makeup and perfume and took pleasure in baiting homosexuals, only to turn viciously on them when they showed an interest. He particularly liked to shock people; his slogan was "Don't argue. Destroy."

Although he referred to Gudrun, as to all women, as a cunt, she called him "Baby." When Baader raved at his comrades (as he frequently did until at times he foamed at the mouth), Gudrun was always there to mop up the mess.

She seemed to have little sympathy or time for Ulrike and joined Baader in ridiculing the journalist in front of other comrades. When Ulrike spoke of her concern for her abandoned ten-year-old daughters, Gudrun would airily say how she too had abandoned a child. Later on, Gudrun arranged for the Meinhof twins to be taken to a Palestinian orphanage camp in Jordan, and Ulrike seems to have concurred with this decision. The twins' father just managed to rescue the girls en route.

However annoying and bourgeois Gudrun and Baader found Ulrike, it was excellent for propaganda purposes to have in the ranks a woman who was a household name.

Around these three revolved at different times twenty to thirty others, at least half of whom were women. When Baader was arrested Gudrun and the other women followers planned and executed his escape from prison. Gudrun had included one man in the rescue party, but he unfortunately panicked and shot a prison guard. When Baader was freed it seems he did not waste any congratulations or thanks on the women; it was the marksman whom he clapped on the shoulder.

The freeing of Baader in May 1970 heralded the birth of the Baader-Meinhof group, whose aim was ultimately to achieve world revolution, and an overthrow of capitalism to be replaced by a Marxist society. Particularly singled out for targets were American bases in Germany as a protest against the Vietnam War, and the police and judges as upholders of a corrupt consumer society. The membership also wanted to expose West Germany as still very much a Nazi-run state, believing that many of those in authority were former members of the party. The group's motto, or one of them, was "to destroy the thing that destroys you."

In their first twelve months, they carried out bank robberies, stole cars, and broke into government buildings to obtain false papers. The group had a particular predilection for BMWs, and in time the car became known as the "Baader-Meinhof Wagen." The best driver among them was Astrid Proll, who later fled to England, and was arrested there.

Many of the offenses were carried out by women; in the early seventies the police always knew when a bank raid had been perpetrated by Baader-Meinhof because witnesses would report that some of the robbers were women. Gudrun, it seemed, was the group's purse holder and account keeper, while Ulrike found flats for the comrades, drawing heavily on her circle of friends and acquaintances.

The more I learned about the Baader-Meinhof group, the more it seemed that the women had been the key players. I asked Bommi Baumann, who had known most of them, if this was the case. He grinned a little ruefully: "To tell the truth, the RAF women could have done it on their own. But many of them were already in couples when they joined."

Initially, the group enjoyed considerable support from a wide range of individuals. "German society then was totally frozen," explained Bommi. "Just look at the people who got caught for hiding us, giving us their apartments. Some of them were highly respected professionals, capitalists. It would have been possible that Herrhausen, who was killed by this generation of the RAF, would have given us a donation. Lots of people like him were involved; even the bourgeoisie. Everyone felt as we did: that something had to change." The group's members were viewed as modern-day Robin Hoods or, as Astrid Proll once put it, "You have got to remember that we were very well-armed social workers."

In the group's second year of existence, however, its actions changed, and many supporters fell away. Baader-Meinhof had launched a bombing campaign in the course of which four American soldiers were killed and over forty people were injured, including civilians. Public sympathy evaporated, and after a huge police hunt most of the gang's active members were caught.

It was not the end of the group—far from it. From inside their jails, they continued to organize their comrades through the offices of sympathetic lawyers. Then the "second generation" of the RAF was born, young people mainly drawn from a group called "Red Aid," which had been set up to protest conditions the prisoners were being kept in.

Again, women played a major role. Inge Viett, who was to go on to become one of the leading lights in the movement, allegedly took part in the murder of a Berlin judge in 1974, along with Barbara Meyer and another woman. Ms. Viett had been trained in guerrilla warfare in the Middle East and, when she was captured in 1975, had no intention of languishing in jail. She and three other women escaped by sawing through the prison bars, and she took refuge in France. She apparently used her time there to help reactivate a French revolutionary group, Action Directe. They later drew up a plan of joint attack with the RAF, choosing NATO as their main target.

Other women had carried on the fight for the prisoners in her absence. On the day that the Baader-Meinhof trial was supposed to begin, six people stormed the German embassy in Stockholm, demanding the release of the defendants. Hanna-Elise Krabbe, older sister of Friederike, guarded the hostages with a submachine gun while her colleague planted explosives. Four people died, including two of the terrorists, and the building was recaptured by the police.

The trial went ahead, with the prisoners all placed together on one floor of Stammheim prison, next to the courthouse. Arguments broke out among them, and Ulrike Meinhof found herself increasingly isolated and taunted by Gudrun and Baader. The final straw came when Gudrun told the court that the RAF had not been responsible for one of the bombing attacks (on a publishing house in which seventeen workers had been injured). Ulrike had masterminded this incident and, four days later, she was found hanged in her cell.

The new RAF knew nothing of the bullying that had been going on in the prison; to them, Ulrike Meinhof's death was not suicide but murder committed with the knowledge of the authorities. In retaliation they murdered the federal prosecutor general.

The verdicts—life sentences—for the people they idealized only made the new RAF commandos more determined to gain their comrades' release. They decided to kidnap a prominent business-man and hold him hostage. Among the candidates on the kidnap list was the head of the Dresdner Bank, not least because one of the commandos had close family ties with the man. Susanne Albrecht had known the Pontos for many years—indeed Jurgen Ponto was her sister's godfather. The Albrecht parents were old friends of the banker's and his family, and to Susanne he was "Uncle Jurgen"; she had even stayed overnight at their home. For several years, Su-sanne had worried her parents: she had become a university drop-out after meeting a young man who was in an RAF cell. He had introduced her to the RAF circle, and when Ponto's name was suggested, she became the most crucial member in the group. It was decided that she should go home to her parents and arrange a visit to Ponto's house.

To Herr Albrecht, a maritime lawyer, and his wife, it was the return of the prodigal daughter. Susanne appeared to be a reformed character: she was pleasant, calm, and, as her mother afterward recalled, was quite happy to sit knitting in the evenings. A few days after her return home she mentioned that she would like to continue her interrupted studies at Frankfurt, where the Pontos lived. Su-sanne told her parents that there was a very good language school there that she wished to attend. Her parents were only too pleased to call Ponto on her behalf and arrange for her to meet him.

On the appointed day, Jurgen Ponto and his wife were sitting on the sun terrace when the doorbell rang. Over the intercom came a voice: "It's Susanne."

She had brought two friends, a young man and a girl, and they presented Ponto with a bunch of flowers. He left them talking to his wife while he went to fetch a vase. The young man followed, suddenly drew a pistol and aimed it at him. The two men strug-gled, the gun went off, bringing Susanne's companion running into the room. She fired five shots at Ponto, three into his head; he died that night. The communiqué claiming responsibility for his death jeered: ". . . we didn't realize clearly enough how powerless such characters, who set off wars in the third world and wipe out whole nations, are in the face of violence when it confronts them in their own homes." It was signed, "Susanne Albrecht, RAF commando."

This action did cause particular outrage. That a woman who was virtually a relative of a target could use that relationship to gain entry to his home, bringing his killers with her, seemed beyond the bounds of human decency.

However many headlines the Ponto murder had created, the fact remained that it was an action that had failed. The new RAF generation, whose core consisted of five women and five men, still needed to kidnap a prominent person. The next target they chose was Dr. Hanns-Martin Schleyer, president of the Employer's Association and of the Federation of German Industry. He was a difficult target, as he knew he was on the kidnap list, and had a retinue of bodyguards. But as he was being driven to work one day, a young woman pushed a pram in front of his car, and his chauffeur slammed on the brakes. The other members of the RAF commando shot dead the chauffeur and bodyguards and dragged Schleyer to a waiting van. He was held captive for forty-three days, then killed.

Earlier on the same morning, the bodies of Gudrun Ensslin, Andreas Baader, and another Baader-Meinhof member were found in their cells. There was speculation that they had been murdered, but it is far more likely they died by their own hands as part of a suicide pact.

Their successors have carried out twenty-one major actions, including bombings and assassinations and are, according to the German anti-terrorist squad, "the best organized and most important group in western Europe." The current RAF generation, the fifth, has learned from the mistakes of its predecessors and spends many months planning an attack. In June 1990, a commando came close to kiling the head of the Federal police force; and in April 1991 the group succeeded in assassinating the chairman of the agency responsible for de-nationalizing state-owned firms in the former East Germany.

The German authorities do not know if those people on the wanted poster are still carrying out such attacks, or if there is now a new RAF network whose identities are as yet unknown. What is known is that the "hard core" numbers only ten to twenty people, at least half of whom, it is confidently believed, are women.

The name of Astrid Proll is well known in Britain because she lived as a fugitive in London for four years before being arrested. When she was finally discovered, she was public enemy number one; she was wanted in Germany on charges of attempted murder of two policemen. A floor in Brixton prison was cleared for her; shifts of prison guards were changed regularly to ensure maximum security, and at her court hearings, marksmen encircled the buildings and streets. She was extradited to Germany but the charges were dropped.

In 1987, after being a free woman in Germany for several years, she applied to the Home Office for permission to visit Britain. She was turned down three times; the authorities considering that her past made her still too dangerous a woman to be allowed in. She finally won on appeal and now is free to visit friends, but she has never been permitted to enter the United States to see her mother.

The myth of the terrorist woman clings to her, and probably always will. The fact that the charges of attempted murder were dropped by the German courts after it was discovered that the two policemen had fabricated the evidence against her, does not seem to matter. Once a "gun girl," as the British press called her, always a gun girl.

She actually did not do very much. She was a member of Baader-Meinhof for a year—the first year, when they drove around in fast cars, robbed banks, and were popular heroes. She was arrested before the violence escalated into bombings and murder. Yet her year with the group has done more than make her notorious and a persona non grata; it has scarred her emotionally.

When I first met her in the office where she now works as picture editor for a magazine in Hamburg, she was charming and assured me that she had "no barriers in talking about it." The interview we had later was a trifle hurried and squeezed into her extended lunch hour, but she said she had no objection to me coming back to talk to her again. A day and a time were fixed, but between these meetings the RAF killed Herr Herrhausen. It shook her; she had thought the RAF had ceased to be (there had been no major attacks for three years), but she still agreed to see me. However, when I arrived in Hamburg and called her, she had changed her mind. "Your questions are strangling me," she cried. "I can't talk about it."

Bommi Baumann, one of her closest friends, who has served two prison sentences for terrorist activities (he made bombs), informed me that she had been so distressed at Herrhausen's death that she had decided never to talk about her past again. He supplied some of the information about her.

She had been nineteen years old when she met Gudrun and Baader in Berlin in the late sixties. She was studying photography, but much of her time was spent participating in the protest movements that had originated in America, then swept through Europe.

The protests were chiefly against the Vietnam War, the atom bomb, and, in West Germany, the presence of American troops. Berlin was one of the centers in Germany for demonstrations and debate; the city had a large population of students and radicals, who could live cheaply in the plentiful supply of large empty buildings, many still in a state of disrepair from the war. There were several communes, drugs were consumed, and those who wished to do so could enjoy a Bohemian lifestyle.

Astrid Proll was a dedicated young woman, often seen in demonstrations. She was also committed to a new protest movement— women's rights. She lived in a women-only commune in Berlin with two other women who were, like her, later to join the faces on the "Wanted Terrorists" posters. The three were part of a women's subculture growing in Berlin at the time. They called themselves, not without some humor, the "Militant Black Panther Aunties." Astrid developed through feminism to revolutionary violence in a similar way to Susanna Ronconi.

According to Bommi, the Aunties were a pretty hair-raising bunch. "They ran around, stealing like mad, stealing for the sake of it. They had no interest in the things they took, and didn't keep them. They were 'domestic hash rebels,' and a lot of LSD was taken, too. They went around saying they had no possessions, not even their clothes were their own. 'We only have hashish,' they said. 'If the police come, then we get violent.' "

Women's rights, he added, were treated very seriously in those days, and male guerrillas, mindful of SCUM, accorded their female comrades considerable respect. Besides, there were so many things that the women could do that the men could not: "Women can get closer to the target. If a man in a high position, perhaps knowing that he may be a target for terrorists, is approached by a woman, he may think, She is a prostitute. Women can go straight to the target's doorstep; sometimes they do it in pairs, two women, saying they are lost. If two men approached him, he would be suspicious."

Bommi was a leader of a revolutionary group known as "The Second of June Movement," which was overshadowed by Baader-Meinhof, although it was responsible for a number of killings and attacks. He described how Berlin at that time was a "melting pot" of ideas and revolutionary anger, which were poured forth at certain bars in the city. It was at one of these bars that Bommi met Gudrun and Baader. He was most impressed by the young woman, but considered Baader a horror. "He was aggressive, rude, and not very intellectual. He ranted all day. Gudrun, of course, well, she had a very high opinion of him, but by some miracle, Astrid liked him too."

Several other young women who were dedicated feminists also joined Baader's group; how did they react to being called cunts?

Bommi shrugged: "He was screaming around the whole day; you just ignored him. Anyway, Gudrun was always there, behind him, to clean up his shit.

"All the women involved in the group were quite intelligent. I mean, they were not the normal sort of girl you would meet on the dance floor. They were pretty interested in technical things. Inge Viett, for instance; she was fantastic at repairing cars, and Astrid was the best driver, and good at mechanics. They were all pretty male-dominated; I mean they had male characteristics.

"Gudrun was really good at finances and organizing; she kept everything together. Astrid got involved when Gudrun was canvassing for people to help spring Baader out of prison. I don't know, she had this way of talking to people. She was an extremely intelligent woman; very into it, fanatical, and she could talk."

The interview I had with Astrid took place in a bar near her work. I had contacted her through another journalist who was a friend of hers, and she had agreed readily enough to an interview. She liked the British, she said. Her office was open-plan and not the best place; she took me in her car to the bar.

She was in her middle forties, with a rather caved-in appearance, reminding me slightly of Alazne, the ETA woman who had suffered so much. But Astrid seemed very much in control of herself, and the situation; it was only later that I realized how disturbing she found her past. She appeared relaxed as she described the conditions that had led to the birth of Baader-Meinhof.

"It had a lot to do with the postwar conditions in West Germany. We, the young generation, decided that we would never participate or keep quiet about something that was bad in society, as our parents had done. We hated our parents because they were former Nazis, who had never come clean about their past.

"The Nazism had never been acknowledged; there had been no

time to mourn. In the fifties there was the cold war; in the sixties, the cultural upheaval. We grew up with the American culture and their army sitting here, as the occupiers. It began with student protests. At the time we felt that the state was the oppressor, and that we had the right to use violence because we were the state's victims. But of course they managed to turn it around, so that we became the guilty ones and society the victims.

"After the war, a lot of Nazis went straight into business again. They were everywhere—every second person was a Nazi, and they held powerful jobs in business and in the judiciary; the Nazis just continued their careers. At the height of the RAF, there were, I suppose, twenty to thirty activists, and there was a lot of sympathy for us because everyone knew someone who was either involved or supported people who did. It was something that everyone felt they had a responsibility to resolve."

She had been born in Kassel, near the border of what was then East Germany, in 1947. Her brother, Thorwald, was six years her elder, and their father was an architect. When Astrid was a young teenager, their parents were divorced, and custody was awarded to their father; their mother, the court ruled, had, by leaving them, not "properly attended to her parental duties." Here was another example of a woman who had lost a parent at an early age, and who then had chosen a violent path.

Thorwald was already in Berlin studying art at the Free University when Astrid arrived to start her course in photography. Both she and Thorwald lived in communes and frequented the radical bars. When she first met Baader, she thought him "a cocky youth," but one who had charisma. "He convinced me that armed struggle was the way to bring about a new age."

In 1968 Thorwald joined Gudrun and Baader in their first "action against the state"—setting fire to department stores in Frankfurt, in protest of the Vietnam War. The three were immediately arrested and sentenced to three years in prison; but after a year they were released on bail, pending appeal. The appeal was rejected, and the three arsonists went on the run to Paris.

From a hideout in the city, Baader telephoned Astrid and told her to bring him books, papers, and his Mercedes. She was delighted to join the runaways. She smiled rather sadly: "You must understand that then the most fantastic thing in the world was not to be a rock star but a revolutionary." She clearly had enjoyed this first stage of the outlaw life; it was exciting, rebellious, and fun. She loved driving and fast cars, and the prospect of going underground with fugitives was exciting.

When she joined her brother and the others in Paris they went on a spending spree, eating huge meals at restaurants and taking photographs of each other. Thorwald estimated that in just two days they went through about $700. They disagreed about what to do next: Astrid wanted to go the Middle East and be trained in the Palestinian guerrilla camps; whereas Gudrun thought it better to lie low for a while. The forceful Gudrun won. Astrid was sent off to Amsterdam to buy false papers and passports, and with these the group decided to go to Italy.

Any thought that Astrid was involved just because of her brother's influence was dispelled at this juncture. Baader had decreed that Thorwald was not made of revolutionary material, and that he should be dumped by the others. His sister agreed, and the three left him waiting by a fountain until he realized the truth. He went back to Germany, served his sentence, and got out of the revolution. Today he is a married man with children. I asked Bommi why Thorwald had not warned his younger sister to do likewise. Bommi shrugged. "Perhaps he did not get the chance." Astrid was a strong-minded woman, even at that age, and she wanted to be a revolutionary more than anything else in the world.

She drove the other two to Italy, where they stayed for several weeks with friends. During this time they decided that they had to return to Berlin to set up a military underground. Astrid and Baader stole a car in Rome, and she drove it back to Germany on her own, with Baader and Gudrun following a few days later. They began to select comrades for the struggle, occasionally meeting at the large home of the journalist who had interviewed Gudrun in prison, Ulrike Meinhof.

Two months later, Baader was arrested and sent back to prison; the women of the group planned his escape.

There were six of them. Astrid and another woman were to be the getaway drivers. Ulrike was to convince the prison authorities that she was writing a book on young offenders with Baader, and that they needed to do some research at a library near the prison. Two other women were to pretend to be doing research at the library, thus enabling them to open the door to Gudrun Ensslin, who would burst in with a gun to free her lover.

Guns were needed for the operation, and Astrid and another woman were dispatched to buy them at a bar frequented by right-wing extremists. They bought two pistols with silencers for about $900. Then there was a discussion among the women—Gudrun felt it was necessary to have at least one token man in their team. She selected a candidate with previous criminal convictions for the dramatic rescue that she would lead into the library. The plan worked perfectly, except the man mistook the loaded pistol in one hand for the air gun in the other and shot a guard. Baader was sprung from custody, and Ulrike's days of agonizing about leaving her children were over—now she was a fugitive from justice.

Astrid took part in several bank raids and burglaries on government buildings to obtain false papers; she was also an excellent car thief. As their actions increased, so did the police hunt for them. I asked her what it was like, being hunted as outlaws. Was she armed?

"We carried guns, but didn't think we'd ever hurt anyone. At first it was just a game; we were all very young. It was exciting, I suppose, because it was dangerous, but at the same time there was fear. We all felt that we had an existential quality to our lives; nobody knew what they were getting into. Sometimes the whole fight seemed to be between our small group and the big, political group that was part of the state. The press and the police were one hundred percent against us—a very typical German attitude."

She paused, then added quietly, "I will never be part of any group again." Groups, like the one she joined, ruined your life.

After seven months of raiding banks and stealing cars, over half the membership had been arrested. The women of the group, excluding Gudrun, tried to convince Baader that his policy of "hitting" banks in towns they did not know was dangerous—and likely to lead to more arrests. Baader screamed abuse at them, calling them cunts, for shouting at "their menfolk." It was, he yelled, what women's liberation had brought them to. It seems he felt threatened by all these extremely able women around him, realizing that they could do it on their own.

I wondered why he had allowed so many of them into his group if he saw them as such a threat to his own position, and then realized that with their practicality, technical expertise and stamina, he needed them.

Astrid inadvertently launched the biggest police hunt yet for her comrades. On a February night, she and a young man were stopped by two police officers in Frankfurt, who wanted to examine their identity papers. "They were trying to arrest me; I was with a friend and we escaped. They said I shot at two policemen, but I didn't even have a gun on me. No one was injured, and we got away, but they really framed me on those charges. I think they wanted to make our escape into a big thing because we had got away. I don't know why they made up the story—perhaps it was so that they could increase the money the security services got. Every different police organization in the country wanted to catch us; they all wanted the money, and to be the most important."

According to the police officers, although their stories differed even at her first trial, Astrid and the young man produced pistols and fired at them, before they both ran off. Unknown to the police officers, a counterintelligence man had also been following the pair, and he wrote a memo about the incident, saying that Astrid Proll did not produce a gun, nor had the young man fired his.

The memo, however, was not produced for eight years, and posters went up of Astrid Proll, warning that she was armed and dangerous. A few months later she was caught.

A gas station attendant at a garage in Hamburg recognized her from the wanted poster. He summoned the police, and although she tried to escape in the car, she was surrounded by armed officers and arrested. She was to spend nearly three years in prison, two of them before her trial. A few months after her arrest, the remaining members of the group were also picked up, and Ulrike Meinhof was sent to the same jail as Astrid. The two women were, however, kept totally separated, and each spent long periods in total isolation. Ulrike realized that her daily walk, accompanied by two prison guards, took her near Astrid's cell, and one day called out her name. After that, the guards always put on a vacuum cleaner or ran a bath so that the women could not communicate.

Astrid and the other prisoners were, for periods of several months, subjected to "acoustic isolation," a form of torture. "By the time of the trial, I was very ill. My nerves and blood circulation had given up. Very exceptionally, because of this breakdown, I was granted temporary release.

"I was sent to a clinic and had to report to the police, but knew that I had to get out. I could not have stood any more of those prison conditions, so I escaped from the clinic and went underground."

There was a network of sympathizers and supporters who spirited her out of the country to Italy, where she stayed for a couple of months—but she found their attempts to help suffocating; it seemed more like orders than helpful advice. "They told me exactly what to do. 'Do this, do that,' and they were trying to help, thinking they knew best, but they were running my life. I could have stayed in Italy but I did not feel at home there. In Italy, women are a certain type, and I would always have stood out."

Moreover, she felt after her three years as a terrorist prisoner that she somehow looked different from other people. "I felt special, a terrorist.

"The idea that you are special because you have been a special security prisoner, and therefore stand out from other people, is very difficult to shake. You feel that if anybody looks at you, they know you are a special security prisoner.

"The people who were sheltering me made lots of suggestions about where I should go next, but it was I who decided on England. I had never been there before, although I had visited America with my mother when I was young, so I knew the language. I also knew that London was full of tourists, and I thought it would be easy to hide there. I thought of Paris, too, but overall London seemed to be the best idea for me because I could understand the sort of society I was in and knew how to act.

"I thought I would go there, not to stay, but just for a bit. I had been given an address in London, and I went there. I was very needy; I felt very unsafe and insecure, very shaky. I felt desperately that I had to meet people who could support me. Gradually I met some that I could trust and began to feel a little better. It helped that I could read a newspaper. I was free to act for myself for the first time in a long time."

A few RAF sympathizers in London sheltered her for some months, and then she met a young man at a party who was prepared to marry her. They went through the ceremony, but afterward hardly saw each other again—even squatting in different houses in the East End of London. Technically, though, she was now Mrs. Anna Puttick. She explained: "My aims for marriage were very different from his or any other person's. The most important thing was that I would get somewhere where I could live without the pressure of using illegal papers." Her husband, Robin, left England two years later and went to a religious community in India, where she presumes he still is.

With her marriage document, she was able to obtain a national insurance card, and thus armed, could look for work. For five months she was a gardener, tending Clissold Park and London

Fields in Hackney, where she was squatting. Then she took a job as a fitter's mate in a toy factory before enrolling in a government training course in car mechanics. She also attended evening classes in welding twice a week at Hackney College and was well qualified for her next job—as a teacher in car mechanics at the North London Vehicle Repair Workshop. The workshop was funded by a government grant, and it was aimed at training the young and unemployed. "I felt very safe there," she recalled. "I enjoyed the work; I found it very therapeutic to be doing something so practical. When I was in prison in Germany I wanted so much to learn a trade, become an engineer—it was what I had dreamed of.

"But a lot of the kids on the training scheme nicked cars, and we had more and more policemen turning up to question them. I got very annoyed with the kids and tried to make them stop stealing. Usually a colleague dealt with the police, but they were already interested in me because they thought it was so strange that a woman should be working in a garage."

For several months, though, she remained undetected. Her colleagues remembered her as "a good lass," and someone who went out of her way to help people. She was a good mechanic, said one, who also remembered she was very much a "woman's libber"—even to the point of hoping that Margaret Thatcher would win the election, although Astrid appeared to be so left-wing. The only odd thing about her, the man continued, was that she was cagey about where she lived and would not give her address to the workshop manager. "I knew her as Anna, and I would say she knew nothing about violence. Some of the lads could be a bit rough, and if there was any trouble, I'd step in and help her out. She couldn't handle it."

When a book of the Baader-Meinhof gang, *Hitler's Children*, came out, some of her friends warned her that her photograph was in it and was a very good likeness. She was terrified: "I knew that if I was arrested again, nothing would mean anything anymore. I had had four years of peace to learn something in Britain. When I was arrested, I think one of the policemen who used to come to the workshop had identified me from the photograph in the book."

She was in the workshop when twelve plainclothes policemen stormed in. She was flung against a locker and searched, then taken to London's most security-intensive police station, Paddington Green. For a year she was kept in prison, fighting extradition to Germany, and the newspaper headlines eagerly followed her court appearances: ARMED POLICE WATCH AS TERROR GIRL CHATS TO FRIENDS FROM DOCK; MY HUSBAND DIDN'T KNOW WHO I WAS, SAYS ASTRID; HOW BRITAIN CHANGED ME, BY THE TERRORIST. And of course, there were many articles on her lesbianism.

Astrid remembered those days and shuddered. "I was taken to Brixton prison, where once more I was a top-security prisoner. I was isolated and watched all the time by two women guards. There was another Category-A woman prisoner brought in—it was terrible. The two of us were a sort of training ground for the guards because they had not had Category-A women at Brixton before. They had no special quarters for us, so they emptied the top floor in the men's prison. We had the whole place just for us two. There was a new crew of women warders every month, so nobody felt comfortable and everyone was on edge.

"I was made very aware once more that I was viewed as the most serious of criminals. The lawyer I had was very nice, but his face went white when he saw the charges that the police in Germany were bringing against me—attempted murder on two counts. At first I felt very lost, and all the friends and support I had in England did not seem to matter. To me, Germany was like one big prison—a place I never wanted to return to. I knew I was facing prison for the rest of my life."

She was doubly fearful about returning to Germany where a year before her friends had died at Stammheim, events she described as "terrible tragedies." The suspicion that the deaths had not been suicide but the work of the German security services played on her mind, and she was convinced that if she was extradited, she too would die, one way or another. As it turned out, she was freed almost immediately on her return to Germany, the court ruling that she had already served a long enough sentence for bank robbery and stealing documents. She smiled: "I think the Germans did that to astonish the English and show them how good they were.

"But the RAF had already shown, by the way the authorities treated them in prison, that Germany was a fascist state. After the terrible events at Stammheim, things changed a bit. In the seventies, the whole of Germany was holding its breath about the RAF; but a year later the Green Party became prominent, and the German left-wing newspapers started. The atmosphere changed. People were not talking about imperialism but about other things—ecology, women's rights. The RAF," she said firmly, "was a movement of its time, and that time had now passed; what we were talking about was really history." She was incorrect of course, as the death of Herr Herrhausen showed.

After being released, it took her several years to reestablish herself, but the experiences she had gone through had left permanent scars. "It was the beginning of a nightmare," she said. "I was thirty-five, with no skills, no money, and no friends. It took me a long time to recuperate. I have seen a lot of people come out of prison; some go straight ahead with their lives but others are unable to do so, and with them it takes time to start again. I lived in Frankfurt for a while and tried to get back into the car repair business, but it was no use; it seemed dirty, terrible, and heavy. Only in the last few years am I really beginning a new life." Eventually, in 1988, she completed a film course at the art school in Hamburg and got her job at *Tempo* magazine.

It is not a publication to her taste, being similar she said to the fashionable British alternative magazine *The Face*. "A lot of the people it is aimed at hate the Baader-Meinhof group because they feel overshadowed by them. They want to do something themselves, and they resent what we did and look upon what happened back then as solely a cultural thing."

She paused. "We fought society from the outside; they consider it is best to fight from within."

She was beginning to look tired. "It does exhaust me, talking about it," she admitted. But she was beginning to hope that finally she was being allowed to bury her past.

The German authorities are convinced she has completely broken with terrorism; Herr Christian Lochte of the Hamburg Office for the Protection of the Constitution described it as "fantastic" that she has severed all contact, yet has not become a traitor to her former comrades. He was trying, he told me, to help her in her struggle to be allowed entry to the United States to see her mother. "I admire her very much; she has a very strong and independent personality. She has found her own way out of the past without being forced by anyone. Nothing is more impressive than to come to the conclusion that a very strong woman is ready to fight for peace because that woman's role as a fighter would be very bad."

Although she has severed all contact with her past, Astrid still feels strongly for her former comrades who are serving lengthy prison sentences in Germany. In 1987 she made her first public appearance at a meeting of the German Green Party on the origins of urban terrorism and the need to rehabilitate repentant prisoners.

She referred to the "isolation torture" still endured by RAF prisoners and urged that the government should put all the prisoners together in one jail.

She admitted that the supporters of the current RAF—the fifth generation, she supposed—still idolized "the oldies"—the ex-prisoners like herself and those serving sentences, as martyrs. She sighed. She does not want to be a martyr to anyone or for anyone. "There are a lot of people who feel guilty about the number of RAF people sitting in prison today, many of them for life. It was very easy to get a life sentence then for being a member of the RAF. Lots of them did hardly anything. Perhaps when they got arrested they shot at a policeman and although nobody was injured, they got life anyway. It was crazy."

Was it all worth it? I got the impression that Astrid thought not, that the price for those wild days of fighting the system had been too high. She considered the question: "Now I think that the RAF was a sort of rehearsal; it was a movement of its time. I don't know if it was necessary."

How did she remember her dead comrades? "If Ulrike Meinhof had been freed and become a politician or a mother, she would have been remembered for that." She has a reminder of Ulrike every day that she goes to work—one of her twin daughters, Bettina, works alongside her at *Tempo*.

Although the Red Army Faction is viewed by the German law enforcement agencies as the major terrorist threat, there are other groups whose philosophy has led to murder, bombings, and kidnapings.

The Militant Black Panther Aunties, which Ms. Proll belonged to, had a fairly short-lived existence, but from them grew another militant feminist movement, the Red Zora. This group was formed in the late seventies, and its membership was composed almost entirely of women. The attacks it carried out were related not only to feminist issues but also to industries and organizations considered guilty of harming the public.

They believed that human life should not be harmed, but in 1981 they killed a sixty-one-year-old politician as he lay asleep in bed. Herr Heinz Karry could hardly have been a more unpopular figure: he wanted to built a nuclear waste processing plant, extend Frankfurt Airport, and build a new road system. Those women who had broken into his house were not supposed to have killed him, though, and Red Zora issued a statement apologizing for his death.

Much more in keeping with their style of attack was a spate of bombings on several marriage bureaus in 1983. The bureaus were advertising a vacation-honeymoon package in Thailand to German men: "Come to Thailand," the advertisements ran, "where hundreds of young, pretty girls are waiting for the right husband." The bombings of such establishments took place at night and without injury; Red Zora claimed that as the government had refused to stop such practices, which showed contempt for women, women had to act for themselves. In the course of the campaign, Red Zora also bombed the Philippines embassy in Bonn, for "complicity" in the trade.

Their most recent action took place when they simultaneously set fire to eleven department stores that, a Red Zora statement declared, were selling clothes made in South Korea, where the women workers were not being paid proper wages. The group was particularly active in the eighties when it carried out nearly 250 actions, but since the capture of most of its leaders in 1987 there have only been four attacks.

Women have also played major roles in the neo-Nazi movement in Germany. In 1988 Sibylle Vorderbrugge emerged from prison, having served eight years of a life sentence for the murder of two Vietnamese boat people, bomb attacks, arson, and membership of a terrorist group. She was thirty-two years old, and part of her sentence had been served in the same isolation wing of Stammheim prison where members of the RAF served their time. The beliefs she had held, however, could not have differed more from those of her fellow prisoners.

The group she had joined in 1980 was led by a notorious neo-Nazi called Manfred Roeder, who claimed that one of Hitler's admirals had named him as the führer's successor. He was a fifty-five-year-old lawyer, and in the previous five years had gathered around him a small group of men and women who believed that he was the new führer. Their task was to rid Germany of foreigners.

I tried to interview Ms. Vorderbrugge, but she refused to see me, having told her story already to the German *Quick* magazine. She was trying to rebuild her life and did not want to be reminded of her past.

In a series of articles in the magazine, she claimed that she had been led on to more and more serious racist attacks, culminating in murder, because of her love for Roeder. None of it was really her fault, she implied, because she had been so much in love with the man. "It was as if I was blind," she was reported to have said.

It all seemed too easy an explanation and it was frustrating not to have questioned her, not least because she appeared to be the only woman who fitted into the theory that women were dragged into violent groups out of love for a man.

According to the articles, she had first become involved in neo-Nazism after talking to a colleague at the hospital where she worked as a medical assistant. The colleague, a young woman called Gabriele Colditz, had asked Sibylle to give her something to read; Sibylle had given her *The Diary of Anne Frank*. Gabriele tossed it aside, describing it as "a lying fairy tale." She then went on to "enlighten" Sibylle, telling her about the "Auschwitz Lie," and the "truth" about Nazi war crimes.

Over the next couple of months, she gave Sibylle a selection of Nazi publications and tape recordings of speeches made by Roeder. Sibylle was deeply impressed by the speeches and begged Gabriele to introduce her to the speaker. As soon as she met Roeder, she was mesmerized, she claimed, and dreamed about "spending a night with him."

Roeder eventually fulfilled her wish, and the two became lovers. As Sibylle became more infatuated, he encouraged her to become part of his network. His group, The Freedom Movement of the German Realm, had already bombed an Auschwitz exhibition and a hostel for asylum seekers. Gabriele and her father, who was a doctor, had been involved in the attacks. Sibylle claimed that suddenly violence appeared to be justifiable in order to realize Roeder's vision of a pure Germany.

Roeder demanded more violence; he wanted asylum hostels blown out of the sky, he declared. Sibylle was determined to earn his admiration.

She had resigned from her job and become Roeder's secretary. This had necessitated her moving in with him at his home, called the Reichshof. It was a turn of events that did not please Frau Roeder, a mother of six. Sibylle worked without pay, bringing her savings of about $5,000 for the movement's funds, but her presence created understandable tensions, and she moved out after two months.

For her first mission, bombing a house for refugees, she was teamed up with a male comrade. The explosion caused considerable damage, but Roeder was not satisfied; he wanted to gain international attention for his cause.

A week later she and two men bombed a hotel for Eritrean refugees near Stuttgart, injuring three. Her lover was pleased with her and Sibylle herself was quoted as saying, "It took hold of me like an intoxication. Of course I realized that people would be injured, but I didn't like to picture it in my mind. Roeder was happy, and I was happy because he was." Her next attack resulted in the deaths of two people. She had read in a Hamburg newspaper that a new hostel for asylum seekers had been opened in the city. She telephoned Roeder for permission, and, according to her, was given express orders to carry out a bombing. At midnight Sibylle and her male comrade threw Molotov cocktails into the hostel, where thirty-four Vietnamese boat people were sleeping. A fireball exploded, and two Vietnamese men, aged twenty-one and eighteen, were burned to death in the inferno.

Sibylle was deeply shocked at what she had done, but was reassured by Roeder that her actions were necessary. He dismissed the deaths as simply being those of "half-apes," and Sibylle's initial guilt transformed itself into a feeling of heroism. She went on to plan further attacks against charities that helped foreigners, but before she could cause any more deaths, she was caught after spraying racist graffiti on a wall.

Herr Christian Lochte, the Hamburg director of the Office for the Protection of the Constitution, considered that Ms. Vorderbrugge was a good example of how women become very dedicated to a cause; much more dedicated than men. Herr Lochte, a former judge, started working for the office in 1972, during the hunt for the Baader-Meinhof group, which he virtually masterminded. He became its head in 1980, and his work clearly fascinated him. "We are not interested," he told me, "in catching terrorists. We are interested in studying them, doing surveillance so that we can learn about them."

Ms. Vorderbrugge, he went on, confirmed what he had always said about women terrorists: "One day she had never heard of the neo-Nazis, the next she was a terrorist. One day she had no interest in the subject; the next she was a hundred percent terrorist; she became a fighter overnight." This total dedication to a cause, to the exclusion of all else, even family ties and upbringing, was also demonstrated, he believed, in the case of Susanne Albrecht.

He considered that if Susanne had been a man, she would have tried to convince her RAF comrades that they should pick another target to kidnap—anyone other than her Uncle Jurgen. As it was, Herr Lochte said, "Her attitude was to achieve the goal, to go straight ahead without any interruptions, any faltering. This attitude is not possible with men.

"Susanne was so swept away with emotion and ideology that she did not care what happened. This can happen with men, too, but not to such a radical degree—to sweep away all obstacles in your path without thought of the consequences. A young man would behave differently, he would try to find another way out of the problem. Susanne, though, did not have any levels or stages to overcome. She was immediately ready to do it and went underground afterward. Her parents, who had been so pleased to have her home, have not heard from her since."

This greater dedication to their cause, and the ability to achieve the required result, heedless of any other factors, are qualities that make women far more dangerous than men if they decide to join a revolutionary or terrorist group. Herr Lochte's theory seems to ring true, although in the case of Susanne, according to the account that is given below, she had to undergo virtual brainwashing before she agreed to take the commando team to the Pontos'.

Women would not hesitate, Herr Lochte continued, to shoot if they were cornered—a conclusion he has come to after many years' observation. "For anyone who loves his life, it is a good idea to shoot the women terrorists first.

"From my experience, women terrorists have much stronger characters, more power, and more energy than men. There are several examples where men who have been cornered have waited a moment before they fired, but the women shot at once. It is a general phenomenon." I asked why he thought this should be; why women would not hesitate where men would.

His explanation was that women had more to overcome just by being in a terrorist group in the first place; they had to fight sexism as well as the enemy, and the best way to prove they were equal was to show that they were even more ruthless than the men. "I believe that the question of how women find their own role in the world of men plays an important part in the terrorist world; it has a lot to do with emancipation.

"Among the left-wing circles the question of the women's role is much more important than in other sections of society. So the RAF women have an extra challenge compared to the men—they have to prove themselves as women as well as terrorists, and in order to do this they have to become better than the men. They have to be more aggressive and show greater strength than the RAF men because they are fighting the men as well." He pointed out that Astrid Proll was a red flag to Baader because she was so strong, and he feared her for it.

One gained the impression from talking to Herr Lochte that he admired the women terrorists he had studied over the previous twenty years. Most terrorist groups are fairly unstable, and he believed that the most important qualities a woman member could bring were practicality and pragmatism. He compared the underground terrorist movement with a nation at war: "In wartime women are much more capable of keeping things together. This is very important for a group of terrorists, for their dynamics. Especially a group like the RAF, where there are a lot of quarrels about strategy, about daily life. Women come to the forefront in such a group, because they are practical."

In the early days of the RAF it was Gudrun Ensslin who was in charge of the money, and Ulrike Meinhof who found flats for the group; one of many examples of this trait.

Herr Lochte gave his own example, from everyday life, to illustrate his point: "There was a television program shown here recently about a woman who had founded a computer company. Her staff comprised of fifteen employees, twelve of whom were women. She was asked why this was, was she a feminist? No, she said, her employee policy was based on substantial differences between men and women. Women understood things better and faster than men, and were more pragmatic. They not only learned faster, they worked faster.

"The men, though, wanted to play with the computers, experiment, and create something new. She said: 'With that attitude, I couldn't exist. I can only get the job done with women.'

"There is more than an element of truth when you relate that to men and women terrorists. For the daily business, women are far more pragmatic."

Not only that, he continued, the women he had studied were not afraid to use their instincts, whereas the men would waste time in debate. He illustrated his point by describing what he had learned about the dynamics of a group that his office had monitored for several months.

"We did surveillance on a group in Hamburg for about six months, including tapping their telephones. The head of it was a man who is now in prison. He and two women, Christa Eckes and Margrit Schiller, were the leaders. There were other men and women but these three were the important ones. In the end, from tapping the phones, and from other sources, we learned that they were planning a bank raid and had them arrested. But before that we managed to gather a lot of very good information about the roles of different members within the group.

"We learned that they only had a leader for two or three days to find a solution to a particular problem; then there would be no leader for a long period. The role was always held either by the man or Margrit Schiller—it went between the two of them. The leader had to have a strong personality. It was interesting that when they discussed taking a major step, Margrit Schiller was always ready to move further forward and faster than the man. She also always had the support of the other women in the group. The man was only strong when they were discussing an operation in which they had to be very careful not to be caught.

"On one occasion, they were discussing whether they should accept two new members. Schiller decided immediately. 'Well, they are OK; we should accept them,' but the man was very afraid. He, however, gave logical reasons, whereas she just said, 'It is my feeling that these two are OK.' She was very quick to form an opinion on people, relying purely on her emotions."

Women revolutionaries, therefore, are stronger, more dedicated, faster, and more ruthless than men, and added to all these qualities are able to keep a group together, run it, and carry out any mission given to them. Was there anything else? "Women are able to stand more suffering," he said. "They have much better nerves than men, and they can be both passive and active at the same time." There was no doubt, at the end of the interview, which sex Herr Lochte feared more.

In 1991 the total number of people being hunted by the German police for terrorist offenses, including those whose faces appeared on the wanted poster, were twenty-two, thirteen of whom were women. Many of the fugitives were believed to be living in Iraq or Lebanon, where they had found shelter through contacts originally made with Palestinian guerrillas. There was considerable fear at the start of the war with Iraq that those who had been protected by Saddam Hussein's regime would be called upon to step up terrorist attacks in Europe.

A great deal of information on the extent of the succor offered to these people by Iraq was supplied by five women and three men who were arrested during 1990 after the fall of the Berlin Wall. They told how they had been spirited out of what was then West Germany to Baghdad, where they stayed in houses provided by the Popular Front for the Liberation of Palestine (PFLP, Leila Khaled's organization). Several of the RAF, by the time they reached the Iraqi capital, had decided to leave the revolution to others; these included Susanne Albrecht and Inge Viett.

After the killing of her Uncle Jurgen, Susanne Albrecht collapsed, crying continuously. She had never imagined that he would be shot; the aim was only to kidnap him and hold him until the German government gave into their demands. According to the story of one of her former comrades published in *Stern* magazine, Susanne had needed a lot of persuasion before she agreed to exploit her relationship with the banker and her own family. She told the man that for several days she had been subjected to "forced" debate on the subject by her comrades, a "kind of brainwashing," before she eventually gave in. When the intended abduction escalated so suddenly to murder, she had become hysterical—and a danger to the safety of the rest of the group.

A male comrade was detailed to take her away from Frankfurt, across the country toward Holland, but it was difficult to travel with a woman who was shaking uncontrollably and crying incessantly. She was quickly escorted to an Eastern bloc country and from there to Baghdad, where she handed her passport over to the authorities. She was taken to a PFLP house and hidden, but her total emotional collapse rendered her a danger to other members of the RAF who were also living there.

Over the next weeks, more RAF escapees joined Susanne at the house, among them Brigitte Mohnhaupt, who had taken part in Ponto's murder. Brigitte became leader of the Baghdad RAF in exile, and she quickly classified Susanne as an "unreliable," someone who had to be removed if the group's standing with their PFLP hosts was to survive.

According to the article in *Stern* the leader of the PFLP was told that Susanne had to go, and he set about finding a safe haven for her and a few other "unreliables." Cuba, Angola, Nicaragua, and the Eastern bloc countries were all possibilities, but East Germany, as it was then, seemed the obvious choice because there would be no language problems. The PFLP man had good contacts with certain members of that country's regime (including, it seems, with those who had access to the East German leader, Erich Honecker) and with the feared secret police, the Stasi.

It was agreed that the fugitives should be given new identities, jobs, and homes by the Department of State Security. In ones and twos, the ex-revolutionaries made their way to Paris, where there was an RAF headquarters, before being brought to East Berlin.

In 1979 Susanne Albrecht was one of the first to be sent there. She was given the name of Ingrid Becker, who had been born in Madrid, and a job as a teacher of foreign languages. She was told by the Stasi man appointed as her guardian that she should answer any curious questions about her past by saying that her parents had thrown her out of her home and she did not want to talk about it. Four years later, Susanne married a physicist and in 1984 gave birth to a son, Felix.

Although protected and cosseted by the Stasi, Susanne was officially still being hunted as much in East Germany as in the West. In 1986 her wanted photograph appeared in a television program about the RAF, and a colleague at work recognized her. The family was spirited away to Moscow, where they remained until it was deemed safe for them to return to East Berlin.

Today, the German anti-terrorist squad cannot understand why Susanne Albrecht did not flee when the Berlin Wall fell. Perhaps it was because she had nowhere else to go, was too tired to run, or believed that the Stasi would protect her. They did not; in June 1990, following a tip-off from a former Stasi officer, she was arrested in front of her flat in East Berlin. She was prepared, she assured her captors, to give information about her former comrades' whereabouts; she felt so guilty about her past.

Inge Viett was also identified by an East German who saw her photograph on a wanted poster in Berlin. After sawing through her prison bars and escaping to Paris, she had lived undetected until in 1981 she shot at a French policeman.

He had stopped her as she rode through Paris on a motorbike without a helmet. Apparently all he had had time to say before she opened fire was, "Just a minute." The trigger-happy Ms. Viett was whisked off to Baghdad by her comrades, but she had already decided that enough was enough; she was no emotional wreck as Susanne had been, she just wanted out. She felt she had done more than her fair share anyway; she had remained at large in France, a dangerous place for a woman whose picture seemed to be every-where, and had performed her task of improving the French rev-olutionary group, Action Directe. Even the excitement she had apparently derived from standing in front of her wanted poster while other people stood staring at her photograph, little realizing who was standing beside them, had palled. According to *Stern*, Ms. Viett told the new RAF leadership in Baghdad that she had no inclination to subject herself to the discipline and self-criticism the group demanded; she wanted a new life.

One was provided for her, as for Susanne, by the Stasi. In 1983, she appeared in a suburb of Dresden under a new name. She worked as a photographer for state security and settled into the law-abiding life of an East German citizen, even declaring her am-bition to one day run a pizza house.

In 1985, she was recognized and had to move to Magdeburg, but she spent another five years at liberty, working in a factory where she was the union representative. Her colleagues remem-bered that she was the only one in the workplace who was not at all pleased by the pro-democracy movement.

Six days after Susanne Albrecht's arrest, the police arrived at her flat in Magdeburg; she went with them quietly.

The arrests of these two women and the other former RAF per-sonnel were something of a coup for Germany's anti-terrorist squad. Its headquarters are located in the spa town of Wiesbaden, in the Black Forest, in a series of modern buildings at the top of a hill. Security measures are stringent as the headquarters are an obvious target for attack: the buildings house a computer, known as the Kommissar, which has been programmed with every available piece of information on any person suspected of having connections with the RAF. It is said to contain over ten million pages of data.

In contrast to the impressive efficiency and unsmiling, armed security guards, the windows of the buildings are decorated with the silhouettes of swallows. It is not, however, for aesthetic pur-poses—but to stop birds flying into the glass. The room for the meeting I was to have with the anti-terrorist squad was located along so many identical corridors, up and then down so many flights of stairs, that even my guide got lost. Eventually the office was located, a stark room where on the notice board were stuck the photographs of two Irish women, Pauline Drumm and Donna Maguire, who had been arrested as suspected members of an active service unit in Europe. Maguire has since been acquitted of any involvement in the shooting of two Australian tourists in a Dutch town.

The three men in the room, including the head of the squad, were far more interested in the arrest of the suspects they had been hunting for thirteen years. They had gleaned quantities of fresh information from those detained on the organization of the RAF and had learned which people had been directly responsible for the murders and bombings of the past. There was only one person who had not given a statement, Ms. Viett, who maintained that she would talk, but at her trial and not before.

It was toward the end of the interview that the squad's head, who had spent the previous two hours repudiating any suggestions that RAF women differed in their actions and motivation from RAF men, smiled a little sheepishly. "Now here," he admitted, "in the role of giving information, there is a difference between the men and women."

Under a new law that had just been passed in Germany, criminals who were willing to give new evidence at their trials about the offenses they or others had committed, could expect a reduction in sentence. The three men detained in the East, it seemed, had immediately started to bargain for reduced sentences by promising that they had new information to divulge; the five women, on the other hand, would initially say nothing. "The women said, what we did, we did—and we won't tell you anything; the men had no objections. When a newspaper wrote that one of the women had agreed to supply information, she became very upset and cried and said that it was not true.

"Eventually, all of them agreed to give evidence to us—even Ms. Viett, who will not talk now but has said she will at her trial. Even so, there is still a difference between the men and women. The men have this new law at the forefront of their minds; the women are not interested in it, in getting reduced sentences. The men said, 'We will talk so we do not get such heavy sentences'; but the women are ready to talk because they feel guilty. That is the difference: the men immediately turned the situation to their advantage; the women have not sought to do bargains."

There was also a difference in the way in which the sexes gave their statements, he went on. "My impression was the women were less spontaneous about the information they gave. Before they spoke about the incidents they had knowledge of, they reflected a lot and tried to make sure everything that they said was absolutely correct. The men, however, did not bother about the accuracy of what they told us; they made a lot of mistakes and a lot of superficial statements."

I wondered whether the women's reluctance to speak initially, followed by their determination to ensure that their statements were correct, was related to a deeper commitment to the group than their male comrades. Some of the women I had interviewed, for example Susanna Ronconi of Prima Linea, had revealed that many men in her movement had joined because "it was the macho thing to do," and therefore had a relatively shallow allegiance to the group.

The head of the squad conceded that RAF women were, "just like women in any job," more personally involved with their cause than men. He declared: "Women's mentality is to be fully committed to their job, much more than men, who think it is, after all, only a job.

"Women are also more enthusiastic than men about social matters; they want to solve social problems. They have the same motives, targets, reasons as men for terrorist actions, but they are a bit more emotional about their convictions. When we talk about their motivation, they make remarks about their fight for social improvements."

One felt that it had been a difficult task for the man to spend all morning trying to analyze the contrasting roles of the men and women he hunted. Women had played such an important part in terrorism for so many years that it was, as he said, "very normal to us that women engage in terrorism"; it had a lot to do with German women's superior emancipation status. Was it possible, I asked, that in his view, as women in other countries caught up with the advanced state of German women's liberation, there could be an increase of women in the field of terrorism throughout the world? He grinned. "Yes, it may be that that will happen; that numbers of women terrorists will increase around the world as women become more emancipated. But that is only an opinion."

Conclusion

Twenty women, some living thousands of miles apart, all united by one factor: that they have been prepared to use violence to achieve their ends. One, Leila Khaled, was successful and escaped; the IRA volunteer and the Intifada fighters are still engaged in their battles; the others have been jailed; some of them are repentant, others not. For me, they engender a wide range of emotions: pity for some at wasted lives; fear of others because I know that the death of an individual means little to them and can be wiped from their minds by that comforting phrase, "casualty of war"; horror at some of the actions they described; admiration for those fighting against heavy odds; and puzzlement at the paradoxes they pose.

Some are or were living in circumstances so appalling that one could see only too clearly why they fight: the Intifada women for instance. Some belong to causes that are rooted in history, while others have engineered the wars in which they fight. Some are victims and others aggressors, and some a mixture of the two. The unique case of Miss Kim shows beyond doubt that there is no level of violence that a woman will not commit.

It would have been surprising if these women had nothing in common. In fact, they shared much. Sometimes, as in the case of the IRA volunteer and the fourteen-year-old Intifada fighter, who both spoke of the "ordinary" lives they were glad to leave behind but also of a sense of the limitations their new lives imposed, expressed almost identical opinions. In general, though, the similarities were less precise.

The majority of those interviewed came from societies in which women are repressed: Catholic countries—Spain, Ireland, Italy—where women are expected to be mothers and the nurturers of God-given life; and Arab cultures, where women are still largely relegated to the role of the second-class citizen, the servants of men. North Korea could hardly be a more repressed country, and even in Germany, where women's emancipation is apparently so advanced, one recalls the description of the "frozen" society out of which the Baader-Meinhof group emerged.

All the women have broken the taboo, not just in repressive societies but the world over, against violent women. That alone makes them extraordinary and points to an innate independence of spirit. Having broken that taboo, most have no intention of being relegated to the kitchen sink or being put back on the pedestal of the mother Madonna once the battle is won.

Feminism, for all but two of these women (Miss Kim and Leila Khaled), is something they hold dear, although they may have arrived at a feminist position from different beginnings. It seems that in the nationalist struggles—Irish, Basque, Palestinian—women not only set out to be combatants, they also hoped to win an equal role for their sex in the new society they were fighting for. As a result of their activities, they came to realize that they were certainly equal to men on the frontline. The women of ETA so proved themselves in this respect that, with the approval of their male comrades, they set up a women's movement. One thinks also of the Bill of Equal Rights drawn up by the Intifada women, and the acknowledgment by IRA women that the struggle for equality should go hand in hand with the nationalist fight.

Both the women from the revolutionary groups, Susanna Ronconi and Astrid Proll, began as militant feminists and had then moved on to join men in a wider battle against society.

Is there any significance in the fact that so many of the women are feminists? Certainly the head of the German anti-terrorist squad seemed to think so, when the reason he gave for the numbers of German women terrorists was "female emancipation." But only a tiny proportion of feminists turn to violence; and it is a widely held feminist view that men are violent and love fighting whereas women do not.

But the reason these women turned to violence must lie in a combination of circumstances: they see themselves as victims not only of what their male comrades would call "political oppression" but also of male oppression. Italian men could beat their wives *legally;* Basque women also suffer from the macho self-image of the Latin male. German women, whose voice was never heard in Hitler's Germany, have had to share the national guilt of his crimes against humanity. The key awareness is of being a *double* victim, with oppression having to be fought on two fronts. In that light it is perhaps more surprising—and this is the view of many criminologists and psychiatrists—that more women are not violent. They certainly seem to have more to be angry about.

All the women, excepting Miss Kim of course, are proud of what they have achieved. They did not necessarily get a kick out of killing, although Leila Khaled showed a dubious glee in recounting how she had terrified her victims, but they were pleased that they were able to fight on equal terms with men. They have proved that a woman is just as capable as a man of learning how to make bombs, plant them, and detonate them, and is just as likely to be a good shot with a gun.

It does not matter how weak or physically insignificant a woman is, she is as fearsome as any imposing male figure if she has a gun in her hands and knows how to use it. Two of the women are very small: Txikia and, by her own account, Leila Khaled, although she did not appear to me as being particularly small when I met her. It was Txikia whose eyes shone as she talked of the power of the gun and how it cut through all that dreary paperwork; and Leila Khaled was most memorable when describing the thrill she derived from being in absolute control—with the help of her weapons. Susanna Ronconi also talked vividly of how carrying a gun made her feel strong, protected, less vulnerable in her daily life.

Did these women who had been violent find it more difficult to kill or injure than men? No. Susanna Ronconi commented that she had met many men who told her that they would not have been able to kill in the way she had done. She does not believe that violence is a male preserve. Other women echoed her opinion. Some people can kill and others cannot. It does not matter if you are a man or a woman.

Are these women somehow warped, or mad, or evil? Has something happened to them to make them such misfits in the world of women? One does not question interviewees on the quantity of their body hair, but it was perfectly obvious that all these women are intelligent and articulate, rather than otherwise. Nor did they appear to want to be men. It was notable that the question that most often provoked anger was whether they had been hauled onto the frontline by their boyfriends. It was as if I was suggesting that they were not capable of taking such a step themselves.

As to whether they are suffering from mental disorders, this is not something I am qualified to judge. Sometimes they did seem to be disturbed by certain questions. For example, Amaia of ETA did not appear ever to have thought out the consequences of her actions. She denied being responsible for killing people in one breath, only to express in her next her satisfaction that she had killed "the bastards." This has been described by a clinical psychologist, Oliver James, who had made a study of the violent psyche, as an example of "splitting," or the coexistence of two opposing attitudes to the same subject. Splitting is a common mental process in the violent person, according to Mr. James. It is a schizoid mechanism, which can be a symptom of schizophrenia, although someone who is schizoid is not necessarily schizophrenic. Had Amaia's actions driven her to the point of madness? She did not appear to be a woman teetering on the edge, but she may have unresolved problems with her past.

Susanna Ronconi struck me as someone who has worked out all the problems of her violence for herself. She honestly described how she believed herself to have been in a schizophrenic state after witnessing her first murders. In warfare parlance, this would be called shell shock or posttraumatic stress disorder. Susanne also admitted that she had felt she was putting aside the "life preservation force" when she killed. It was one of the reasons, she went on, that "it is impossible to go on doing it for a long time; you will eventually have a personal crisis." Her crisis came upon her in prison, and she survived it.

Miss Kim, who became deeply depressed as the realization of what she had done came home to her, was given the hand of religion to help her through. She was also fully supported by a team dedicated to making her a new person. She had appeared absolutely in control of herself, perhaps too much in control. One of her minders remarked that she had never shown any emotion whatsoever toward anyone in the two years she had known her. She also has no sense of self, possibly not surprising in a victim of brainwashing. Mr. James thought it significant that this lack of identity was coupled with a beautiful physical appearance—"a striking external presence in contrast to the void within." He said Miss Kim had many of the symptoms of a "borderline personality." "This is someone who appears to live much of their life at second hand, an 'as if' existence, only feeling real when acting a role."

Leila Khaled's inability to put herself into her victims' shoes, and her apparent dissociation from the rest of mankind, is also disturbing. Yet she is functioning very well as a mother and stateswoman.

She is one of the three women in this book who had lost a fully functioning parent before the age of fourteen, either through death, illness, or separation. Mr. James found this significant. According to studies, women who lose a parent before fourteen are far more likely to become depressed.

Depressed or not, I certainly did not feel that I was ever in the presence of a madwoman, which is not to say that occasionally I did not shudder at some of their words. The ETA woman, Gloria, with her warning that the children of the Civil Guard were as much targets as their fathers, certainly shocked me.

Nor did the women seem to be "evil" or totally heartless either. Some of them were a bit irritable; some of them said some horrible things; but they did not behave like monsters. I remember the agonized look on the face of the former IRA woman when she asked: "Do you think we rejoice when a busload of young Yorkshire soldiers gets blown up?" They are undoubtedly used to answering moral accusations, but that does not make their responses untrue. They sincerely believe that when innocents are killed, it is a tragedy of war.

Perhaps another question should be addressed: do these women possess qualities that make them particularly good fighters, and are these qualities peculiar to women alone?

It was Susanna Ronconi who made the point that violence is linked to maternity. "It is the woman who gives life; it is the woman who also takes life."

Motherhood and the maternal instinct are certainly issues that run through the interviews. Many of the women felt guilty about what harm they might be causing emotionally to their children in neglecting them for the cause. The two Intifada mothers come into this category, as did Leila Khaled—who had the extra burden of having to protect her children from assassination simply because they were her children. For Rita O'Hare, the former IRA woman, it was the fear of her children being harmed that prompted her to go on the run, and it was the thought of them that made her fight for her life when she was shot.

Many of the other women who were not mothers nevertheless have given considerable thought to motherhood and what it might mean to their future as fighters. Mary Doyle, the former IRA woman, agonized over going on a hunger strike in case it made her sterile, but still went ahead with the protest. The ETA guerrillas said that few mothers would become fighters because of fear of what might happen to their children, and that this fear resulted in commando women putting off childbirth. Ulrike Meinhof and Gudrun Ensslin resolutely abandoned their children in favor of the revolution, and Ulrike went a step further by agreeing to send her young daughters to a Palestinian orphanage, where they stood a good chance of being trained as fighters themselves.

Susanna Ronconi, pregnant by a comrade when she had only just started as a revolutionary, had an abortion. When she spoke of the group she had formed, the loyalty she owed it surpassing her loyalty to her lover, it was almost as if she was speaking of a mother's love for her child. The Intifada mothers actually referred to the uprising as their son, their favorite child for whose sake other children might be sacrificed. When Leila Khaled saw children about to board the flight she was to hijack, she hesitated, and then called to mind all the thousands of other children who were depending upon her. It was as if the women were capable of projecting maternal instincts onto the cause. A mother will turn killer to protect her young, and if such projection of maternal instincts is possible, it may go some way to explaining why many of the women seemed to be so much more dedicated, single-minded, and determined than their male comrades.

Susanna Ronconi pinpointed another difference between men and women guerrillas. She used to laugh at the men who had a gun fetish and had joined the movement to enhance their macho image. Women, she said, "put far more of themselves and their whole entities into the experience." Consequently, fewer women than men were prepared to betray their comrades when caught. Their commitment was that much deeper, since it had not been engendered by such casual and superficial considerations.

The head of the German anti-terrorist squad agreed with her. He gave the example of the differences between the RAF men and women who had been captured after the fall of the Berlin Wall. The women had been far more reticent about giving information than the men. The police concluded that when they did decide to talk, it was for reasons of guilt over their past actions—not to get themselves a reduced prison sentence, as in the case of their male comrades.

Along the same lines, Txikia argued that women have to give far greater thought to joining an ETA commando unit than men: they have so much more to lose. "There is the very strong possibility you will lose your family, your home, and of course, all security. . . . [Men] know that whatever happens to them, their wives will still look after the children. But if a woman does the same thing, she must cut all those ties and abandon those feelings."

Women commandos, having given up so much and broken a powerful taboo, will put everything into the fight. The German anti-terrorist chief thought that in "ordinary" life women were more committed than men anyway: "Women's mentality is to be fully committed to their job, much more than men who think it is, after all, only a job."

One can begin to see why a woman fighter should be more feared than a man: she views her cause as a surrogate child—one for which she may have sacrificed authentic maternal feelings—that must be protected at all costs, and she starts off with a capacity for deeper commitment in the first place. Because of these fundamental differences, women may often feel that their political commitment has an emotional edge. Susanna Ronconi said that she was "not that lucid" when the group she had formed began to crumble and her lover left her because he felt all was lost. "I felt too torn apart by duty and sentiment," she recalled. The tears welled up in Aida's eyes as she spoke of the Intifada as her son, and of the suffering that she and others endured. This great emotional attachment to the cause was a dangerous thing, in the opinion of Christian Lochte of the Hamburg Office for the Protection of the Constitution. One reason why he thought that "Shoot the women first" was a good piece of advice was that in his experience women tended to act on emotional instinct—an easier and readier motive for killing than a set of political beliefs alone.

He also felt that women make more resolute fighters than men because they are naturally accustomed to pain. Txikia made this point, too, adding that women are less likely to break under torture. Another source of this resolute determination may be the need to compete with male counterparts. Herr Lochte again: "The RAF women have an extra challenge. They have to prove themselves as women as well as terrorists, and in order to do this they have to become better than men. They have to be more aggressive, more powerful, and show greater strength than the RAF men because they are fighting the men as well." This echoes the comment made by a woman from the Italian Red Brigades to the effect that if a woman shows any hesitancy or expresses doubts, her wavering is taken far more seriously than it would be in the case of a male colleague. Women, then, have to be doubly tough, constantly on their guard against any emotion that might be construed as "feminine weakness," and this might further explain why they are on occasion more ruthless. Newly acquired power and status, especially if vulnerable and on trial, is heady and exciting in itself, and may induce overreaction in a crisis.

A criminologist, Mrs. Frances Heidensohn of Goldsmiths College, London, pointed out that women are not taught the rules of violence as children: "There are subcultures that are predominantly masculine, such as gangs, where boys learn the rules. It is not true that women are not clubbable, but when women join these groups they may feel out of it because they do not know the rules that the men learned in childhood. They may wish to compensate for this, and be keen to do dreadful things to prove they are as good as the men. Many middle-class girls have not learned the rules about fighting, so a woman may feel that by being violent she is working her passage into the group."

There were several examples of women being apparently more ruthless than men: the Action Directe woman who kept shooting at the police when her boyfriend had surrendered without a whimper; Leila Khaled, who did most of the terrorizing while her male comrade stood silently beside her; and the IRA woman, Marion Coyle, who remained cold and steely toward her kidnap victim while the "tough" IRA man established a rapport.

It seems then that women, familiar with pain but unfamiliar with violence, and fearful of internal criticism, may overstep the mark in a determined effort to prove themselves. Miss Kim and Leila Khaled were both proud of being chosen for important missions and expressed the desire to carry out the task perfectly. The ETA woman, Amaia, seemed to me to be protesting too much when she declared: "If women decide to do an action, they will do it for themselves! They don't have to prove anything to men."

Being a guerrilla presents far more conflicts to a woman than to a man. The women pay the cost of being viewed not only as brutal animals, but also as "unnatural." Mrs. Heidensohn suggested this theory to me, but interestingly it was Amaia who first mentioned it. The Spanish police, she claimed, "wanted to punish us more for daring to be involved in the armed struggle. They cannot accept that women can do these things." As Mrs. Heidensohn put it, such women are guilty of "double deviance."

Not only can they expect harsher treatment from society, they are also seen as poor candidates for rehabilitation. Mrs. Heidensohn continued: "There is a whole genre of women rescuing men from themselves, but the stigma for a woman accused of a crime is very profound. In India a woman criminal is sometimes killed by her family. As a man you are allowed to sow wild oats, but for a woman association with crime means an unstable sex life. The man can meet a good woman who will sort him out, but a woman is unlikely to be taken on by a good man."

The lives of the women proved her right, for few had been allowed to forget their past. Astrid Proll, despite the fact that she was not really violent, will always be seen by some as the "gun girl." And who would ever really trust Miss Kim again?

Several of the women seemed to be aware of the irreversible step they had taken in choosing to be violent. One sensed that they felt, having stepped over the mark, they had nothing more to lose. If this is truly how they feel, then they are indeed likely to be more dangerous adversaries than men.

Society seems more afraid of violent women than men, as if they were more threatening than men. Indeed they are, for if women usurp the traditionally male role of aggressor, and if they do it successfully, men fear that their ultimate weapon—their physical superiority over women—is gone. The whole basis of society might crumble as a result of these dangerously unleashed women running amok. Men would be emasculated; the Society for Cutting Up Men, so popular among German women guerrillas, would triumph.

Perhaps this accounts for the degree of anger the ETA women described in the reactions of the police when one of their number slipped through a police trap by pretending to be engrossed with a lover. According to Amaia, they were "absolutely fucking furious, much angrier than if it had been a man who had got away."

Another element of this fury is the shame that attaches to a man outwitted or—even worse—defeated in combat by a woman, especially if "feminine wiles" have been used to make the man look silly and gullible. It is recognized that by playing on what is traditionally expected of them, women can be more effective than men in the kind of underground wars described in this book. No one could have expected the pretty and dainty Miss Kim of bombing an aircraft. Bommi Baumann pointed out that a male target is much less likely to run off when approached by two women than by two men. Mary Doyle observed that a woman pushing a pram does not look remotely threatening, so if a pram is to be used to plant a bomb a woman has to do the job. The ETA women used to exploit the macho attitudes of the police to their own advantage by protesting, when arrested, that their boyfriends made them do it. Even today, they claimed, a certain type of woman—well-dressed and elegant—can still dupe the police. One can imagine police recruits being warned not to trust any woman, no matter how innocent or elegant she might seem; but it is not hard to see how difficult it could be to train men to regard women as dangerous.

I spoke to a retired SAS man, who had killed many times. The victim he remembered most clearly, the one he had nightmares about, was a young Asian woman he stumbled across in the jungle. "She was pointing a gun at me and was just about to fire. I had to kill her, but momentarily I stopped and thought, It's a woman!" If the woman had been a little quicker herself, she could have used that moment of hesitation to kill him. She would have won that encounter not by virtue of being better trained or more ruthless, but simply because of the male attitude toward women.

Why do women, who have so little to gain and so much to lose, ever become guerrillas? Political motives apart—and these are certainly strong in most cases—power seems to be an important motive. For however brief a period, and no matter that it may mean a shortened life, these women have the opportunity to become the equal of men. The violence they are supposed to swoon at is theirs to use, and it empowers them in a way few women can experience, particularly if they come from repressive societies. Astrid Proll spoke of the existential quality of the Baader-Meinhof gang—the feeling that the exercise of power was expressive of something vital and life-enhancing. Susanna Ronconi explained, "You felt you were able to influence the world about you instead of experiencing it passively." As revolutionaries, such women do not have to bother with traditional expectations of womanhood, and that must be a liberating feeling in itself. "What have fashion and knitting patterns to do with me?" demanded Leila Khaled. For as long as they take their places at the frontline, these women can expect to be treated as political beings capable of actively pursuing their beliefs, of attempting to change society. As fighters, some of them, like the men, may make history. They may become the role models for a new generation of women, and also the object of male fantasies—not, it must be said, that any of them seemed consciously to seek this end.

Ambition for fame, the image of heroism—these motivations are as potent for women as for men. Although the women I spoke to often denied being members of an elite, that is clearly how they are regarded. The Basques admire the "armed spearhead" that is ETA. Bana, the young Palestinian stone-thrower, earned the hero-worship of her school friends. Susanna Ronconi referred to the "heroic dimension" of her activities. Even Astrid Proll, who so desperately wanted to bury her past, admitted the glamour and glory of her Baader-Meinhof days.

It does seem that a woman who makes a conscious decision to use violence for political ends is likely to be more highly motivated than a male counterpart. If her sacrifice is greater, her will to make that sacrifice worthwhile will be stronger. If expectations of her abilities are lower, she will have a great deal more to prove. With the progress of female emancipation, these motivations may lose some of their compelling force, though the view of violent women as especially aberrant appears to be well entrenched. Certainly the women I spoke to wanted above all to be seen as equals, and it was significant that being called names that derided them *as women* evoked more fury than anything else: one thinks of Susanna Ronconi's reaction to being called a tart—I got the impression she would rather have been called a murderer. To this extent, the British Anti-Terrorist Squad's view that the women they encounter are no different from the men will suit the women in this book just fine.

ABOUT THE AUTHOR

EILEEN MACDONALD is a free-lance journalist who writes for a variety of British publications. She spent two years researching this book, traveling to the Far East, the Middle East, Europe, and Ireland. She lives in London.

ABOUT THE TYPE

The text of this book was set in Janson, a typeface designed by Anton Janson, who was a punch cutter in seventeenth-century Germany. Janson is an excellent old-style book face with pleasing clarity and sharpness in its design.